Women Rights and Law: The Exigent Horizons

Women Rights and Law: The Exigent Horizons

Dr. Shashi Nath Mandal
Dr. Tapan Kumar Samanta

NAMYA PRESS.com

Published by
Namya Press
213, Vardhan house, 7/28, Ansari Road,
Darya Ganj, Delhi - 110002.
Email: namyapress@gmail.com

Edition	:	First Published in 2020 (Namya Press)
Title	:	Women Rights and Law: The Exigent Horizons
Editor	:	Dr. Shashi Nath Mandal & Dr. Tapan Kumar Samanta
ISBN	:	978-93-91010-10-2
MRP	:	₹ 600.00
Copyright	:	© Dr. Shashi Nath Mandal 2020 All rights reserved

Acknowledgement & Dedication

This academic work is a result of co-operations from many learned persons and luminaries of the academia. The work is the composite work of both the authors. They are immensely indebted to the Almighty for all blessings, showered for the completion of the work. The authors are grateful to all fighters of women's right throughout India.

The work titled on 'Women Rights and Law: The Exigent Horizons' is dedicated to all the women fighters, who have served the society and sacrificed their life for the cause of women rights.

Dr. Shashi Nath Mandal
Dr. Tapan Kumar Samanta

The 1st January, 2020, Burdwan, West Bengal

Preface

Rights and protection of women, in every respect, is necessary not only for the development of the society but for the proper development of our country also. Though we have completed 74 years of our independence still, the position of women in the Indian society is not better than that of the depressed classes in general. They are able to enjoy few rights independently, but still subjected to various restrictions and atrocities. What their status is in practical ritualistic and there is a hard reality about it. Numerically almost half of the total population, women in India has been the subject of economic exploitation, social injustice, appalling poverty, humiliation and discrimination of various kinds through centuries. In our country still, women are trained from the mother's lap that they had to be an embodiment of service and sacrifice, and had to accept the male as her master and benefactor, though the arrival of a separate school of Feminism has brought changes, but miles to go in India. Educationally backward, socially and economically dependent, this crippled creature, which has assured, the unique pride of motherhood of man and unparallel influence in the shaping of the society, has lived through suppression, exploitation and ill-treatment at the hands of men in most of sphere. Actually, background of the Indian society and that of the Indian women have been reinforcing each other, as it were in a vicious circle. Without a drastic change in the living conditions and mental make-up of the women in India, advancement of the larger society towards the goal of progress and prosperity will remain unfulfilled. Women development is contingent on the general development of the country as a whole. Women problems cannot be tackled piecemeal, in isolation from men. Today, inequality has effected all aspects of social life of in India. Unequal treatment meted out to the women follows from such in egalitarian social structure and division of labour. Indian women were never conscious about their position because of their century-old feelings of subjugation and so called inferiority. The denial of educational opportunities had made them submissive to male domination. Whatever progress has been achieved in the field of individuation has been marked and marred by condescension on the one hand and extreme liberation on the other. A woman is a person in her own right and is entitled to an identity, independent of her father, brother, friend or her husband. She is in quest of attaining and asserting this identity. More or less two third of the India's women are still illiterate despite grandiose government plan and propaganda. In-spite of plethora of legislations for empowering and protection of women, it has been observed that there is a big hiatus between the law and the actual application of the law. Protection of women in work place and economic independence were among the priority steps towards real emancipation.

Keeping in mind the need of a work on issues relating to women and their rights recognized under various laws including labour sector and scope of legal protection only the present book on 'Women Rights and Law: Exigent Horizons' has been thought of by the authors and taking reference of various research work and study the book has been penned by the authors.

In this book, we have tried to put forward the various issues which are responsible for the existing position of women in India. The endavour has been made trough this book to analyse the areas and the forums which can take part in identifying women's rights and protection issues and in developing the position of women including Legislative, Executive and Judicial approach.

The book contains eleven very relevant chapters bearing various areas and scopes of the subject rights from its historical development, international initiatives, constitutional position, legislative endeavors, judicial efforts, personal laws, criminal laws and a few palpable shortcomings and very pertinent necessities have also been gathered and placed for the advance students and learners. The book shall be a wonderful instrument to understand the existing position and future challenges in the matter of position of women, their existing rights and challenges on enjoyment of their rights in totality in all areas including labour sectors in India. Several shortfalls, precautions proposals have also been discussed for the advanced learners and researchers, which are the product of critical study of the authors in the relevant field from long time.

—Dr. Shashi Nath Mandal

—Dr. Tapan Kumar Samanta

The 1st January, 2020, Burdwan, West Bengal.

Contents

Abbreviation

AIR	:	All India Reporters
Art.	:	Article
CEDAW	:	Convention on the Elimination of All Forms of Discrimination again Women
CSW	:	Commission on the Status of Women
ECOSOC	:	Economic and Social Council
GWA	:	Guardian and Wards Act
HAMA	:	Hindu Adoption and Maintenance, Act
IDA	:	Indian Divorce Act
ILO	:	International Labour Organization
IPC	:	Indian Penal Code
Lab I C	:	Labour & Industrial Cases
LAB L J	:	Labour Law Journal
NCW	:	National Commission for Women
NHRC	:	National Human Rights Commission
NOW	:	National Organization for Women
SCC	:	Supreme Court Cases
SHRCs	:	State Human Rights Commissions
U.K.	:	United Kingdom

UDHR	:	Universal Declaration of Human Rights
UN	:	United Nations
UNESCO	:	United Nations Educational Scientific and Cultural Organization
USA	:	United States of America
Vs.	:	Versus

List of Cases

CHAPTER

1 Women and Law

"Yatra Nariyastu Pujyante Ramante Tatra Devata,
Yatraitaastu Na Pujyante Sarvaastatra Falaah Kriyaah"[1]

1.1 Introduction

Our religious scriptures confer upon us the duty to accord due respect to women. The *slokas* cited above means *"wherever women are given their due respect, even the deities like to reside there and where they are not respected, all action remains unfruitful."* This clearly shows the basic understanding of our mindset in the Vedic period but in the passage of time things have got lots of degrading evolution and the position of women in the society became worsen, the Indian society became male dominated society. From the position of 'worship' the women became the subject of torture and sex in different fields of the society, which make the subject mare challenging in the society. The challenge is not limited to one country or state but is very pertinent globally.

We know that, Women have a unique position in every society, whether developed, developing or underdeveloped. This is particularly due to various they play during various stages of their life, as a daughter, wife, mother and sister etc. In-spite of her contribution in the life of every individual human being, she still belongs to a class or group of society

1 Manusmriti 3.56

which is in a disadvantaged position on account of several social barriers and impediments. She has been the victim of tyrant at the hands of men who dominate the society. The position of Indian woman is no better compared to their counter parts in other parts of the world. On one hand she is held in high esteem by one and all, worshipped, considered as the embodiment of tolerance and virtue. But on the other hand she has been the victim of untold miseries, hardships and atrocities caused and perpetuated by the male dominated society. The vulnerability of the women as a class has nothing to do with their economic independence. The women has been a victim irrespective of her the victims of social barriers and disadvantages of varying kinds. A report of the United Nations Organizations points out that women constitute half of the world population, perform nearly two-thirds of work hours, receive one-tenth of the world's income and own less than one-hundredth percent world's property.

In India almost half of the Indian population is women. They have always been discriminated against and have suffered and are suffering discrimination in silence in the civilized as well as the primitive society. Even though self-sacrifice and self-denial are their nobility and virtue, yet they have been made the victims of all indignities, inequity and discrimination, from time immemorial. Dr. B. R. Ambedkar the father of the Indian Constitution and a social reformer, fought for the down-trodden class of the society including women. According to him, women of our country have always been discriminated against on the basis of sex. Even Manu has stated that day and night women be held by their subjection. Dr. Ambedkar criticized Manu for conferring inferior status upon women. Women have always been meted out ill-treatment in every walk of life. In spite of effort made by Dr. Ambedkar to provide social justice to the down-trodden and weaker sections including women, women have been pushed into the funeral prayers of their husbands. They could not hold property, were always treated as inferior to man.

The exploitation and discrimination of women has been multifaceted, all around and all pervading. There has been hardly any job, employment or engagement in which women were not given wages less than the men, even when they have been engaged in the same type of work and for the same duration. Despite the constitutional mandate that women will not be discriminated in any sphere, discrimination has continued. The social justice enshrined in the constitution enjoins the sate that exploitation of weaker section of the society should cease. And despite the constitutional guarantee of equality of sexes and constitutional mandate of social justice, rampant discrimination and exploitation of women continues. The incidents of bridge burning, women haltering, molestation and rape, and brazen ill treatment of women is on the increase. Their discrimination and exploitation in father's house and in in-law's abode and at work place are still the order of the day.

We know that the principle of Gender Justice is enshrined in the Indian constitution on its preamble, fundamental rights, fundamental duties and directive principles. The constitution not only grants equality to women, but also empowers the state to adopt measures of positive discrimination in favour of women but the illiteracy and lack of social awareness making these provisions dormant and sometime useless particularly for unprivileged women, which is a real challenge before law.

This intense craving, coupled with avarice, made the middle classes seek new avenues for getting rich quickly. They restored to coercion and blackmail by compelling young birds' parent to dish-out money, and more money after marriage. Thus women, who has been traditionally regarded as the preserver of social order and the standard-bearer of decency and social morality, is now subjected to inhuman and immoral treatment in case her parents failed to meet the ever-increasing demands of her husband and his parents. Needless to say, such treatment of women, which is the outcome of dowry syndrome, is a bolt on our society. Bride burning is still going on in our society.

1.2 Position of Women in the Pre-Constitutional Period

The Vedic period as golden days for women when they like men participated in all the social fields and took active part in each and every sphere of human life. The women enjoyed full freedom and equality with men during those periods. They had studied in Gurukul and equally enjoyed learning Vedas. The girl belonging to higher societies were allowed even to undergo 'Upanayana' rite. The great women as Ghosa, Apala, Visvara, Lopamudra, Gargi, Matreyi, Indrani, Yami and many others had distinct qualities of art, dance, music and even fighting in the battle too. In Vedic period there was no custom of 'purdah'. The women had similar rights in their selection of life partner in marriage. In those periods, custom of polygamy was very rare and as confined to the ruling class only. The systemof dowry was also prevalent in royal and rich families but it was not in the shape of demand. The widows were allowed to marry again or could enter the recourse of 'Mioyoga' (levirate). The position of women deteriorated during the period between 1500 B.C. to 500 A.D. during this period which is known as post Vedic Period, certain limitations and restrictions were placed on the rights and privileges of women and suddenly the status of women suffered a setback and they were confined to the four walls of their houses. The 'upanayana' rities for the girls were completely abandoned during the period 500 B.C. to 500 A.D. which can be approximated to the period of early smritis, the epic Ramayana and Mahabharata and early puranas. The law makers restricted the freedom of women only in deeds and speeches and the society slowly become polygamous. The marriageable age of girls was reduced and there were deprivation of women in various areas during the puranic and epic period. Sita was exited and even was forced to prove her chastity before all persons present.

Draupadi was humiliated in the court. Ahilya was converted into a statue when the in-laws of MeeraBai attempted to put her to death. In those days, sons were treated as the hope of the family as in the observance of epics of Ramayana and Mahabharata and the women had only one duty to obey their husbands blindly.

The situation worsened in the real sense only since the Gupta period as dowry emerged as an institution, widow remarriage was not allowed, women had no right to property and life had to be spent in penance and austerity.In the medieval period, the position of women became worse than under the Gupta period. In this period female infanticide, child marriage, purdah, Jauhar, sati and slavery were the main social evils affecting the position of women. Women are largely uneducated and remained confined to their homes. During the British period, some of the social problems which attracted the attraction of British administrations and enlightened the social reforms were 'sati', infanticide, child marriage, the prohibition of widow marriage & overall deplorable status of Indian women.

1.3 Position of Women in the Post Constitutional Period

India got its full Constitution in the year 1950 which was the result of result of social conditioning of the then period. The constitutional framers given lots of provisions for the protection and advancement of women from violations. It contains Article Part III i.e. from Article 12 to 35 as the Chapter of Fundamental Rights and Part-IV, the Chapters of Directive Principles of State Policy, more specifically Articles 14,15,16,23,24,39 mainly provided for the protection of women. Beside these, Article 40, 243,243-234-ZG added through 73rd Amendment of the Constitution and later on 93rd Amendment of Constitution provided the special provision for the participation of women in the local administration.

It is an established fact that women have got a unique position due to variety in role they play during various stages of their life, for example, as a daughter, wife, mother, sister etc. In-spite of her contribution in the life of every individual she belongs to a class or a group of society which is in a disadvantaged position due to several social barriers and impediments. She has always been the victim of tyrant at the hand of her male counter who dominates the society, particularly in India. Upto the beginning of the present century she has been the victim of untold miseries, hardship and atrocities subject to some exceptional situations where held in high esteem by everyone, worshiped and considered the God of the tolerance and virtue.

Since the long period of Britishers the position of Indian women degraded at high rate. Consequently, from the beginning of the 20th Century social reformers like Raja Ram Mohan Roy, M.N. Roy, Rishi Arabinda, Vidyasagar etc. initiated the issue relating to women protection and development with their reachable strength. As a result anti-women development practices started decreasing and laws to protect women from exploitation started increasing which continues till day. Besides constitution of India some remarkable laws to protect women in general are IPC, Cr. Pc, Abolition of Sati, Immoral Traffic (Prevention) Act, The Pre Natal Diagnostics Technique (Regulation, Prevention and Misuse) Act, 1994, Dowry Prohibition Act, Legal Services Authorities Act, Medical Termination of Pregnancy Act, Protection of Women from Domestic Violence Act. But these laws are mainly empowered and protected women theoretically, but practically their position has not been improved upto the projection as dreamed for.

Due to the passage of time the society developed women have still been subject to lots of bias and restrictions on the ground of weaker sex. The violation in not limited only in their domestic life, it expanded to every sector of their life including place of work, wages and remuneration etc. The legislature took the responsibility to provide safeguard to the women through labour legislations. Special emphasis have been given on some principles like equal remuneration, equal pay for equal work, special working conditions for women in the factories and industries, payment of service benefits and compensations through various labour legislations like Equal Remuneration Act, Payment of Gratuity Act, Employees Compensation Act, Factories Act, Industrial Dispute Act, Maternity Benefit Act including latest law, the Sexual Harassment of Women at Work Place (Prevention, Prohibition and Redressal) Act 2013. The purpose behind the above mentioned law in this paragraph has been to ensure women protection, but it has measurably failed due to various reasons and the women are still the subject of inequality, torture, harassment(physical and sexual) and social atrocities throughout the country.

1.4 Women Protection under the Existing National Laws

These are some of the factors that prompted the legislature to make various laws to give the women their due share. The constitution of India prohibits any discrimination solely based on the ground of sex in general and in the matter of employment. This prohibition of gender-based discrimination has been given the status of a fundamental right. We know Part III of the Constitution of India deals with the fundamental rights. The provisions from Articles 12 to 35 are applicable to all citizens irrespective of sex. However certain provisions protect the rights of women. Under the constitution the State has been given power to make laws relating to women and children, but such shall not be violative of Article (15) of the constitution. Article 15 (1) prohibits gender discrimination. Right to equality[2] means the equality of opportunity, equality before law, equal protection in the laws, not discriminating any person on the ground of sex, religion, caste and place of birth and no discrimination in the matter of public employment on the ground of sex only as provided under Article 16 of the Constitution. Further, Article 23 is an important right to us. This Article prohibits traffic in human beings and forced labour is prohibited. Article 32 to 35 deals with the right to Constitutional Remedies that is approaching Supreme

---

2 Article 12 & 13 Article 14 to 16 of the Fundamental Rights under Indian Constitution.

Court for enforcing fundamental rights. Again, in the case of ***Ms. Githa Hariharan Vs. Reserve Bank of India***[3]. Supreme Court gave a landmark decision. The decision was Mother can act as a natural guardian during the lifetime of father. Part IV of the Constitution containing Articles 38, 39 (a) (d) and (e), 42, 44 and 45 deal with the welfare and development of women.

Various other laws have been enacted to deal with the personal matters like marriage, divorce and succession etc., of the women. Unfortunately, only a few such laws could be codified and made uniform. The criminal law may also contain numerous provisions to deal with the crimes committed against women; enactments like the Dowry Prohibition Act supplement the existing criminal laws to combat the civil of dowry. Number of labour and industrial laws provide for the protection and welfare of the women, which include maternity benefit, prohibition of employment of women in dangerous activities and crèche facilities for the children of working women. In order to curb the immoral and anti social practice of prostitution, the Immoral Traffic (Prevention) Act has been enacted. The female feticide and infanticide have assumed dangerous proportions and the discrimination of sex of the fetus which became possible due to the advanced scientific inventions, abetted the Commission of these inhuman acts. The parliament has passed the pre-natal Diagnostic Techniques (Regulation and Prevention of misuse) Act 1994 to arrest this undesirable trend. These legislative measures aforementioned are only illustrative in nature and not at all exhaustive.

In order to curb the pervading evil of dowry, the Dowry Prohibition Act 1961was passed. However, this Act could not arrest the rising fide of violence against women. Indian Penal Code also supplemented with drastic provisions. Section 304 B of the Indian Penal code defines dowry death in the following words:

3 AIR 1999 (S.C.) 2894.

"Where the death of a woman caused by any burns or bodily injury or occurs otherwise than under normal circumstances within seven years of marriage and it shown that soon before her death she was subjected to cruelty or harassment by her husband or any relatives of her husband for or in connection with any demand for dowry, such husband or relative shall be deemed to have caused her death.......".[4]

Section 113 B of the evidence Act lays down that if soon before death such a woman has been subjected to cruelty or harassment for or in connection with any demand for dowry, the court shall presume that such person has committed dowry death. The meaning of "cruelty" has to be gathered from section 49 B of IPC.

The exploitation and discrimination of women have been multifaceted, all round and pervading. The worst exploitation is located in wages and remuneration. There are many establishments where many women workers are working with the men workers. They are getting less payment in comparison with the male workers though they are engaged in the same type of work and pay for the same duration. The principal of equal pay for equal work is contained in clause (d) of Article 39 of the Indian Constitution, is now playing a vital role in this regard. Further, the equal pay for equal work finds its place in the Directive principal of state policy and it is an accompaniment of equality clause enshrined in Article 14 and 16 of the of the constitution of India. The Equal Remuneration Act, 1976 provides for the payment of equal remuneration to men and women workers and for prevention of discrimination, on the ground sex against women in the matter of employment and for matters connected therewith or incidental thereto. The Act ensures against discrimination in recruitment and promotion of men and women.

To protect the working women, another important Act, i.e. Maternity Benefit Act 1961, was enacted to regulate the employment of women in certain establishments for certain periods before and after child birth and to provide

4 304 B of Indian Penal Code, 1973

for maternity benefit and certain other benefits. This Act extends to the whole of India except the State of Jammu and Kashmir.

We know that the right of Industrial workers to receive gratuity has long been recognized by the Tribunals, yet the law of land relating to payment of gratuity was very vague and uncertain before passing the present Act, i.e. Protection under the payment of gratuity Act 1972. There was a good of disparity in the various schemes for the payment of gratuity. The Employees' Compensation Act 1923 is one of the earliest measures adopted to benefit the labourers. It was passed in 1923 and enforced on 1st July 1924. Since then, a number of amendments have been made from time to time so as to suit the changing needs and conditions of the employees. Another important Act to protect the women workers is, Protection of Women under 'The Factories Act, 194'. This Act was amended in the year 1954 to prohibit the employment of the young persons including women during the night shift.One of the evils the modern society is the sexual harassment caused to the women particularly the working women by their male counterpart and other members of the society for this recently parliament has passed The Sexual Harassment of Women at Workplace (Prevention, Prohibition and Redressal) Act, 2012 after a long gap of the guidelines given by a Division Bench of Supreme Court speaking through Chief Justice J. S. Verma (as he then was) in ***Vishaka Vs. State of Rajasthan***[5]. Child marriage has been one of the biggest injustices committed against a child. In the process of child marriage, we have deprived the young girl to be an educated and a capable citizen and also deprived a new generation of children from getting care by a well informed and healthy mother. The potential loss to society, both socially and economically, will be hard to quantify but it would be enormous. Women have historically always constituted an exploited class in the society. The English Common Law created wife as the chattel of husband. Since then law has tried to address the problems of the status of women by means of legislation.

5 AIR (1997) 6 SCC 241.

Legal Service Authority Act-1987 was passed to provide free and competent legal services to the weaker sections of our society in order to ensure proper justices for the poor and needy people and to see that they are not denied of such rights. We can refer an interesting case in this connection; ***Kesavananda Vs. State of Kerala***[6].

We are living in the 21st century, i.e., in the modern era. It could hardly be denied that women of our country are the weaker section of our society till date. LokAdalats are playing a vital role to protect the women's right in our country.

After fifty-sixth year of the Republic of India, the parliament has enacted an important Act to provide more effective protection of the rights of women under the Constitution, who are victims of violence of any kind within the family and for matters connected therewith or incidental thereto. That Act was entitled as – "Protection of Women from Domestic Violence Act 2005". This Act is very important Act of our Country to protect the women from domestic violence, but honest implementation of this Act is necessary. Despite of these Acts there are no protective Acts for the Domestic servants (men & women) who are working, usually, morning to night at his/her master's house year after year. Many men and women workers are working in many hotels, food plaza and Big Bazar etc. They are working from 8 a.m. to 8 p.m. There is another important Act to protect the women to save their lives, e.g. Medical treatment of pregnancy Act 1971.

1.5 Women under Five Year Plan

From the fifth-five year plan (1974-78) onwards there has been a marked shift in the approach to women's issues from welfare to development. In recent years, the empowerment of women has been recognized as the central issue in determining the status of women. The eighth-five year plan (1992-1997), with human development as its major focus, renewed the emphasis on development of women. It sought to ensure that benefits of development from different sectors

6 AIR 1973 SC

do not by-pass women. In the 9th-five year plan (1997-2002) made two significant changes in the conceptual of planning for women. First, 'Empowerment of women' became one of nine primary objectives of the Ninth Plan. Second, the plan attempted 'convergence of existing services' available in both women – specific and women-related sectors.In the 10th-five year (2002-2006) plan continued with the major strategy of 'Empowering Women' as agents of social change and development. It adopted a sector-specific 3-fold strategy for empowering women viz. Social Empowerment, Economic Empowerment and Gender Justice.

Forty Eight Percent (48%) of the total Indian population is female. 'Inclusive and integrated economic, social and political empowerment with gender justice' is how the Eleventh plan envisions empowerment of women.Over the years, women's empowerment has received wide policy support. However, question still remains about how far we have been able to achieve these objectives and address the need of women belonging to different social groups and regions of the country.

1.6 Women and Protective Commissions

The Parliament of India has realized the importance of a monitoring institution to examine and investigate all the matters relating to the safe guards provided for woman under the Constitution and other laws. This realization has led to the enactment of the National Commission for Women Act, 1990 which came into force with effect from 31-01-1992, which has been burdened with the laborious responsibility of reporting to the Government as to the efficacy and effective implementation of the safeguards for improving the conditions of woman by the Government and for monitoring the socio-economic development of women in all walks of their life. Unfortunately, the Commission can make only recommendations and send the same to the respective authority for action. It has no Judicial Powers for making it an effective instrument for providing relief to woman and distress. Justice V. R. Krishna Iyer, aptly remarked that a National Commission for Women has "*hardly any teeth or nail*"[7].

Apart from above we have had a number of commissions and committees on women's problem. Reports have piled, numerous suggestions have been made, and many solutions had been offered. The result is that, their role as a housekeeper and keeper of children and that of second fiddle to man, unchanged.We need total transformation of the man's mind, and the outlookof the society towards women should be drastically changed, for the emancipation of women and that is our goal.Problems of women are problems of the society, as well as the country as they constitute 50% of the total population of our country.

1.7 Women and Panchayati System in India

Though the Panchayati Raj Institutions have been in existence for a long time, it has been observed that these institutions have not been able to acquire the status and dignity of viable and responsive people's bodies due to a number of reasons including absence of regular elections, prolonged supersessions, insufficient representation of weaker sections like Scheduled Castes, Scheduled Tribes and women, inadequate devolution of powers and lack of financial resources.

Article 40 of the Constitution which enshrines one of the Directive Principles of State Policy lays down that the State shall take steps to organise village panchayats and endow them with such powers and authority as may be necessary to enable them to function as units of self-government. In the light of the experience in the last fifty years and in view of the short-comings which have been observed, it is considered that there is an imperative need to enshrine in the Constitution certain basic and essential features of

7 Justice V.R. Krishna Iyer on the role of National Commission for Women.

Panchayati Raj Institutions to impart certainty, continuity and strength to them.

Accordingly, it is proposed to add a new Part relating to Panchayats in the Constitution to provide for among other things, Gram Sabha in a village or group of villages; constitution of Panchayats at village and other level or levels; direct elections to all seats in Panchayats at the village and intermediate level, if any, and to the offices of Chairpersons of Panchayats at such levels; reservation of seats for the Scheduled Castes and Scheduled Tribes in proportionto their population for membership of Panchayats and office of Chairpersons in Panchayats at each level; reservation of not less than one-third of the seats for women; fixing tenure of 5 years for Panchayats and holding elections within a period of 6 months in the event of supersession of any Panchayat; disqualifications for membership of Panchayats; devolution by the State Legislature of powers and responsibilities upon the Panchayats with respect to the preparation of plans for economic developments and social justice and for the implementation of development schemes; sound finance of the Panchayats by securing authorisation from State Legislatures for grants-in-aid to the Panchayats from the Consolidated Fund of the State, as also assignment to, or appropriation by, the Panchayats of the revenues of designated taxes, duties, tolls and fees; setting up of a Finance Commission within one year of the proposed amendment and thereafter every 5 years to review the financial position of Panchayats; auditing of accounts of the Panchayats; powers of State Legislatures to make provisions with respect to elections to Panchayats under the superintendence, direction and control of the chief electoral officer of the State; application of the provisions of the said Part to Union territories; excluding certain States and areas from the application of the provisions of the said Part; continuance of existing laws and Panchayats until one year from the commencement of the proposed amendment and barring interference by courts in electoral matters relating to Panchayats.

In 1992, when the 73rd and 74th Constitutional Amendments introduced local self-governance, it was an unparalleled step to consciously empower women as decision makers with 1/3rd of the seats reserved for women, It came into force with effect from April 24, 1993.

In this place, Gandhi had aptly favoured the panchayati raj and his dream got translated with the passage of the Constitution (73rd Amendment) Act, 1992, which introduced the three-tier Panchayati Raj system by inserting the to ensure people's participation in rural reconstruction in general and that of women in particular.

1.8 Women Protection and International Laws

Discrimination against women was so extensive that additional means for protecting the human rights of women were seen necessary. After the United Nations charter came into force, the most important task before the United Nations was the implementation of the principles of the Universal respect for and observance of human rights could be fulfilled only if provision was made for an International Bill of Rights and for its implementation. Ultimately Universal Declaration of Human Rights was adopted in 1948 and two International Covenants were adopted in 1966. Many International Conventions and International Declarations were held upto 2008. The General Assembly of the United Nations had adopted the convention on the Rights of women on 20th December 1952 which came into force on 7th July, 1954. Another convention was held on the Elimination of All Forms of Discrimination against Women, in the year 1979 on 18th December, 1979. From this Convention it was reiterated that the state parties to the International Covenants on Human Rights are under obligation to provide equal rights to men and women in civil, political, social, economic and also cultural field. On 7th December, 1967, the General Assembly of the United Nations adopted the Declaration on Elimination of Discrimination Against Women. It reaffirms the principle of equality of right of women in worldwide scenario. Further the

General Assembly of the United Nations adopted Declaration on the Elimination of Violence Against Women in the year 1993. Notably this declaration is the first of its kind which exclusively dealt with the Elimination of Violence against Women and intended to protect fundamental right of freedom of women.In addition to the above, in the year 1995, the Fourth World Conference on Women was held in - Beijing. In its thirty-seventh session the commission on the women expressed a serious concern relating to women's rights.

Besides the United Nations and other international bodies the South Asian Association for Regional Co-operation (SAARC) consisting of seven South Asian countries, has adopted a Convention on preventing and Combating Trafficking in women and children for prostitution, in its eleventh summit in Kathmandu in January 2002. International Labour Organization (ILO) was established after the First World War on April 19, 1919 as an autonomous institution by the treaty of Versailles and was associated with the League of Nations. Its original Constitution formed part of Treaty of Versailles. On October 9, 1946 the amending instrument was signed at Montreal which is known as the I.L.O. Instrument of Amendment 1946. The I.L.O. has been working for the improvement of Labour standards and conditions throughout the world since last seventy five years. International Labour Organisation now playing a vital role worldwide in connection with the labour problems.

1.9 Position of Women in India

Women in India enjoy right to equality. However, in order to improve their status further, the Constitution provides under Article 15 (3) that State may make special provisions for women. Consequently, a number of legal provisions aimed of securing equal status for and removing discrimination against women have been made. For instance, the Constitution was amended in 1992 to reserve 33 percent of the seats in their favour in ***panchayets***[8] and ***minicipalities.***[9] The Amendment

8 Article 243 D – Inserted by the Constitution, seventy third Amendment Act, 1992.
9 Article 243 T – Inserted by the Constitution, Seventy fourth Amendment Act, 1992

is regarded as a major step for socio-economic empowerment of the women in India. The Constitution has also cast the duty on every citizen to renounce practices derogatory to the dignity of women.[10] It being a part of Directive Principles of State Policy, is not enforceable in a court of law but if the State makes any law to prohibit any act or conduct in violation of this duty, the Court would upheld the law as a reasonable restriction of the fundamental rights.

Indian Courts on the basis of above Constitutional provisions have regarded a number of rules and regulations as discrimination against women and consequently, unconstitutional. For instance, in ***C. B. Muthamma Vs. Union of India***[11], validity of the Indian Foreign Service (Conduct and discipline) Rules of 1961 was challenged which provided that no married woman member of the service shall obtain the permission of the Government in writing before the marriage is solemnizes and at any time after the marriage a women member of the service may be required to resign from service, if the Government is satisfied that her family and domestic commitments are likely to come in the way of the due and efficient discharge of her duties as a member of the service. The Supreme Court held that the Provisions in Service Rules requiring a female employee to obtain the permission of the Government in writing before her marriage is solemnized and denying right to be appointed on ground that the candidate is a married women are discriminatory against women. The Court however, held that equality of opportunity in matters relating to employment does not mean that men and women are equal in all occupations and all situations. In ***Air India Vs. Nargesh Meerza***[12], the Supreme Court struck down the provision of the rules which stipulated the condition that services shall be terminated on her pregnancy as unconstitutional. However, restriction on Air Hostess not to marry within four years of service was held reasonable.

10 Article 51-a(e) Inserted by the Constitution, forty-second Amendment Act, 1976.
11 AIR Supreme Court 1979.
12 AIR 1981 Supreme Court.

In ***Maya Devi Vs. State of Maharashtra***[13], the requirement that a married woman should obtain her husband's consent before applying for public employment was held invalid and unconstitutional. It was observed that such a requirement is an anachronistic obstacle to women's equality. In ***Prativa Rani Vs. Suraj Kumar***[14], it was held by the Supreme Court that it cannot be said that upon entering into matrimony the Stridhan property of the married women has to be placed in the custody of her husband.

In ***Gita Hariharan Vs. Reserve Bank of India***[15], the Supreme Court while interpreting the word 'after' used in Sec. 6 of the Hindu Minority and Guardianship Act, 1956, held that the mother could be the guardian in be absence of the father.

In ***Vishaka and Others Vs. State of Rajasthan***[16], a writ petition was filed before the Supreme Court by certain social activities and NGO's with the aim of preventing sexual harassment of working women on all work places through judicial process, to fill the vacuum in existing legislation. The immediate cause for the filling of the petition was an incident of alleged brutal gang rape of a social worker in a village of Rajasthan. It was observed by the Court that there is no domestic law to check the civil of sexual harassment of working women at all work places, and therefore the contents of International Conventions and norms are significant for providing guarantee of gender equality and right to with human dignity. International Conventions and norms are to be taken into consideration in the absence of enacted domestic law and when there is no inconsistency between them.

The Court observed that each incident of sexual harassment of women at work place results in violation of fundamental rights of 'Gender Equality' and the 'Right to life and liberty'. Since, neither civil nor penal laws in India

13 I.S.C.R. (1986).
14 AIR (1985) Supreme Court.
15 AIR 1999 Supreme Court.
16 AIR 1997 Supreme Court.

provide specific protection to women from sexual harassment in work places, the Court laid down the guidelines and norms, for effective enforcement of the basic human rights of gender equality and guarantee against sexual harassment and observe more particularly against sexual harassment at work places or other institutions, until a legislation is enacted for the purpose:

It shall be the duty of the employer or the responsible persons in work places or other institutions to prevent or defer the commission of acts of sexual harassment and provide the procedures for the resolution, settlement or prosecution of acts of sexual harassment by taking all steps required.

All employers or persons in charge of work place should take following steps to prevent sexual harassment (a) express prohibition of sexual harassment as defined at the work place should be notified, published and circulated in appropriate ways; (b) the rules/regulations of Government and public sector bodies relating to conduct and discipline should include rules/regulations prohibiting sexual harassment and provide for appropriate penalties in such rules against the offender; (c) as regards private employers, steps should be taken to include the aforesaid prohibitions in the standing orders under the industrial Employment Act of 1946; (d) appropriate work conditions should be provided in respect of work, business, health and hygiene of further ensure that there is no hostile environment.

Where such conduct amounts to a specified offence under the Indian Penal Code or under any other law, the employer shall initiate appropriate action in accordance with law by making a complaint with the appropriate authority. In particular, it should ensure that victims or witness are not victimized or discriminated against while dealing with complaints of sexual harassment. The victims of sexual harassment should have the option to seek transfer of the perpetrator or their own transfer.

Appropriate disciplinary action should be initiated by the employer of the conduct amounts to misconduct as per relevant conduct rules.

An appropriate complaint mechanism should be created in the employer's organization for redness of the complaint made by the victim. Such complaint mechanism should ensure time bound treatment of complaints.

It should be adequate to provide, where necessary, a Complaint Committee, a special counselor on other support service including the maintenance of confidentiality. The committee should be headed by a woman and not less than half of its members should be women. In order prevent the probability of any undue pressure or influence from the senior levels, such Complaints Committee should involve a third party, either N.G.O. or other body who is familiar with the issue of sexual harassment. The Complaints Committee must make an annual report to the Government and the action taken by it.

Employees should be allowed to raise issues of sexual harassment at workmen's meeting and in other appropriate forum and it should be affirmatively discussed in Employer-Employee meeting.

Awareness of the rights of the female employees in this regard should be created in particular by prominently notifying guidelines in a suitable manner.

Where sexual harassment occurs as a result of an act or omission by a third party or outsider, the employer or person in-charge will take all steps necessary and reasonable to assist the affected persons in terms of support and preventing action.

The Central/State Governments are requested to consider adopting suitable measures including legislation to ensure that the guidelines are also observed by the employers in private sector.

The court stated that the 'above guidelines and norms would be strictly observed in all work places for the preservation and enforcement of the right to gender equality of the working women'. These directions would be binding and enforceable in law until suitable legislations are enacted to occupy the field[1].

We know that under the umbrella of the Indian Constitution, there are many Acts, Laws etc. for protecting the women as well as the weaker sections of our country. Hence, it will be nice if we go through those Acts, Laws etc. to find out that whether these are sufficient to give protection to the women of our country?

Most of the time, it is said that the Indian laws towards protection of women are young and lacking confirmation of a judicial strategy, particularly from the highest level of judicial system in order to toughening up crime against women. So, some questionsare roaming around the women protection mechanism.Are available laws sufficient for the protection of women and lacking in implementation only? Does the responsibility shifted to the courts, especially to the Supreme Court to take active role in the process of protection of women? Can it be said that Indian Judges have finally accepted their moral and constitution duty to activate the anti women exploitation laws? Whether this portrayed as human rights protection or matter of public interest or pro-women activism does not matter? Is it correct that the organs of the Governments are now ready to take active role in the process of women protection particularly working women?

❑❑❑

CHAPTER

2 Evolution of Women Rights and Protection

2.1 Introduction

In India the history speaks that the women are considered as a divine force but the multi-cultured Indian society placed the women at different positions. Thus, there is no uniform status of women in the Indian society. However, civilization showed the overall upliftment of women's position. The Indian philosophy poses the women with dual character. On the one hand she is considered aggressor and represents 'shakti'.

On the one hand, Goswami Tulsidas in his famous Holy book 'Ram Charit Manas' inscribes women as the right thing for punishment and compared her with drum, ridiculous, sudra and animal but on the other hand Manu believes that the place where women are respected the God himself live there. To suppress women she was devoid of education in a planned way by man dominated Indian society. It was told by Brahmins that if the words of Vedas are heard by women and sudra even by mistake then melted glass should be poured into their ears. This was a pre-decided conspiracy against women for the continuance of male dominance in the society.

To study the position of women before the independence period, it is very necessary to discuss the position of women during the Vedic period, Post Vedic period and Medieval period.

2.2 Position of Women in Pre-independence Period

Position of women can be traced and understood under the following periodical study:

2.2.1 Vedic Period

The position of women was glorious on account of freedom and equality. During this period the women participated in every walk of life. Women studied in gurukul and enjoyed liberty in every sphere. In Upnisad wife regarded as true companion of husband. The wife has been blessed to live as a queen in the husband's house in Rigveda. This shows the high status of women. The wife has called the root of prosperity, enjoyment and Dharma in Mahabharat. The man was not religiously competent to perform religious duties without his wife. There was absence of *pardah* system, right to select life partners. However the system of polygamy and dowry was prevalent in upper class only. There was no prohibition in the remarriage of widow and also no discrimination between a boy and girl. As a result girls were permitted to undergo thread ceremony (Upnayan Sanskar).

2.2.2 Post Vedic Period

During the post-vedic period the women had suffered drastic hardship and restrictions as propounded by Manu, He attempted to set up male dominated society by increasing the authority of men. The birth of a girl was treated as a disaster for the family. Girls were not allowed to undergo thread ceremony (Upnayana Sanskar). During this period pre-puberty marriage system was originated, thus the marriageable age of girls belonging to ruling class were allowed to receive education, training in military science and administration. On the other hand Manu beloved that where the women are respected, there all deities are pleased and where they are dishonoured there all religious activities fruitless.

Surprisingly in the post-vedic period the women's right to property was recognized and the concept of 'Stridhan' prevailed.

2.2.3 Medieval Period

The women position was further degraded during the Medieval Period with invasions on India by Alexander and the Huns. Society observed security threats with invading soldiers roaming countryside.

Consequently women were placed behind the veil. Women were deprived of education and participation in community affairs. During the medieval period the social evils like child marriage, sati, female infanticide mushroomed extensively, further social curse like dowry had become inevitable particularly in Rajasthan. Thus during this period the women were oppressed in every sphere.

2.2.4 British Period

In the British period the position of women had undergone drastic changes mainly due to western impact on the Indian society. The concept of equality, liberty and individual secularism although arose but limited to ruling class. Two major movements took place during the British regime. These are:.

2.2.4.1 Social Reforms Movement and Position of Women

This movement emerged during the 19th century and raised the question of equal status of women. Social reformers showed the concern regarding problems of sati, prohibition on re-marriage, denial of right to property, child marriage and education to women. Swami Vivekananda, Dayanand Saraswati and Anne Besant were of the opinion that the old vedic period should be revived which was ideal for women's status. The father of nation Mr. M. K. Gandhi strongly criticized the system of child marriage, Sati, prohibition of widow's re-marriage and Devdasi system.

2.2.4.2 Indian National Movement and Women

The nationalist movement drew the attention of a large number of people and generated confidence among women to raise their voice against oppressive system. In 1927, All Women's Conference was formed and it proved to a crucial movement towards the right to equality of women.

Consequently a number of legislation were enacted like Widow's Remarriage Act, Child Marriage Act and Hindu Women's Right to Property Act, which intended to eradicate certain social evils. Even, provisions of Industrial laws were appropriately amended to restore the status of women which prevailed during the Vedic period. The establishment of crèches, reduction of working hours, prohibition on night working hours and restriction to work in mines were introduced under the banner of nationalist movement.

It is submitted that during the British period public awareness was created while women's political and social participation attained movement.

2.3 Position of Women in the Post-Independence Period: Women's Movement

Various thinkers have propounded the women's subordination in different perceptions with different approaches. It is true that women have subordination rather lower status in the field of politics, economics and education. Even in society they have been placed below the men. To end this subordination and different perceptions three major ideological movements of women emerged. These are:

1. Liberal Movement
2. Radical Movement
3. Socialist movement

During the ancient times dowry was considered as a custom in our country. The custom however became a social evil with the passage of time. This social evil has taken lives of many innocent brides for its non fulfillment. Deaths of young brides through suicide or homicide following disputes over the dowry are increasingly a feature of Indian society.

Marriages in Indian are usually arranged by parents and the wife become a member of the husband's family, in most cases moves in with them. Since most marriages are arranged with the assistance of third parties, the family generally does not know each other well. Nevertheless, the newly wedded bride is expected to switch her principal loyalty overnight to her husband's family. The husband's family may make little accommodation to the bride, but expect her to adjust to them. Since they are now supporting her, the husband's family believes that she must be considerate to their wishes. If they think she is not, they may feel justified in treating her harshly, even violently. In the early stages of a marriage, a new bride who is being ill-treated by her husband's family may not seek help from her own parents because they will already have counseled her that a period of adjustment to her new situation may be needed. If she does complain, unless the abuse is repeated or extreme, most parents would probably be reluctant to intercede on her behalf with the in-laws or husband. This reflects the Hindu norm that once a girl is married, her parents have only limited rights to a say in her new family's personal affairs. They might also hope that some mutual adjustment might occur between the bride and her new family so that there would be a reduction in harassment and ill-treatment. If the girl returns to her parent's house because of quarrels with her husband, this brings shame on her parents' family and prevents the marriage of any of her sisters. Moreover, she cannot take part in any religious ceremonies without her spouse. For all these reasons an abused wife may not expect much support from her parents and may only get support from her parents and may only get support in more extreme cases. These marriage arrangements reflect the general subordinate and powerless position of younger women, and pattern of domestic violence in India are indicative of this position.

The practice of dowry has its roots in the most common rite associated with a Hindu marriage (the majority of Indians are Hindus), 'Kanyadan', the act or giving the bride to the groom (the word literally means the act of giving or donating a virgin to the groom on an auspicious day). It is recommended in the shastras (certain rules prescribed in Hindu philosophy) that the bride be adorned with jewellary and then given away. According to the shastras, the ritual gift remains in complete until the groom and his parents are given 'dakshina', a token gift in their honour. This supposed to be in recognition of the fact that the bridegroom and his kin deserve to be honoured (and financially compensated) for accepting the girl into their field. The existence of unearned and easy money in our society today has led to an unhealthy competition among people for getting rich fast by hook or by crook. This unwholesome longing has not only encouraged and fostered materialistic tendencies but also considerably undermined our age-old moral values. Sad to say, this social and moral disorder has a devastating effect on middle classes, placed in a situation where they even found it different to afford the bare necessaries of life, they now began to crave for luxuries. This intense craving coupled with avenues for getting rich quickly. They restored to coercion and blackmail by compelling young brides, parents to dish out money and more money after marriage. Thus, women who has been traditionally regarded as the preserver of social order and standard bearer of decency and social morality, is now subjected to inhuman and immoral treatment in case her parents failed to meet the ever-increasing demands of her husband and his parents. Needless to say such treatment of women, what is the outcome of dowry syndrome, is a bolt on our society.

Despite of the above, now in this twenty first century conditions prevailing in the societies are not much different. Still now in our society, we find a prevalent practice, particularly of poor parents to prevent the birth of female child. The most astonishing statistics shows that in a famous hospital in Mumbai, the pre-sex determination test revealed that during 1990-1995, nearly 8000 pregnant women want to give birth to a female child. But to prevent this 7690 of them under went abortion violating article 21 of the constitution.

In the modern era women are facing serious troubles in the field of industry also. Labour problems specifically for the women labourer of our country, constituted a serious menace to our society and needs solution. The maximum numbers of workers are illiterate and poor and therefore unconscious of their rights. The socio-economic status of the workers is far below the employer's. As such, they could not exercise their free will in negotiating with the employer for employment. The employer is taking advantage of the poor conditions with regard to wages, hours of work, leave etc. The workers are left with no-choice but to accept such terms and conditions because service is the sole means of earning their livelihood.

2.4 Women Rights under International Laws

Gender equality and empowerment of women is recognizes globally as key instrument element to achieve progress in all areas. It is one of the eight Millennium Development goals to which world leaders agreed at the Millennium Summit held in New York in 2000. The charter of the United Nations signed in 1945 is the first international agreement that proclaimed gender equality as a fundamental right. Ever since there had seen many conventions, programmes and goals to help humankind by conferring on them human rights which are "universal, indivisible, interdependent and interrelated".

The 'Preamble' of United Nations lays down "*to re-affirm faith in fundamental human rights, in the dignity and worth of the human person, in the equal rights of men & women and of nations large and small*". It clearly demonstrate the UN objectives about the position of women.

Article 1 of the charter lays down that one of the purposes of the United Nations is *"to achieve international co-operation in solving international problems of economic, social, cultural or humanitarian character, and in promoting and encouraging respect for human rights and for fundamental freedoms for all, without any distinction as to race, sex, language or religion."*

Article 8 of the charter lays down that the United Nations shall place no restrictions on the eligibility of men and women to participate in any capacity & under conditions of equality in its principal & subsidiary organs.

Article 13 of the charter throws reflection for promoting international co-operation in the economic, social, cultural, educational and health fields, and assisting in the realization of human rights and fundamental freedoms for all without distinction as to race, sex, language or religion.

Article 55 of the charter speaks for universal respect & observance of human rights and fundamental freedoms for all without distinction as to race, sex, language or religion.

The principle of equal rights of men & women has been incorporated in the *Universal Declaration of Human rights. Article 1* of this Declaration lays down that "*all human beings are born free and equal in dignity and rights*". *Article 2* of the Declaration lays down that "*everyone is entitled to all the rights and freedom set forth in this Declaration, without distinction of any kind*". Including sex. It clearly provides that all the rights and fundamental freedoms incorporated in the UDHR are available equally to both men & women without any distinction. This is the basic principle and as such has been incorporated in both the international covenants i.e. *International covenant on Civil & Political right* and *International Covenant on Economic, Social & Cultural Rights.* In addition, the principle of equal rights of men and women, has been found mention in the following international human rights instruments:

1. The commission on the status of women (1946)
2. Convention concerning for equal remuneration for men and women by Indian Labour Organization (1951)

3. Convention on the political rights of women including the right to vote (1952)
4. Convention for suppression for traffic in person and of the exploitation of the prostitution of others (1949)
5. Convention on the nationality of the married women (1957)
6. United Nation Convention on consent to marriage, minimum age for marriage & registration of marriage (1962)
7. International convention on the Elimination of all forms of Racial Discrimination (1965) (ICERD).

2.4.1 Women Rights and Impact of CEDAW in India

As per a U.N. Report of 1980 women constitute fifty percent of world's population. They perform two-third of work hours but receive one-tenth of world's income and own one-hundredth percent of world's property. They constitute more than half of the Indian population inspite of large-scale female infanticide. Due to lack education and societal subdued status which appears to them as normal, many do not even realize that they are entitled to equality, let alone freedom from abuse and exploitation.

The Vienna Declaration on Elimination of all forms of Discrimination against Women (CEDAW), 1979 ratified by United Nations on 18.12.1979 takes note of the discrimination against women and mandates ass member States to take all appropriate measures including legislation to modify or abolish gender-based discrimination in the existing laws, regulations, customs and practice. All forms of discrimination on ground of gender are violative of fundamental freedoms and human rights. The General Assembly of United Nations on 04.12.1986 adopted resolutions on 'Right to development' recognizing the right of every woman to develop. At the local level, The Constitution of India prohibits discrimination only on the basis of sex. Further it empowers the state to take all necessary steps for the upliftment of women. In ***Government***

A.P. Vs. P.B. Vijay Kumar[1] for the first time the Supreme Court laid down that Article 15 (3) can be read into Article 16 to sustain any special provision favouring women. The reasoning is as follow.

"*...........The ambit of Article 16 (2) is more limited in scope than Article 15(1) because it is confined to employment or office under the State. Article 15(1), on the other hand, covers the entire range of State activities,..... Since Article 16 does not touch upon any special provision for women being made by the State, it cannot in any manner derogate from the power conferred upon the state in this connection under Article 15(3). This power conferred by Article 15(3) is wide enough to cover the entire range of State activity including employment under the State. ....To says that under Article 15(3), job opportunities for women cannot be created would be to cut at the very root of the underlying inspiration behind this Article. Making special provisions for women in respect of employment or posts under the State is an integral part of Article 15(3). This conferred under Article 15(3), is not whittled down in any manner by Article 16*"

The concept of equality of women does not mean that the State is denied the right to provide preferential treatment for women in all State activity. In ***Mutthamma Vs. Union of India,***[2] and ***Air India Vs. Nargesh Meerza***[3] the Supreme Court struck down discriminatory service conditions requiring female employees to obtain government permission before marriage and denying married and pregnant women the right to be employed.,

By displaying activist role in ***Vishaka Vs. State of Rajasthan***[4] (noticing the legislative and executive vacuum to prevent sexual harassment at the workplace), the Supreme Court relying on the provisions in the Beijing Statement of Principles of the Independence of the Judiciary, 1995 CEDAW, 1979, and the protection of Human Rights Act 1993

1 AIR 1995 SC 1648 : 1995 SCC (4) 520
2 AIR 1979 SC 1868 : 1980 SCR (1) 668
3 AIR 1981 SC 1829 : 1982 SCR (1) 438
4 AIR 1997 SC 3011 : (1998) BHRC 261: (1997) 3 LRC 361

held that women have right to gender equality to work with dignity and to a working environment available and protected from sexual harassment or abuse. It was categorically held that every incident of sexual harassment at the work place results in violation of fundamental right to life and liberty. The same view was reiterated in ***Apparel Export Promotion Council Vs. A.K. Chopra,***[5] and it was further held that sexual harassment is misconduct in service law making the delinquent person liable for dismissal.

Hence, it is crystal clear that the judiciary has been very prominent in this dedication to protecting the rights of women. However, reality is still to be quelled. The declaration of rights by the judiciary is definitely the first step. But it is a very long way away from achieving these rights in substance. In spite of the influx of women into virtually all sectors, they are still abused and exploited (even sexually) at all levels. The employment statistics show that in agricultural sector of our country seventy percent of the labour is women. The dominant classes of the rural areas seldom treat agricultural labourers as human beings and at slightest opportunity they exploit them. In payment of wages and supply of food etc. the women are discriminated. In blue color and white color employment sectors there is increasing presence of women as employees at all levels. The insult verbally or by sign language is tolerated by women in silence for the fear of losing respect in the society. All the cases of harassment are not reported.

At the same time, even in the face of this stark reality, it cannot be denied that the judiciary has often preempted legislation in areas where declaration of rights and protection of interests are deeply needed. The judiciary has been staunch in its punishments of rapists and perpetrators of domestic violence and dowry harassment. They have come down heavily on discrimination of women in all fields. The judiciary has truly strived to protect the right to life, liberty and security of the Indian women. Perhaps when this is

5 AIR 1999 SC 625 : 2000(1) SLJ SC 65

achieved more can be accorded to efforts aimed to bring about altitudinal changes and holistic development of Indian women.

2.5 Women Rights under the National Commission for Women Act 1990

It is said that the best way to know about society, a civilization and a culture, try to know as much possible about the women. In India, women have come a long way from the rare women scholars and sages of the Vedic age to the women in different sectors of society and civilization today, such as the armed forces, arts, information technology, politics and a number of similar sectors which have traditionally been male dominated, while simultaneously balancing the roles of wife, mother and daughter. While Indian women have fought against the patriarchal Indian society and triumphed at many levels, cases of rape, dowry deaths, female infanticide, sexual harassment at workplaces, female illiteracy, and similar problems are still rampant in Indian society. Women in India, as is well known, have never been treated well even at home or while at work. The matter has all along been agitated inside and outside the Parliament by Parliamentarians, by common men, by organizations and societies for the welfare of the women. Several Commissions had been set up by the Government to look into the matter of status of women in Indian society. Successive Commissions on women had noted in their repots the unequal status of women obtaining in every sphere of life and had suggested me setting up of an agency to fulfill the surveillance functions as well as to facilitate redressal of the grievances of women. Several women activities and voluntary action groups had also been making persistent demands for setting up of a commission for women. It was in this backdrop that the Committee on the Status of Women in India (CSWI) the establishment of the National Commission for Women to fulfill the surveillance functions and to facilitate redressal of grievances and to accelerate the socio-economic development of women was planned.

The principle of gender equality is enshrined in the Indian Constitution. The Preamble, promotes Equality of status and of opportunity; the Fundamental Rights enshrined in Part III of the Indian Constitution and Directive Principles enshrined in Part IV of the Constitution all promote gender equality. The Constitution not only grants equality to women but has also made special provisions for ensuring equality Thus, as per the recommendations of the CSWI and in order to uphold the mandate of the Constitution and keeping in view the desirability of women at the national level the National Commission for Women Bill, 1990 was introduced in the Lok Sabha on 22nd May, 1990. Later on this Bill became an Act to be known as the National Commission for Women Act, 1990 *w.e.f.* 30-8-1990, and in the line of the Act, the National Commission for Women (NCW), was set up in January 1992, as a statutory body under the National Commission for Women Act, 1990 (Act No. 20 of 1990 of Government of India) to carry out the mandate set by the Act as well as CSWI.

2.5.1 Relevance of National Commission for Protection of Women's Rights in India

Women as a class neither belong to a minority group nor are they regarded as a backward class. India has traditionally been a patriarchal society and therefore women have always suffered from social handicaps and disabilities. It thus became necessary to take certain ameliorative steps in order to improve the condition of women in the traditionally male dominated society. The Constitution does not contain any provision specifically made to favor women as such. Though Art. 15 (3), Art. 21 and Art. 14 are in favor of women; they are more general in nature and provide for making any special provisions for women, while they are not in themselves such provisions. The Supreme Court through interpretive processes has tried to extend some safeguards to women. Through judgments in cases such as ***Bodhisattwa Gautam Vs. Subra Chakraborty***[6] and the ***Chairman Rly Board Vs.***

6 AIR 1996 SC 922

Chandrima Das[7] Case, where rape was declared a heinous crime, as well as the landmark judgment in ***Vishaka Vs. State of Rajasthan,***[8] the courts have tried to improve the social conditions of Indian women. But these have hardly sufficed to improve the position of women in India. Thus, in light of these conditions, the Committee on the Status of Woman (India) as well as a number of NGOs, social workers and experts, who were consulted by the Government in 1990, recommended the establishment of the apex body for woman.

2.6 Women Rights and Human Right Protective Institutions

The setting up of a national institution is one of the most effective means to perform the various functions relating to the implementation of human rights. Such an institution raises human rights awareness through education, training, research and conduct impartial investigation into alleged violations. It may also prove or secure effective redress either by negotiation with the government concerned or may assist the victims by providing relief through a court of law. The domestic institution of human rights may also influence the legislators to preserve human rights in the widest sense of the term. It may also monitor government compliance with treaty commitments.

The idea of the creation of an impartial institution of human rights in the States was initiated by the UNESCO in as early in 1946. The Secretariat in the Memorandum, 'Supervision and enforcement of Human Rights' in 1947 had suggested for the creation of such a body in the states.

In 1966, the General Assembly adopted a resolution for considering the advisability of the proposal for the creation of a national commission on human rights to perform certain functions pertaining to the observance of the Covenant on Civil and Political Rights and the Economic, Social and

7 AIR 2000 SC 988
8 AIR 1997 SC 3011

cultural Rights and the Economic, Social and cultural Rights.[9] The commission in 1970, agreed that the question of the establishment of the national commission of human rights should be decided by each government in the light of the traditions and institutions of its own country.[10] The commission in 1978 again emphasized the need for the creation of a national institution. But all these attempts went in vain. States paid little head towards them. Many States opined that such an Intuition may condemn the action of the state's executives and judiciary if the occasion would demand.

The World Conference on Human Rights in 1993 realising the importance of such an institution or commission, stated that the World Conference on Human Rights urges Governments to strengthen national structures, institutions and organs of society which play a role in promoting and safeguarding human rights.

India has shown keen interest in the past in establishing or strengthening a national institution for the promotion and protection of human rights before the Third Committee of the General Assembly. It introduced a draft resolution wherein it emphasized the importance of the integrity and independence of such national institutions. In the draft resolution it also requested the Secretary- General of the United Nations to submit a report to the General Assembly in two years regarding the functioning of the various kinds of national institutions and their contribution towards implementing human rights instruments. The interest shown by India in the establishment of a national institution for the protection and promotion of human rights was laudable. The interest shown in the international forum implied that it was in favour of establishing such an institution. However, at that time no such institution was established.

In early 1990(s) India felt the need of establishing a commission as a positive response to the criticisms of the

9 General Assembly Resolution 2200 (c) XXI, dated December, 1966.
10 Report of the Commission on Human Rights of 26th Session, Dec. (1970)

foreign Governments in the Context of political unrest and violence in Punjab, Jammu & Kashmir, North-East and Andhra Pradesh. In addition to the pressure from the foreign countries, pressure was added from the domestic front as well for the creation of a National Human Rights Commission, because of the awareness among the people for the protection of human rights. All this led the Government to decide to exact a law to establish a Human Rights Commission.

2.6.1 Protection of Women under Protection of Human Rights Act 1993

The Human Rights Commission Bill was introduced in the look on May 14, 1992. The bill was referred to the Standing committee of the parliament on Home Affairs. However, in view of the urgency of the commission due to the pressure from foreign countries and from the domestic front, the president of India Promulgated and ordinance on 28th September 1993, for the creation of a National Commission on Human Rights (NCHR) and commissions at State level, after having made certain amendments, this bill was passed by both the Houses of the Parliament to replace the Ordinance. After receiving the assent of president on January 8, 1994, this bill converted into an Act. The purpose of the enactment of the Act is to provide for the constitution of a National Human Rights commission, State Human Rights Commission in States and Human Rights Courts for better protection of human Rights and for matter connected therewith or incidental thereto.

Section 2(d) of the Act defined the expression 'human rights' by stating that human right means the rights relating to life, liberty, equality and dignity of the individuals guaranteed by the constitution or embodied in the international Covenants and enforceable by courts in India. The above definition limits the scope of the functioning of NHRC, India ratified the two covenants-International Covenant on civil and Political Rights and Economic, Social and Cultural Rights, but these covenants in the Act are purely cosmetic. The decisive words are: *"and enforceable by courts in India"*. These words limit human rights strictly to the fundamental rights embodied in Part-III of the Constitution which are enforceable by the Courts in India. The fact is that they are more limited than human rights in the covenants. Further the Commission's mandate does not extend to those human rights which have been recognized in international treaties signed and ratified by India besides the fundamental rights. A pertinent question arises as to why the commission was established for the protection of fundamental rights when they being constitutional rights are enforceable before the courts?

It appears that the main purpose of the enactment was to provide better protection of human rights. At the time of passing of the Bill there was growing concern in the country and abroad about issues relating the human rights. Having regard to this Government was reviewing the existing laws, procedures and system of administration of justice with a view to bringing about greater accountability and transparency in them and devising efficient and effective methods of dealing with the situation. It was thought that the commission would provide immense help in this regard. Wide-ranging discussions were held in a number of conferences and seminars and after taking into account the views expressed therein, the Bill was brought before the Parliament.

The Act set up a National Human Rights Commission and the State Human Rights Commission in the States and the Human Rights courts in the districts.

The protection of Human Rights Act was enacted in 1993 to provide for the Constitution of NHRC, the State Human Rights Commission and Human Rights Courts in districts with a specific purpose i.e. for 'better protection of Human Rights'. Here, a question also arises : has the NHRC been able to protect the human rights, or to say, has it achieved the purposes for which it was enacted ? No doubt, the NHRC has made an enquiry into thousands of complaints of the violations of human rights; if has also investigated a number of serious cases of human rights violations, and it has submitted reports to the Government wherein it has made a number of recommendations suggesting measures to be taken to curb the human rights violations but the Commission has been least effective to protect human rights. It is so because the Commission is simply an investigative and recommendatory body. Further, the commission does not have powers of prosecution. The National Human Rights Commission, therefore, does not have teeth. It does not provide any remedy other than what has already been provided under the Constitution by way of fundamental rights.

In order to remove the deficiency and to make it a more effective instrument for the protection and promotion of human rights in the country, the NHRC has set up an advisory committee headed by the former Chief Justice of India, A.M. Ahmadi to suggest revisions to the Protection of Human Rights Act 1993. The seven members Committee[11] submitted its report on October19, 1999 wherein it recommended for the financial autonomy of the National and State Human Rights Commissions, and for the change in the composition of the NHRC with two judicial and three non-judicial members of whom one should be a woman. The Committee also recommended some valuable suggestions for making the Act more effective. The recommendations of the Committee were accepted by the commission in February, 2000.

The Commission after discussion formulated its views on the amendments that are required to be made to the Act keeping in view major impediments and structural inadequacies experienced by the Commission.

It is to be noted that situation for protection of human rights is not likely to improve even if the propound amendments are accepted by the Government[12].

11 Other members of the committee are justice Rajender Sachar, Former Chief Justice of Delhi High Court, Mr. P.C. Bala Krishna Menon, former Chief Justice of Himachal Pradesh High Court, DR. Rajiv Dhawan, Senior Supreme Court Advocate, Prof. N.R. Madhava Menon, member of the Law Commision of India, Dr. Ramaiah Former Law and Justice Secretary and Sankar Sen, D.G. Investigation Division in the NHRC.

12 Annual Report of NHRC of 1999-2000

It the denials of human rights are analyzed, one would find that the complex political, economic, social, psychological and moral factors are responsible to a large extent. The factors along with many other deep-rooted customs and superstitions may be regarded as fundamental causes for the denial of human rights. So, the first and the primary task in furthering the human rights is the study of the real situations, practical problems and actual obstacles.

It is true that no national institution or human rights Commission, however effective it might be, can provide food, shelter, clotting, education and health facilities to the wanting millions. It is the duty of the Government to provide these basic rights which are essential for the promotion of the human dignity. A culture of human rights can be achieved by making people aware of their rights.

In India the full realization of human rights is a distant dream. It cannot be easily or quickly achieved. Although recent years have seen remarkable efforts of the Government to promote human rights like many other developing countries, much has to be done for the better protection of human rights. Struggle for human rights mush continue with greater vigour. Although other social and economic problems like poverty[13] , illiteracy, unemployment, population growth and law and order have surpassed the importance due to human rights, all efforts are required to made to make the people aware of their rights. The strong will and determination, for the promotion of human dignity and worth will certainly make the human rights movement a great success.

Women and the growing violence against them have become pervasive in the society. The patriarchal system of the society and the approach and attitude of men towards women as downtrodden has fuelled and developed violence and various crimes against women. Despite having so many enactments and legislations at the international and regional level which

13 About 26 percent of India's populations live in abject poverty, According to world Bank Standard ($1 per day/per capita income) about 525 million people in India are living below poverty line.

deal with women, the oppressed and poor conditions of women have not been improved and they are still facing all types of atrocities, violence and abuses. This proves the failure of the legislative, executive and judicial machinery in the country to protect the women from the hands of perpetrators and also fails to provide respect to women in the patriarchal form of society. The inequality status prevalent between the men and women cannot be bridged by just enacting and enforcing legislations unless public support is sought for. It has also been clear from the situation that century old practice existing in the society cannot be eliminated in few days. It will take a lot of time to make people understand and realize their rights, equality and humanity and make them aware of their development through education, awareness programmes etc. These legislations enacted are not supported by the will of the people. They public is not aware of such steps which have been taken for the upliftment of women in the society and hence it faces great resistance and opposition from the conservative thought of the society. To improve the status of the women in the society, prevent the violence against women and protect them is the need of the hour. Since the conservative social thinking is deeply rooted in the society, there is a need that such legislations should to be enacted with the support and strong public willingness and opinion.

❑❑❑

CHAPTER

3 Global Initiatives for Protection of Women Rights

3.1. Introduction

The United Nations, from the very day of its inception from 1945 till date worked to secure women's legal equality. The United Nations have chalked out a comprehensive programme by means of various conventions to uplift and develop the status of women in the field of education, politics including the position in social life with the formation of the Commission on Human Rights and the Commission on the status of Women in 1946 and the adoption of the Universal Declaration of Human rights in 1948. It was found that in many parts of the world the women have constantly been denied equality in law and also in practice. They are compelled to live under male dominated world and are subjected to variety of discriminations. As a result the United Nations hasincorporated a series of treaties and conventions to achieve the equal the equal legal, social and political rights of women worldwide.

The Commission on the Status of Women, a functional Commission of the Economic and Social Council, was established in 1946. The membership of the Commission originally fifteen and expanded to 21 in 1961. Since 1991, the Commission has 45 members. The Commission meets once in two years in Vienna to examine Women's progress towards equality throughout the world. Its functions primarily to prepare recommendations and to make reports to the Economic and Social Council on the promotion of women's rights in political, social and educational fields. It also makes recommendations to the Council on problems requiring attention in the field of women's rights. It also drafts and develops proposals to give effect to those recommendations aimed at improving the status of women in law and practice.

The Commission recognized that women could not make progress in any field unless they shared decision making power with men. In 1449, the Commission initiated work on the Commission on the Political Rights of Women. The Convention, the first legal instrument dealing exclusively with women's rights was adopted by the General Assembly in 1952. The Commission was also helpful in adopting the Convention on the Elimination of All Forms of Discrimination Against Women by the General Assembly in 1979. The Commission made efforts to prepare a Convention on the Nationality of Married of Women which was adopted by the General Assembly in 1957. In addition to above, the Commission has focused on many topics relating to women such as role of women in development, family planning, education and economic rights of women.

3.2 Women, Human Rights and Universal Declarations

Human beings are rational beings. They by virtue of their being human possess certain basic and inalienable rights which are commonly known as human rights. Human rights being essential for all round development of the individuals in the societyshould be necessarily protected and be made available to all the individuals. They need for protection has arisen because of inevitable increase in the control over men's action by the governments which by no means can be regarded as desirable. The consciousness on the part of the human beings as to their rights has also necessitated the protection by the States. It has been relished that the functions of all the laws whether they are the rules of municipal law on that of international law should be protect them in the interest of humanity.

One of the achievements of the contemporary international law is to recognize human dignity and honour. The individual has come of age in International Law. It has been also realizedthat the International protection of the individuals against the State should no longer be entrusted to the State as his guardian *in litem*. This is clearly reflected from a number of conventions of varying scope which have been adopted under the auspices of the United Nations Organization in the last fifty eight years or so. A number of declarations adopted by the United Nations or its specialized agencies also go to prove that their members have pledged themselves to achieve the promotion of Universal respect for and observance of human rights and fundamental freedoms. States themselves are conscious of the rights of the human beings. They in order to protect the rights have made regional agreements by making conventions.

3.3 The Achievements of the United Nations in the field of Women's Right Since 1948

The charter of the United Nations had expressed the desirability of promoting and encouraging respect for human rights and fundamental freedoms for all without distinction as to race, sex, language or religion. But the basic question on which there existed difference of opinion was that what those rights and freedoms are? The Universal Declaration of Human Rights in 1948 laid down a number of rights as a common standard of achievements of all peoples and for all nations. However, rights enshrined therein were not legally binding on States since it was not an international agreement. The Declaration simply stipulated the basic principles of human rights and freedoms. The two Covenants - International Covenant on Civil and Political Rights and International Covenant on Economic, Social and Cultural Rights – were legally binding instruments but they are no means the only human rights treaties drafted and adopted under the auspices of the United Nations. A number of conventions have been adopted under the auspices of the United Nations to prevent the commission of certain acts because of their being inhuman and because their commission is against the dignity and worth of human persons such as genocide, apartheid, slavery and slave trade, forced labour, torture, cruel, inhuman and degrading treatment or punishment, and traffic in persons. The United Nations has been successful in the adoption of the conventions specifically some of these aspects are as follows:

1. Universal Declaration on Human Rights, 1948;
2. Convention of the Political Rights of Women, 1953;
3. Convention of the Nationality of Married Women, 1957;
4. Declaration on Elimination of Discrimination Against Women, 1967;
5. Convention on the Elimination of All Forms of Discrimination against Women, 1979;
6. Declaration on the Elimination of Violence Against Women, 1993;
7. Optional Protocol to the convention on the Elimination of Discrimination against Women, 1999;
8. Commission on the Status of Women.

3.3.1 Universal Declaration on Human Rights, 1948

The Preamble clearly declares as the common standard of achievement of all peoples and all nations. If this declaration is to be construed as a recommendation a question arises as to whom this recommendation has been made. It is not addressed either to the Members or to the States or to the Government. According to Kelsonthe Declaration is intended to be a "Common standard of achievement for all peoples and all nations, and that the duty society shall strive to", thus, the General Assembly recommends to every individual and every organ of the society to do something with respect to the Human Rights laid in the declaration.

Thus, the Preamble of declaration shows the importance and necessity of having faith in the fundamental human rights and dignity of individual including men and women.

According to Article 1 of the said declaration- all human being are born free and equal in dignity and rights. They should act with understanding and spirit of brotherhood.

According to Article 2 of this declaration-everyone is entitled to all the rights and freedom set forth in this Declaration without discrimination of any kind such as race, colour, sex, language, religion, political or other opinion, national or social origin, property or other status. Therefore, no discrimination shall be made on the basis of the political, jurisdictional status of the country to which a person belongs.

Article 3 of the said declaration deals with the right to life, liberty and security. This Article says that everyone has right to life, liberty and security of person irrespective of the country or territory he/she belongs. Further Article 7 of the said declaration provides that all are equal before law and are entitled without any discrimination, to equal protection of law.

Article 16 of this declaration provides that men and women of full age without any limitation due to race, nationality or religion, have the right to marry and to form a family. Thus, the rights to marry, form a family and dissolution of marriage and also marriage shall be entered into only with the free and full consent of the intending parties. It has been affirmed that the family is a basic unit of society which is entitled to protection by the State.

3.3.2 Convention of the Political Rights of Women 1953

The General Assemble of the United Nations had adopted the Convention on the Rights of Women on 20th December,

1952 which came into force on 7th July, 1954. In view of the charter of United Nations, the convention emphasizes regarding recognition of the principles of equality in the public employment and also representation of men and women equally in the Government of his/her country or indirectly by means of freely chosen voting system.

By virtue of Article I of the said convention, the women shall be entitled to vote all elections on equal terms with men and there should not by any discrimination on any ground. Women shall be eligible for election to all elected institutions as provided under Article II of the convention. According to the Article III of the said convention women shall be entitled to hold public office and perform public functions on equal terms with men.

3.3.3 Convention of the Nationality of Married Women 1957

Commission on the status of Women prepared draft of the Convention in 1957 which was adopted by General Assembly of the United Nations and was called Convention on the Nationality of Married Women, 1957. Various commitments were undertaken by the contracting parties. Briefly are as under:

1. Article 1: Neither the celebration nor the dissolution of marriage between one of its nationals and an alien, nor the change of nationality by the husband during the marriage, shall automatically, affect the nationality of wife;
2. Article 2: Neither the voluntary acquisition of the nationality of another State nor the renunciation of its nationality by one of its nationals shall prevent the retention of its nationality by the wife of such national;
3. Article 3, Para 1: The alien wife of one of its nationals may, at her request, acquire the nationality of her husband through specially privileged naturalization procedures. However, the grant of such nationality

may be subject in such limitations as may be imposed in the interest of national security or public policy;

4. Article 3, Para 2: The present convention shall not be constructed as affecting legislation or judicial practice by which the alien wife of one of its nationals may, at her request acquire her husband's nationality as a matter of right.

3.3.4 Declaration of Elimination of Discrimination Against Women 1967

On 7th December, 1967, the General Assembly of the United Nations adopted the Declaration on Elimination of Discrimination against Women, 1967.

The Preamble of this Declaration states that despite the existence of various conventions protecting women the discrimination against women continues. This Declaration is pledged to eradicate the discrimination against women in any form. It re-affirms the principle of equality of right of women in worldwide scenario.

3.3.5 Convention on the Elimination of all Forms of Discrimination Against Women 1979

To achieve the provisions incorporated in Article 1, 2 and 55 of the chapter of the United Nations Declaration on the Elimination of discrimination against Women, 1967 was adopted by the General Assembly of the United Nations which consequently paved the way to the adoption of the Convention on the Elimination of All Forms of Discrimination against Women, 1979.

By means of the said Convention it was reiterated that the state parties to the International Covenant on Human rights are under obligation to provide in equal rights to men and women in civil, political, social, economic and also cultural field.

The State Parties to the convention were fully convinced that discrimination is an important factor causing obstruction in the development and advancement of women with men at National and International level. It was realized that to achieve equality of women with men it is indispensable to bring awareness in the society across the world because it is needed most in the present scenario.

3.3.6 Declaration on the Elimination of Violence Against Women 1993

The General Assembly of the United Nations adopted Declaration on the elimination of Violence against Women, 1993. Notably this declaration is the first of its kind which exclusively dealt with the Elimination of Violence against Women and intended to protect the fundamental rights of freedom of women.

Article I of this Declaration describes Violence as:

'any act of gender based violence that results in or is likely to result in physical, sexual or psychological harm or suffering to women, including threats of such acts, coercion or arbitrary deprivation of liberty, whether occurring in public or private life'.

Thus, this definition of 'violence' includes not only physical or sexual but psychological harm caused on women.

3.3.7 Optional Protocol to the Convention on the Elimination of Discrimination Against Women, 1999

By means of this Protocol it was realized by the State parties to the Convention on the Elimination of all Forms of Discrimination against women, 1979, that there is an urgent need to gear up by all the adequate means ensure full and equal enjoyment of freedom by women of all human rights.

In this context India, who is one of the signatories to this Protocol, has shown parliamentary endeavour in the relevant field, as a result in the year 2005, the Parliament has pleased the enactment to be called the Protection of Women from the domestic Violence Act. However, we are yet to experience its effect in crime graph of domestic violence against women.

Unfortunately, as the crime statistic to be relied India is one of the leading countries in such type of crime.

3.3.8 Commission on the Status of Women

In 1946 the Economic and Social Council established its functional Commission is having the main functions as under:

To prepare and its recommendation relating to measures that are to be taken in promotion of the rights of women in the field of education, politics, civil, social and economic; and

To make recommendation on the matters which are of urgent nature in the field of women's rights.

At present the commission is consisting of 45 members whereas at its inception there were only 15 members. It would be pertinent to refer some relevant important International conferences, namely:

1. Vienna Conference
2. Beijing Conference

3.3.8.1 Vienna Conference

Notably, the commission on the status of women has made significant contribution in the field of women's rights, from its very inception. In 1975, the First world Conference on women was held in Mexico City which raised the themes of Equality, Development and Peace at the International level. However, in 1980, the Second World Conference was held in Copenhagen which added the themes of Education, employment and Health. The Third world Conference on women was held in Nairobi to review and access the achievement during the period commencing from the year 1976 to 1985. From March 29th to 7th April 1989 the Conference was held at Vienna, the commission on the status of women in its thirty-third Session emphasized that serious endeavours must be made to propel the campaign for advancement of women and their rights as the development and advancement of women's rights have been slowed down. During Vienna Conference the Commission on the status of women pledge unanimously on the elimination of various against women and realized that it is a major hurdle to the achievement of equality, development and peace.

3.3.8.2 Beijing Conference

From 4-15 September, 1995 the Fourth World Conference on Women was held in Beijing. In its thirty-seventh Session the Commission on the women expressed a serious concern relating to women's rights.

Therefore a number of U.N. sponsored International Conference on Women proposed programmes in the field of human rights of women.

3.4 Women Under South Asian Association for Regional Co-operation (SAARC)

Besides the United Nations and other international bodies the South Asian Association for Regional Co-operation (SAARC) consisting of seven South Asian countries, has adopted a Convention on Preventing and Combating Trafficking in women and children for Prostitution, in its Eleventh Summit in Kathmandu in January, 2002. Under Article 3 of the said Convention it is provided that State Parties to the Convention shall take effective measures to ensure that Trafficking in any from is an offence under their respective criminal law.

It is submitted that we are yet to achieve desired result in spite of various Conventions. The position of women is really deplorable in the developing countries and India is one of them. In my view the root cause of women's poor status in Indian society is lack of education and economic dependence of women. To raise the women's position in the society, it is essential to make them educated and self- employed.

The existing international conventions on human rights no doubt cover a variety of human rights and fundamental freedoms of individuals but the international community presently facing some new problems which were not even anticipated at the time of the proclamation of the Universal Declarations of Human Rights or at the time of adoption of the International Covenants. For instance, the right to a clean and safe environment is regarded as human rights but the right does not find place neither in any international convention nor in any regional convention. An international convention is required to be adopted under the auspices of the United Nations in this regard as environment degradation jeopardizes the survival of mankind and is also likely to affect the future generation. Similarly, the invasion of information technology on privacy and established moral and ethical standards, and the far reaching implications of artificial procreation made possible by genetic engineering pose new threats to human rights. International co-operation, a powerful engine of the system for the promotion and protection of human rights, is very much required to adopt conventions on these rights so that human beings can live with dignity.

3.5 United Nation and Women

The advancement of women has been a focus of the work of the United Nations since its creation. The Preamble of the charter of the United Nations sets as a basic goal to reaffirm faith in fundamental human rights, in the dignity and worth of the human persons, in the equal rights of men and women.

In the year 1946 the commission, on the status of women, was established to deal women's issues. The Universal Declaration of Human Rights had affirmed the principle of the inadmissibility of discrimination and proclaimed that all human beings are born free and equal in dignity and rights and that everyone is entitled to all the rights and freedoms set forth therein, without distinction of any kind, including distinction based on sex. However, there continued to exist considerable discrimination against women primarily because women and girls face a multitude of constraints imposed by the society not by law. It violated the principle of equality of right said respect of human rights.

The General Assembly on November 7, 1967 adopted a Declaration of Discrimination[1] against women. In order to implement the principle set forth in the Declaration, a Convention on the Elimination of the all forms of discrimination against women was adopted by the General Assembly on December 18, 1979. The Convention often described as an 'International Bill of Rights for Women', came into force in 1981. As on June 16, 2006 the Convention had 183 State Parties. General Assembly Resolution 2263 dated November 7, 1697.

A Convention on the Political Rights of Women was adopted on December 20, 1952 by the General Assembly through a resolution 640 (VII), which came into force on July 7, 1954. Women shall be eligible for election on equal terms with men, without any discrimination, and shall be entitled to hold public office and to exercise all public functions.

Although the International Bill of Human Rights laid down a comprehensive set of rights to which all persons, including women are entitled, additional means for protecting the human rights of women were seen as necessary because the mere fact of their 'humanity' has not been sufficient to guarantee women the protection of their rights. The Preamble to the convention guarantees the protection of their rights. Explains that, despite the existence of other instruments, women still do not have equal rights with men. Discrimination against Women continues to exist in every society.

The convention under Article 1 defines the term discrimination against women as any distinction, exclusion or restriction made on the basis of sex which has the effect or purpose of impairing or nullifying the recognition, enjoyment or exercise of women, irrespective of their marital status, on a basis of qualify of men and women, of human rights

1 CEDAW

and fundamental freedoms in the political, economic, social, cultural, civil or any other field (Article 1).

Hence, the convention under Part III lays down a number of fields where state parties are required to take steps to eliminate discrimination against women which includes the following:

3.5.1 Education

The convention under Article 10 conditions for careers and vocational guidance as to that of men. They shall be provided same access to studies for the achievement of diplomas in educational establishments of all categories in rural as well as in urban areas. This equality shall be provided in pre-school, general, technical, professional and higher technical education as well as in all types of vocational training. Women shall have access to the same curricula, the same examinations, teaching staff with qualifications, teaching staff with qualifications of the same standard and school premises and equipment of the same quality as to that of men, they shall be provided same opportunities as to men in matters relating to scholarship and other study grant. They shall have same opportunities for access to programme of continuing education including adult and functional literacy programmes. They shall have the opportunities to participate actively in sports and physical education.

3.5.2 Employment

The Convention under Article 11 provided that States Parties shall take appropriate measures to eliminate discrimination against women in the field of employment providing same rights, in particular (a) the right to work; (b) right to same employment opportunities; (c) right to free choice of profession and employment; (d) right to equal remuneration including benefits and equal treatment in respect of work of equal value as well as equality of work; (e) the right to social security particularly in cases of retirement, unemployment, sickness, invalidity and old age and other incapacity to work, as well as the right to paid leave; (f) right to protection of health and safety in working conditions. There shall be no discrimination against women on grounds of marriage or maternity.

3.5.3 Health Care

Article 12 of the Convention provides that States Parties shall take steps to eliminate discrimination against women in the field of health care, access to health care services, including those related to family planning.

3.5.4 Economic and Social Life

Article 13 of the Convention provides that discrimination against women shall be eliminated in other areas of economic and social life. They shall be provided, the same rights as to that of men in particular (a) the right of family benefits; (b) the right to bank-loans, mortgages and other forms of financial credit; (c) the right to participate in recreational activities, sports and all aspects of cultural life.

3.5.5 Rural Areas

Article 14 provided elimination of discrimination against women in rural areas. State Parties are required to ensure such women the right:

- to participate in the elaboration and implementation of development planning at all levels;
- to have access to adequate health care facilities, including information counseling and services in family planning;
- to benefit directly from social security programmes;
- to obtain all types of training and education, formal and non-formal, including that relating to functional literacy, as well as the benefit of all community and

extension services, in order to increase their technical proficiency;

- to organize self-help groups and cooperatives in order to obtain equal access to economic opportunities through employment or self-employment;
- to participate in all community activities;
- to have access to agricultural credit and loans, marketing facilities, appropriate technology and equal treatment in land and agrarian reform as well as in land resettlement schemes; and
- to enjoy adequate living conditions.

3.5.6 Equality Before Law

Article 15 of the Convention provides that 'States Parties shall accord to women equality with men before the law'. Women shall have equal rights to conclude contracts and to administer property and State Parties shall treat them equally in all stages of procedure in counts and tribunals. States Parties agree that all contracts and all other private instruments of any kind with a legal effect which is directed at restricting the legal capacity of women shall be deemed null and void. Further, the State Parties shall accord to men and women the same rights with law relating to the movement of persons and the freedom to choose their residence and domicile.

3.5.7 Marriage and Family Relations

Article 16 provides that States Parties shall take all measures to eliminate discrimination against women in all matters relating to marriage and family relations. Women shall be provided:

1. the same right to enter into marriage;
2. the same rights and responsibilities during marriage and at its dissolution;

3. the same rights and responsibilities as parents, in matters relating to their children. In all cases the interests of children shall be paramount;
4. the same rights to decide freely and responsibility on the number and spacing of their children and to have access to the information, education and means to enable them to exercise their rights;
5. the same rights and responsibilities with regard to guardianship, word ship, trusteeship and adoption of children;
6. the same personal rights as husband and wife, including the right to choose a family name, a profession and an occupation;
7. the same rights for both spouses in respect of the ownership, acquisition, management, administration, enjoyment and disposition of property, whether free of charge on for a valuable consideration.

States Parties to the convention condemned discrimination against women in all its forms and agreed to pursue by all appropriate means to eliminate discrimination against women and to this end they undertook:

1. To embody the principle of equality of men and women in their national constitutions or other appropriate legislation if not yet incorporated there in;
2. To adopt appropriate legislative and other measures prohibiting all discrimination against women;
3. To establish legal protection of the rights of women on an equal basis with men;
4. To refrain from engaging on any act on practice of discrimination against women;
5. To take all appropriate measures to eliminate discrimination against women by any person, organization or enterprise;
6. To repeal all national panel provisions which contribute discrimination against women.

3.5.8 Implementation Procedure

The convention under Article 17 made a provision for the establishment of Committee on the Elimination of Discrimination against women for the purpose of considering the progress made in the implementation of the provisions of the convention. The Committee shall consist of eighteen members (at the entry into force of the Convention) and twenty three members (after ratification or accession to the Convention by thirty five states). The members shall be experts of high moral standing and shall possess competence in the field covered by the Convention. The experts shall be elected by the States Parties from among their nationals and shall serve in their personals capacity.

The State Parties shall report periodically to the committee a report on the legislative, judicial, administrative or other measures which they have adopted to give effect to the provisions of the Convention. The Committee examines reports submitted by the States Parties and makes its suggestions and recommendations based on their considerations. It may also invite United Nations specialized agencies to submit reports for consideration and may receive information from non-governmental organization. Thus, the committee acts as a monitoring system to oversee the implementation of the Convention. The Committee shall report annually to the General Assembly through the economic and social council on its activities and may make suggestions and general recommendations based on the examination of reports and information received from the State Parties.

3.6 Optional Protocol to the Convention on Women

The Convention did not provide for individual complaint system. In order to fulfill this deficiency the General Assembly on October, 1999 adopted the Optional Protocol to the Convention on Elimination of All Forms of discrimination against women which would enable victims of sex discrimination, sexual exploitation and other abuses to the Committee on the Elimination of Discrimination against Women against State Parties to the Protocol. Thus, the Protocol would allow to bypass governments to have the Committee to investigate their grievances. As on June, 16, 2006, the Protocol had 79 States Parties.

3.7 World Conferences on Women

The United Nations has organized four world conferences on women. These took place in Mexico City in 1975, Copenhagen in 1980, Nairobi in 1985 and Beijing in 1995. The last was followed by a series of five-year reviews.

3.7.1 The First World Conference on the Status of Women

The first world conference on the status of women was convened in Mexico City to coincide with the 1975 International Women's Year, observed to remind the international community that discrimination against women continued to be a persistent problem in much of the world. 133 governments participated, while 6,000 NGO representatives attended a parallel forum, the International Women's Year Tribune. The conference defined a World Plan of Action for the Implementation of the Objectives of the International Women's Year, which offered a comprehensive set of guidelines for the advancement of women through 1985.

3.7.1 The Second World Conference on the Status of Women

World Conference of the United Nations Decade for Women: Equality, Development and Peace held at Copenhagen during 4 to 30 July 1980. 145 Member States gathered for the mid-decade World Conference of the United Nations Decade for Women in Copenhagen. It aimed to review progress in implementing the goals of the first world conference, focusing on employment, health and education. A Programme of Action called for stronger national measures to ensure women's ownership and control of property, as well as improvements in protecting women's rights to inheritance, child custody and nationality.

3.7.3 The Third World Conference on the Status of Women

The Third World Conference on Women took place between 15 and 26 July 1985 in Nairobi, Kenya, as the end-decade assessment of progress and failure in implementing the goals established by the World Plan of Action from the 1975 inaugural conference on women as modified by the World Programme of Action of the second conference. Representatives of more than 140 Nations attended the World Conference to Review and Appraise the Achievements of the United Nations Decade for Women. The 1985 Conference was to assess the implementation of the action plans adopted by its predecessors. Significance during the conference was the end result of the Forward-looking Strategies for the Advancement of Women being adopted by consensus, unlike the previous two conferences. The conference marked the first time that lesbian rights were introduced in a UN official meeting and the turning-point for violence against women to emerge from being a hidden topic into one which needed to be addressed. Recognizing that the goals of the Decade for Women had not been met, the conference recommended and the General Assembly approved on-going evaluation of women's achievements and failures through the year 2000.

The World Conference marked the end of the United Nations Decade for Women with adoption by consensus of a final document containing strategies, for the rest of the century designed to improve the status of women and integrate them into all aspects of development. This was the third time the United Nations convened an international conference on the status of women.

3.7.4 The Fourth World Conference on the Status of Women

The 1995 Fourth World Conference on Women in Beijing marked a significant turning point for the global agenda for gender equality. This Conference was held to review and appraise the achievements of the UN Decade for Women took place in Nairobi in 1990. The conference's mandate was to establish concrete measures to overcome obstacles to achieving the Decade's goals. The Beijing Declaration and the Platform for Action, adopted unanimously by 189 countries, is an agenda for women's empowerment and considered the key global policy document on gender equality. It sets strategic objectives and actions for the advancement of women and the achievement of gender equality in 12 critical areas of concern:

- Women and poverty
- Education and training of women
- Women and health
- Violence against women
- Women and armed conflict
- Women and the economy
- Women in power and decision-making
- Institutional mechanism for the advancement of women
- Human rights of women
- Women and the media
- Women and the environment
- The girl-child

The Beijing conference built on political agreements reached at the three previous global conferences on women, and consolidated five decades of legal advances aimed at securing the equality of women with men in law and in practice. More than 17,000 participants attended, including

6,000 government delegates at the negotiations, along with more than 4,000 accredited NGO representatives, a host of international civil servants and around 4,000 media representatives.

3.7.5 Beijing Conference and Aftermath

The United Nation has through its General Assembly took initiatives to review the effect of Beijing Conference on the status of women in terms of implementation of resolutions or commitments of participant member states and review of appraisal on the Beijing commitments. Following important reviews have been done till date after the Beijing Conference:

3.7.5.1 Five Year Review in 2000

The General Assembly decided to hold a 23rd special session to conduct a five-year review and appraisal of the implementation of the Beijing Platform for Action, and to consider future actions and initiatives. "Women 2000: Gender Equality, Development, and Peace for the Twenty-First Century" took place in New York, and resulted in a political declaration and further actions and initiatives to implement the Beijing commitments.

3.7.5.2 Ten Year Review in 2005

A 10-year review and appraisal of the Beijing Platform for Action was conducted as part of the 49th session of the Commission on the Status of Women. Delegates adopted a declaration emphasizing that the full and effective implementation of the Beijing Declaration and Platform for Action is essential to achieving the internationally agreed development goals, including those contained in the Millennium Declaration.

3.7.5.3 Fifteen Year Review in 2010

The 15-year review of the Beijing Platform for Action took place during the Commission's 54th session in 2010. Member

States adopted a declaration that welcomed the progress made towards achieving gender equality, and pledged to undertake further action to ensure the full and accelerated implementation of the Beijing Declaration and Platform for Action.

3.7.5.4 Beijing+ 20

In mid-2013, the UN Economic and Social Council requested the Commission on the Status of Women to review and appraise implementation of the Platform for Action in 2015, in a session known as Beijing+20. To inform deliberations, the Council also called on UN Member States to perform comprehensive national reviews, and encouraged regional commissions to undertake regional reviews.

3.7.6 Role of International Bodies for the Protection of Women

The scope and nature to all human beings in respect of race, gender and social status are more specific on the basis of gender. The role of International Human Right Protection plays an important role for the protection of women.

3.7.7 Role of United Nations and Women's Rights

The role of United Nations Character and the Universal Declaration of Human Rights are considered to be the two basic Human Rights instruments and play an important role in order to ensure maintaining the dignity of women.

The two International Covenants i.e., the International Covenant on Civil and Political Rights, 1996 and International Covenant on Economic, Social and Cultural Rights of 1966 reinforces the concept of equality. In addition to these the United Nations Educational, Scientific and Cultural Organization (UNESCO) adopted Conventions concerning problems of women.

Conventions like Political Rights of Women, 1952, Nationality of Married Women-1957, Consent of marriage,

Minimum Age of Marriage and Registration of Marriages, 1962 and the Elimination of all forms of Discrimination against Women, 1979 are related to women.

The Universal Declaration of Human Rights pointed out that "*discrimination against women is incompatible with human dignity and with the welfare of the family and of society, prevents their participation on equal terms with men in the political, social, economic and cultural life of their countries and is an obstacle to the full development of the potentialities of women in the service of their countries and of humanity*".

The Fourth World Conference on Women in Beijing in the year 1995 with the objective of the 'platform for action' was signed and for the commitment to achieve 'gender equality and the empowerment of women'.

The Human Rights Protection Act, 1993 with the objective of 'Empowerment of Women' and to ensure gender equality by removing gender discrimination.

3.8 Women under International Labour Organization (ILO)

The United Nations has been assigned by the charter, the general task of promoting progress and international co-operation in economic, social, health, cultural, educational and related matters. However, it was decided that these task will be mainly fulfilled not by the organs of the United Nations, but by autonomous international organizations established by inter-governmental agreements, outside the United Nations, Specialized agencies are, therefore, performing a number of functions in the economic social, cultural, educational and health field.

One specialized agency is International Labour Organizations (ILO) under the umbrella of the United Nations. The International Labour Organisation (ILO) which was established in 1958 aims for the purpose of equal remuneration for men and women workers for work of value. ILO was established after the first world was on 19th

April, 1919 as on autonomics institution by the treating of Versailles and was associated with the League of Nations. Its original Constitution formed part of the Treaty of Versailles. On October 9, 1946, the amending instrument was signed at Montreal which is cited as the ILO instrument of Amendment, 1946. ILO became the first specialized agency associated with the United Nations when the agreement was approved by the General Assembly on December 14, 1946.

The ILO consists of (a) International Labour Conference Known as General Conference, (b) Governing Body and (c) an International Labour Office (Secretariat). International Labour Conference is the supreme body which meets annually at ILO headquarters in Geneva. Each national delegation is composed of two government delegates, one employer's delegate and one worker's delegate. The Governing Body (Executive Council) normally meets three or four times in a year at Geneva. It elects the Director-General of the International Labour Office (Secretariat) in Geneva is composed of the permanent Secretariat and professional staff. The Conference, the Governing Body and the Office make up ILO.

The ILO has been working for the improvement of labour standards and conditions throughout the world since last seventy five years. It has drafted scores of conventions and recommendations, collectively designed as International Labour Code, covering a variety of subjects, such as relating to employment, unemployment, conditions of employment, employment of women and children, vocational training, industrial health and safety, social security, industrial relations, maritime labour, immigration, freedom for association and trade union rights. ILO conventions are judicial instruments similar to treaties. Member states are requested to submit them to competent legislative authorities to decide whether or not the convention should be put into effect. Although ILO cannot enforce States to accept its standards, it does keep watch over the way conventions are applied in the countries which have ratified them. Member States are required to make regular reports to ILO regarding the adoption of standards and the ways in which the ratified conventions are put into effect.ILO was awarded the Noble Prize for Peace in 1969 in recognition of its activities.

3.8.1 International Labour Organization and Influence on Indian Law

International Labour Organizationsworks for self-employment and working activities ofwomen and recommends many countries for the protection and promotion of Women's Rights. In India also following the principles of ILO following legislations have been enacted to protect the women's rights in various fields.

1. Underground Work Women) Convention, 1935;
2. Night Work (Women) Convention, 1948;
3. Protocol to the Night Work (Women) Convention, 1948;
4. Equal Remuneration Convention, 1951;
5. Maternity Protection Convention, 1952;
6. Discrimination (Employment and Occupation) Convention, 1958;
7. Workers with Family Responsibilities Convention, 1981;
8. Lead Poisoning (Women and Children) Recommendation, 1919
9. Maternity Protection (Agriculture) Recommendations, 1919 and 1921;
10. Night Work of Women (Agriculture) Recommendations, 1921.

3.9 Forced or Compulsory Labour and Women under International Perspective

Forced and compulsory labour constitutions a violation of their rights of man referred to in the chapter of the United Nations and enunciated by Universal Declaration of Human

Rights. In order to suppress it, a Convention was concluded for the Abolition of Forced Labour Convention which was adopted by the General Conference of the International Labour Organization on January 17, 1953.

The convention provided under Article 1, that each member of the International Labour Organization which raffles this Convention undertakes to suppress and not to make use of any form or forced or compulsory labour.

1. As a means of political coercion or education or as a punishment for holding or expressing political views or views ideologically opposed to the established political, social or economic system;
2. As a means of mobilizing and using labour for purposes of economic development;
3. As a means of labour discipline;
4. As a punishment for having participated in strikes;
5. As a means of racial, social, natural or religious discrimination.

States parties to the convention undertake to take effective measures to secure the immediate and complete abolition of forced or compulsory labour.

It may be mentioned that ILO also provides support to the State Parties in their effects to eradicate forced Labour. ILO's Prevention and Elimination of Bonded Labour in South Asia Project is an example of its efforts. However the Convention has not been effective to abolish the forced labour. A study conducted by the ILO in 2001 entitled 'Stopping Labour' reveals that the growth of forced labour worldwide is deeply disturbing.

3.10 Indian Position relating to International Initiatives

We know that India has given equal status to women under its Constitution under Article 14 which provides that *"The State shall not deny to any person equality before the law or the equal protection of the laws within the territory of India"*. The above provision clearly shows that women in India enjoy right to equality and any discrimination against them shall be violence of equality of right and respect for human dignity. The Constitution also provides under article 15 that every female citizen has a right to access to shops, public restaurants, hotels and places of public entertainment and no restriction can be imposed on female citizens with regard to the use of wells, tanks, bathing ghats, roads and places of public resort maintained wholly or partly by State funds. Again, Article 16 of the Constitution provides that these shall be equality of opportunity for all citizens (including women) in matters relating to employment to any office under the state.

In ***Apparel Expert Promotion Council Vs. A.K. Chopra***[2], The Supreme Court observed that the message of international instruments such as the Convention on the Elimination of All Forms of Discrimination against Women and the Beijing Declaration which directs all States Parties to take appropriate measures to prevent discrimination of all forms against women besides taking steps to protect the honour and dignity of women is loud and clear. These international instruments cast an obligation on the Indian State to gender sensible its laws and the Courts are under an obligation to see that the message of the international instruments is not allowed to be drowned. The Courts are under an obligation to give due regard to international conventions and norms for construing domestic laws more so when there is no inconsistency between them and there is void in domestic law.

3.10.1 CEDAW and India

India has rectified the Convention on Elimination of All Forms of Discrimination against Women (1979) on July 9, 1993. Rectification of the Convention obliges India to honour the obligations imposed by the Convention. In ***Madhu***

2 AIR 1999 SC 625

Krishwar Vs. State of Bihar[3], it was held by the Supreme Court that the Convention on the Elimination of All Forms of Discrimination against Women is an integral scheme of the fundamental Right and the directive Principles, Article 2 (e) of CEDAW, International Conventions and the protection of Human Rights Act, to prevent gender-based discrimination and the effective right to life including empowerment of economic, social and cultural rights. Article 2 (f) read with Article 3, 14 and 15 of CEDAW embodies concomitant right to development as an integral scheme of the Indian Constitution and the Human Rights Act. It is therefore desirable that the enabling legislature is enacted to give legal effect to the Convention so that discrimination against women which exists due to legal, social and cultural traditions is eliminated. Rights provided therein will remain meaningless to a large number of women due to their poverty, ignorance and illiteracy.

India has rectified that convention and made two declarations and a reservation. The first declaration reads: With regard to Article 5 (a) and 16 (i) of the CEDWA, the Government of the Republic of India declares that it shall abide by and ensure those provisions with conformity with the policy of non-interference in the personal affairs of any community without its initiative and consent. The second declaration States with regard to Article 16 (2)of CEDAW, the Government of the Republic of India declares that though in principle if fully supports the principles of compulsory registration of marriage, it is not practicable in a vast country like India with its variety of customs, religious and level of literacy. In addition to the above declarations, India made a reservation by stating that it does not consider itself bound by paragraph 1 of Article 29 of the Convention which relates to settlement of disputes through arbitration.

But an interesting matter that the Declaration relating to compulsory registration of decision of the Supreme Court in ***Seema Vs. Ashwani Kumar***[4], wherein the Court held that

3 AIR 1996 SC 1864
4 (2) 2008 1 SCC 180

marriages of all persons who are citizens of India belonging to various religious should be made compulsorily registrable in their states, where the marriage is solemnized.

Further, in order to ensure proper implementation of the provisions of the guidelines laid down in ***Vishaka Case***,[5] the New drafted a bill entitled, 'Sexual Harassment of Women at their Work Places (Prevention) Bill 2004. However, the Bill is not likely to transform into the Act in near future. It is to be noted that the directions issued by the Supreme Court in Vishaka Case have not been followed by the institutions. The National Human Rights Commission in its Annual Report of 2000-2001 has observed that the guidelines issued by the Supreme Court were not being implemented adequately, whether in institutions of the public sector or in those of private sectors. Many institutions have not set up the Complaints Committee required under the judgment to deal with complaints of sexual harassment at the work place.

Although equality of status has been guaranteed to women by the Constitution, it is a myth to millions of women as they are the victims of various kinds of violence within houses, at work places and in the educational system. They are still the subject of suppression. Tall promises for improving the plight of women was made during 2001, which was declared as 'Women's Empowerment Year' but they were far from being fulfilled. National Policy for the Empowerment of Women was placed before a group of ministers but the policy has not been adopted. Seminars were organized on a number of issues affecting the conditions of women, no improvement has been made. They are being discriminated as compared to brothers at home and their male colleagues at work.

3.10.2 International Declarations and the Protection of Women from Domestic Violence Act 2005

The Beijing Declaration and the programme of action had regarded domestic violence as a human right issue and a

5 (1997) 6 SCC 241

serious deterrent to development. In order to provide effective protection of rights of women who are victims of violence of any kind occurring within the family, the Protection of Women from Domestic Violence Act 2005 was enacted by the Parliament.

Domestic Violence has been defined by the Act under Section 3, "*as any act, omission or commission or conduct of the respondent shall constitute domestic violence in case it: (a) harms or injures or endangers the health, safety, life, limb or well-being, whether mental or physical abuse, sexual abuse, verbal and emotional abuse and economic abuse; or (b) harass, harms, injures or endangers the aggrieved person with a view to coerce her or any other person related to her to meet any unlawful demand for any dowry or other property or valuable security; or (c) has the effect of threatening the aggrieved persons or any person related to her by any conduct mentioned in clause harm, whether physical or mental, to the aggrieved person.*"

Any person who has reason to believe at an act of domestic violence has been or is being, or is likely to be committed, may give information about it to the concern protection officer.[6]A police officer, Protection Officer, service provider or Magistrate who has received a complaint of domestic violence or is otherwise present at the place an incident of domestic violence or when the incident of domestic violence is reported to him, shall inform the aggrieved person (a) of her right make an application for obtaining a relief by way of a protection order, an order or more than one such order under this Act; (b) of the availability of services of service provider; (c) of the availability of services of the Protection Officers; (d) of her right to life a complaint under Section 49-A of the Indian Penal Code, wherever relevant.

An aggrieved on behalf of the aggrieved person may present an application to the Magistrate seeking one or more

6 Section 4(1) of the Domestic Violence Act 2005, The State Government shall appoint such number of Protection Officers in each district as it may consider necessary [Section 8 (1)]

reliefs under the Act[7]. The relief sought may include a relief for issuance of an order for payment of compensation or damages without prejudice to the right of such person to institute a suit for compensation or damages for the injuries caused by the acts of domestic violence committed by the respondent[8]. The Magistrate may, after giving the aggrieved person and respondent an opportunity of being hard and on being prima facie satisfied that domestic violence has taken place, pass a protection order in favour of the aggrieved person and prohibit the respondent from (a) Committing any act of domestic violence; or (b) aiding or abetting in the Commission of acts of domestic violence; (c) entering the place of employment of the aggrieved person or, if the person aggrieved is a child, its school or any other place frequented by the aggrieved person; (d) attempting to communicate in any form, whatsoever, with the aggrieved person, including personal, oral or written or electronic or telephonic contract; (e) alienating any assets, operating bank lockers or bank accounts; (f) causing violence to the dependents and others relatives.

How can only be an instrument of change that must be effectively used. The absence of effective law enforcement, results in low rates of conviction, which in turn emboldens the feeling that the accused can get away. It is necessary that deterrent punishments are provided in the statute, and are strictly enforced.

3.11 Traffic in Persons & Prostitution and International Conventions

The prostitution and the accompanying evil of the traffic in persons for the purpose of prostitution are incompatible with dignity and worth of the human person. The United Nations in 1949 consolidated in a single Convention a series of international instruments which were adopted under the auspices of the League of Nations. These included (1)

7 Section 12 (1) the Domestic Violence Act 2005
8 Section 12 (2)

International Convention for the suppression of the Traffic in Women and Children of September 30, 1921; (2) International Convention for the Suppression of the Traffic in Women of Full Age of October 11, 1933 aimed at ending what had been known as the 'White Slave Trade' (WST).

In order to crab traffic in persons a Convention for the suppression of the Traffic in Persons and the Exploitation of Prostitution of Others was concluded on December 2, 1949 under the Auspices of the United Nations[9]. Thus the convention consolidated the conventions adopted under the auspices of the League of Nations.[10] States agreed to punish any person who procures or entices or leads away another person for the purpose of prostitution even with the consent of that person and exploit the prostitution of another person even with the consent of the person.[11] The States Parties also agreed to punish any person who (1) keeps or manages or knowingly finances or takes parts in the financing of a brothel; (2) knowingly lets or rents a building or other places or any part thereof for the purpose of the prostitution of others.[12] Each partly to the convention agreed to take all the necessary measures to repeal or abolish any existing law, regulations or administrative provisions by virtue of which persons are engaged in such activities.

The Convention came into force on July 25, 1951 in accordance with Article 24 of the Convention. As on February 2, 2002, the convention had 74 States Parties. The Parties to the present Convention also agreed to take or to encourage, through their public or private educational health, social and other related services, measures for the prevention of prostitution and for the rehabilitation and social adjustment of the victims of prostitution. It is a matter of serious concern that even after more than a half century since the adoption

9 The Convention was approved by the General Assembly Resolution 317 (IV) adopted on December 2, 1949.

10 International Convention for the Suppression of the Traffic in Women and Children of September 30, 1921 and International Convention for the Suppression of the Traffic in Women of Full Age of October 11, 1933.

11 Ibid

12 Infra

of the Convention, trafficking still continues in a large part of the World. It has been estimated that more than two million people World-wide are being trafficked each year, the majority of whom are Women and Children.

3.12 India and Convention against Torture

Convention against torture was signed by India on October 14, 1997. However, it has not been ratified by it. The National Human Rights Commission has been repeatedly requesting for its ratification, but it is still awaited. The delay has given rise to serious concerns within the country and in major international forums. It is submitted that Article 21 of the Constitution covers the area relating to torture. Further, the right against torture has been judicially recognized by the Supreme Court as a fundamental right and therefore the ratification is not likely to affect much to the Government.

3.13 Trafficking in Women, India and International Perspectives

The Indian Constitution under Article 23 (1) prohibits 'traffic in human being' and any contravention of it, is an offence punishable in accordance with law[13]. However, Article 23 (2) provides that the state may impose compulsory service for 'public purposes' and in imposing such service the state shall not make any discrimination on grounds only of religion, race, caste or class or any of them.

The term traffic in human beings' includes selling and buying of women and children for immoral or other purposes.[14] In 1956, Suppression of Immoral Traffic in Women and Girls Act (SITA) was enacted to prevent sexual exploitation for commercial purposes. The Act also led down that the act of procuring, including or taking away any women with intention to exploitfor the purpose of prostitution is recognized as an offence.

13 Article 23 of the Indian Constitution.

14 Raj Bahadur Vs. Legal Remembrance, 2015 ALL HC 2413, Calcutta, & Basudev Vs. Mittal, AIR 1962 Bom 53.

India has ratified the Convention for the Suppression of the Traffic in Persons and of the Exploitation of the prostitution of others of 1972 on January 9, 1973. In 197, Immoral Traffic (Prevention) Act (ITPA) was enacted to give effect to the Convention. The purpose of the enactment of (ITPA) was to eliminate trafficking from a woman and children for the purpose of prostitution as an organized means of living. The offences under the Act include (a) punishment for keeping a brothel or allowing promises to be used as brothel (Sec.-3); (b) punishment for living on the earnings of prostitution (Sec.-4); (c) procuring, inducting or taking person for the sake of prostitution (Sec.-5); (d) detaining a person in premises where prostitution is carried on (Sec.-6); prostitution in or the vicinity of public places (Sec.-7); reducing or soliciting for purpose of prostitution (Sec.-8) and reduction of a person in custody (Sec.-9).

From the above discussion it is clear that there are constitutional provisions and legislations to prohibit trafficking but the simple mention of the provisions of the ITPA is not at all effective and it has failed to curb trafficking. It may be stated that anti-trafficking measures should be adopted which include the use of rescue, rehabilitation and reintegration of trafficked people into the mainstream. The role of traffickers should also be taken into account in order to combat the menace of trafficking. Measures curb trafficking is required to be taken immediately. The U.S. has threatened to impose economic sanctions against India, if it does not institute measures to check trafficking. If the U.S. carries out its threats, Washington can also vote against bans to India from International financial institutions like IMF and World Bank. India has a dubious distinction of being revenging, sending as well as transit country, in addition to having a fair amount of trafficking within the country. It has been estimated that at least 7,000 are trafficked into India from Nepal every year. They mostly end up in brothels, in metros, condemned to a life of deprivation and future. Further, India is a transit point for women, bound for Pakistan and West Asia. Notable point is that one does not have reliable information on the estimate of the extent of trafficking, the trafficking sautés, and regions from which vulnerable people are trafficked, where they are sent and who forces them into slavery or slave like conditions of work.

The International law is the most remarkable contributors of the legal mechanism for the protection of women working in labour sector besides its effective working for the development of the labour laws and welfare of the labour including women. It has come across lots of challenges and faced the situation with all care and responsibilities towards larger interest of the labour. Going through the existing international laws and policies including the available jurisprudential works, following steps may be helpful in strengthening international law in terms of protection women through labour law. Creative interpretation of existing provision can also be encouraged to protect the victim from further abuse.

Section 107 of the Code of Criminal Procedure can be used to secure peace bonds from the offender, to prevent and discourage the occurrence of violence. Articles 14 and 15 (3) provide unequivocally that women enjoy the fundamental right to equality and cannot be discriminated against on the basis of their sex alone. However, these fundamental rights are enforceable only against the state. In some other jurisdictions, such as South Africa, the non-discrimination clause has been extended to persons and non-state bodies also. It is recommended that the non-discrimination clauses in the Constitution of India be extended from its present application against the state alone to the private sphere. The special protection under Article 15 (3) of the Indian Constitution should be utilized with utmost care, as there were instances where provisions that were intended to help women in actually worked against them, as the line between differentiation and discrimination is very thin and should be drawn with care.

Principles of International law, if not contrary to principles of domestic law, can be used to strengthen the hands of the judiciary where no law exists or to further establish existing law. Additionally, treaties, even if not specifically incorporated into domestic law, can nevertheless be used the courts in several ways, including:

1. As an aid to constitutional or statuary interpretation general;
2. For reviewing administrative discretion by a decision-maker.
3. As giving rise to legitimate expectation that the provisions of the treat will be applied by a decision maker;
4. As a factor to take into account when identifying demands of public policy.

Provisions of International conventions and treaties ratified by India require to be incorporated into the Indian legal system. With respect to domestic violence specifically, the absence of any law on the subject makes it that much easier for the courts to incorporate international principles into the domestic framework since there is no question of conflict between the two. CEDAW, to which India is a party, specifically addresses violence in the 'private' sphere. As the court has already read in provisions of CEDAW with respect to sexual harassment at the workplace into Indian law, there is nothing preventing similar reading in with respect to violence within the family. An overvaulting of the existing criminal legal system is required if the victim of domestic violence is to receive any redressal from the same. At present, the system is oriented towards crime detection and deterrence, and once proceedings are initiated, the victim is nowhere in the picture. However, a shirt of this framework is required so as to make the victim and his/her needs focus of the criminal redressed system.

In Minnesota, USA, a unique experiment was conducted a 'no-drop' policy was adopted with respect to offences of domestic violence. What that meant as that after a complaint was lodged by the wife, the state would go through with the prosecution of the same, even if the victim subsequently changed her mind and turned hostile, until a 'final decision of conviction or acquittal was obtained. Within a year of adopting this policy, it was noticed that the instances domestic violence had declined. As the 'no-drop' policy served as effective deterrent for prospective abusers. A similar policy can be adopted by the state, as even if the prosecution does not result in conviction of the offender, at least a clear unequivocal message is sent out to the public that such crimes are serious and will be treated so by the system.

❑❑❑

CHAPTER

4

Women Rights and Protection under Indian Constitution

4.1 Introduction

Although the constitution of India guarantees equal rights to women as individuals, the state has broadly perceived them as such. Citizenship has long far been exclusively viewed as the domain of men. Womens' identities and lives have been either eluded from or viewed as secondary in the framework of state-citizen relationship. Womens' issues have always been dealt with in the context of family and are, therefore, considered private.

In order to prove its commitment to womens' issues, the state has responded to the criticism and demands by the womens' movement by amending the existing laws and enacting new one like sections 498A and 304B of the Indian Penal Code. But soon the womens' groups believed that laws will prove ineffective as long as there is patriarchal bias in the mindset of the implementers and implementer of the law. They see recourse to law as necessary and in evitable, as it is believed that legally criminalizing a practice would socially delegitimize it, one of the fundamental obstacles in promoting gender equality in development remains at the community level where attitudinal biases often prevent women from realizing their rights. The principle of gender equality is enshrined in the Indian Constitution in its Preamble, Fundamental Rights, Fundamental Duties and Directive Principles. The Constitution not only grants equality to women, but also empowers the State to adopt measures of positive discrimination in favour of women.

4.2 Women under Indian Constitution

The Constitution of India prohibits discrimination based on sex but it equally directs and empowers the government to undertake special measures for women. Though the position of women has improved in the last four decades, but still they are struggling to maintain their dignity and freedom. Presently Indian women are facing the toughest time mentally and physically, mainly due to unawareness and lack of knowledge of legal and constitutional rights of a woman. The Constitution provides many protection rights for women such as Protective discrimination in favour of women, Right to freedom of women, Right of women against exploitation, Rights of women under directives and political representations of women. All these rights are explained below.

The preamble is the key to Constitution. It does not discriminate men and women but treats them alike. The Preamble contains various objectives including the equality of status and opportunity to all citizens. The objective has been inserted with the view to give equal status to men and women in the term of opportunity.

4.2.1 Fundamental Rights

Part-III of the Constitution of India deals with the fundamental rights. The provisions regarding fundamental rights have been enshrined in Articles 12 to 35, which are applicable to all the citizens irrespective of sex. However, certain provisions protect the rights of women of our country. According to article 15(3) of the constitution, discrimination or the grounds of religion, race, caste, sex and place of birth shall not prevent the State from making any special provision for women and children. Under the Constitution, the State has been given power to make laws relating to women and children but such shall not be violative of Article 15 of the Constitution. The Constitution prohibits gender discrimination.[1] The Constitution also lifts that ignominy and permits the state to positively discriminate in favour of women to make special provisions to ameliorate their social, economic and political condition to accord them parity. [2]

Article 15(3) of the Constitution makes special provisions for women and children. It empowers the state to make special legislation in this regard. The features of fundamental rights are as under:

4.2.1.1 Right to Equality

It means the equality of opportunity, equality before law, equal protection in laws, not discriminating against any person on the grounds of sex, religion, caste and place of birth[33] and no discrimination in the matter of public employment on the grounds of sex only as provided under Article 16 of the Constitution.[44]

The Supreme Court has struck down a provision whereby an Air Hostess would have deemed to have retires on pregnancy, as being unconstitutional and violative of Article 14 of the Constitution in the case of ***Air India Vs. Nargesh Meerza.***[55]

4.2.1.1.1 Scope of Article 15(4) of the Constitution

The Apex Court in ***Preeti Srivastava Vs. The State of Madhya Pradesh***[6] Explained the scope and ambit of article 15(4), which was added by the constitution (first Amendment) Act 1951. It enables the State to make special provisions for the advancement of women, as well as scheduled castes and scheduled tribes, not withstanding Article 15(1) and 23(2). The working Article 15(4) is similar to that of Article 15(3).

1 Article 15, 15(1)
2 Article 15 (3)
3 Article 14
4 Article 16
5 AIR 1981 SC1829
6 AIR 1999 SC 2894

Article 15(3) was there from the very inception. It enables special provisions being made for women and children not withstanding Article 15(1) which imposes the mandate of non discrimination on the ground of (among others) Scheduled Caste and Scheduled Tribes.

4.2.1.2 Right to Freedom

Article 19 to 22 of the Constitution deal with the right to freedom. It includes right to freedom of speech and expression, freedom of assembly, freedom to form associations, freedom of movement, freedom to reside and settle and freedom of profession, occupation, trade or business. These 'six freedoms' are not absolute. Absolute individual rights cannot be guaranteed by any modern state. An organized society is the precondition of the civil liberties. There cannot be any right which is injuries to the community as a whole, If people were given complete and absolute liberty without any social control the result will be ruined.[7] At the same time, the restriction must be reasonable from the substantive as well as procedural standpoint.[8]

4.2.1.3 Right Against Exploitation

According to article 23 of the Constitution traffic in human beings and forced labour is prohibited. Again, Employment of the children is also prohibited under Article 24 of the Constitution. "*Traffic in human beings means selling and buying men and women like goods and includes immoral traffic in women and children for immoral or other purposes*[9]". In ***Deena Vs. Union of India***, it was held that labour taken from prisoners without paying proper remuneration was "forced labour" and violative of Art. 23 of the Constitution.[10] In a land mark judgment in ***M.C. Mehta Vs. State of Tamil Nadu***[11], the Supreme court has held that children below 14

7 Wills-Constitutional Law and the United States, 477
8 N.B. Khare Vs. State of Punjab AIR, 1960 SC211
9 Raj Bahadur Vs. Legal Remembrance, AIR 1953 Cal. 522
10 AIR 1983 SC 1155
11 AIR 1997 SC 699

years cannot be employed in any hazardous industry, mines or other works and has laid down exhaustive guidelines how the State authorities should protect economic social and humanitarian rights of millions of children, working illegally in public and private sections. The matter was brought before the court by a publicspirited Lawyer Mr. M.C. Mehta by way of Public Interest Litigation under Article 32 of the Constitution.

4.2.1.4 Right to Freedom of Religion

Article 25 to 28 of the Constitution deal with the right to freedom of religion. The concept of secularism is implicit on the preamble of the Constitution which declares the resolve of the people to secure to all its citizens "*liberty of through, belief, faith, and worship*". The 42nd Amendment Act, 1976, has inserted the word 'Secular' in the preamble. This amendment is intended merely to spell out clearly the concept of 'Secularism' in the Preamble. It only means that in matters of religion it is neutral. The state can have no religion of its own. In should treat all religions equally. In ***S.R. Bommai Vs. Union of India,***[12] the Supreme Court has held that "*Secularism is the basic feature of the Constitution*". The State treats equally all religions and religious denominations. Religion is a matter of individual faith and cannot be mixed with secular activities. Secularism means developing, understanding and respect for different religions. In ***Aruna Roy Vs. Union of India***[13] the validity of the new National Education Policy, 2002, which provided for value based education to school children based on bias of all religions was challenged as violative of Art. 28 and anti secular. The Court held that study of religions in school education is not against the secular philosophy of the Constitution.

Article 25(1) guarantees to every person the freedom of con science and the right to profess, practice and propagate religion. The right guaranteed under Art. 25(1) like other Constitutional Rights is not absolute. This right is, subject to

12 AIR 1994 SC 1918
13 AIR 2002 SC 3176

public order, morality and health and to the other provisions of Part-III of the Constitution. Further, the state is empowered by two sub-clauses (a) and (b) of clause 2 of Article 25 of the Constitution:

1. to regulate or restrict any economic, financial, political or other secular activity which may be associated with religious practice.
2. to prove for (i) Social welfare and reform and (ii) to throw open Hindu religious institutions of a public character to all classes and sections of Hindus. Against Noise Pollution in the name of Religion not allowed, In a significant judgment in church of God (Full gospel) in ***India Vs. K.K. Q.M.C. Welfare Association,***[14] the Supreme Court has held that in the exercise of the right to religious freedom under Arts. 25 and 26, no person can be allowed to create noise pollution or disturb the peace of others. The custom of religious prayer through the use of loudspeakers is not an essential element of any religion.

4.2.1.5 Cultural and Educational Right

We know that the Article 29(1) guarantees to any section of the citizens residing in any part of India having a distinct language, script or culture of its own, the right to conserve the same. A minority community can preserve its language, scrip or culture by and through educational institutions. Therefore, the right to establish and maintain institutions of their choice is necessary co commitment to right to preserve its distinctive language, script or culture. This right is guaranteed to them by Art. 30(1) of the Constitution. According to clause(2) of Article 29, institutions maintained by the State or receiving aid out of State funds on grounds only a religion, race, caste, language or any of them. Art 29 applies only to citizens while Article 30 applies to both citizens and non-citizens. In ***State of Bombay Vs. Bombay***

14 AIR 2000 SC 2773

Educational Society[15] the Supreme Court struck down an order of the Bombay Government banning admission of those whose language was not English into schools having English as a medium of instruction because it denied admission solely on the ground of language.

The protection of Article 29(2) does not apply where the student is expelled from an institution on grounds of indiscipline,[16]or where he is refused admission on grounds of his not possessing requisite qualifications[17].

In ***Bramchari Sidheswar Vs. State of West Bengal,***[18] popularly known as the Ramikrishna Mission Case, the Supreme Court has held that the Ram Krishna Mission established by Swami Vivekananda to propagate Vedanta values as expended by Ramkrishna is not a minority religion separate and distinct from Hindu Religion, but a religious sect or denomination of Hindu Religion and therefore not entitled to claim the fundamental right under Art. 30(1) of the Constitution of establishing and administering educational institutions of their choice. Sri Ramakrishna could be regarded as a religious teacher who expounded and preached the principles of Vedanta on which Hindu religion is founded. A three judge bench comprising Justice Kuldip Singh, Justice N. Venkatachara and Justice Saghir Ahmad set aside a Judgment of the Calcutta High Court which had held the Ramakrishna Mission being a religion distinct and separate from Hindu religion were a minority in West Bengal based on religion.

4.2.1.6 Right to Constitutional Remedies

We know that a declaration of fundamental rights is meaningless unless there is effective machinery for the enforcement of the rights. It is remedy which makes the right real. If there is no remedy there is no right at all. It was, therefore, in the fitness of the things that our constitution-

15 AIR 1954 sc 561
16 Ramesh Chandra Vs. Principal B.B.I. College, AIR 1953 ALL 90
17 Nageshwara Rao Vs. Principal, Medical College, AIR 1962. AP 212
18 (1995) 4 SCC.646.

makers having incorporated a long list of fundamental rights, have also provided for an effective remedy for the enforcement of these rights under Article 32 of the Constitution. Article 32 is itself a fundamental right. Article 226 also empowers all the High Courts to issue the writes for the enforcement of fundamental rights.

Article 32(1) guarantees the right to move the Supreme Court by "appropriate proceedings" for the enforcement of the fundamental rights conferred by Part III of the constitution. Clauses (2) of Art. 32 confers power on the Supreme Court to issue appropriate directions or orders or writs, including writs in the nature of *Habeas Corpus, Mandamus, Prohibition, Quo-Warranto* and *Certiorari* for the enforcement of any of the rights conferred by Part III of the Constitution. Under clause (3) of Art. 32 Parliament may by law empower any other court to exercise within the local limits of its jurisdiction all or of the powers exercisable by the Supreme Court under clause (2). Clause (4) lays that the right guaranteed by Article 32 shall not be suspended except as otherwise provided for the Constitution. Article 32 thus provides for expeditions and expansive remedy for the protection of fundamental rights from legislative and executive interference.

Under Art. 32(1) the Supreme Court's power to enforce fundamental right is widest. There is no limitation in regard to the Kind of proceedings envisaged in Art, 32(1) except that proceeding must be "appropriate" and this requirement must be judged in the light of purpose for which proceeding is to be taken, i.e. enforcement of fundamental rights. It is not obligatory for the Court to follow adversary system. The Constitution-makers deliberately did not lay down any particular form of proceeding for enforcement of fundamentals rights nor did they stipulate that such proceeding should conform to any rigid pattern or strait-jacket formula because they knew that in a country like India where there is so much of poverty, ignorance, illiteracy, deprivation and exploitation, any insistence on a right formula of proceeding for enforcement of fundamental right would become self defeating.

It is clear from Art 32(1) that wherever there is a violation of fundamental right any person can move the Court for an appropriate remedy.[19]

In a landmark judgment in ***State of West Bengal Vs. Committee for Protection of Democratic Rights, West Bengal***[20], the complaint along with a numbers of workers of a political party had been staying in camps of Garpita, District Midnapur, State of West Bengal. They decided to return their homes form such comp. in the way they were attacked by some miscreants numbering 50-60 with fire-arms which resulted in the death of 11 workers and injured many members. The complainant however, managed to escape and lodged the First Information Report with police. D.G.P., West Bengal took over the investigations of the Case. Writ petition under Article 226 was filed in the High Court of Calcutta by the committee for Protection of Democratic Rights, West Bengal, in a 'Public Interest Litigation' allegation that there are months had passed after the incident, yet no serious attempt had been taken to investigate the crime, since, the police administration was in the State's hand which is under the ruling party which was trying to hide the incident to save its image the investigation be handed over to the C.B.I. or an independent agency. The High Court on the basis of the affidavit of the State feel that there is no hope for justice in investigation the crime by the State police and if it is conducted fairly it would be involved with suspicion because all the assailants were members of the ruling party. In view of this the High Court held it appropriate to hand over the investigation to the CBI. Aggrieved by this, the State Government filed a SPL in the Supreme Court.

The main question for consideration was whether the High Court in exercise of its jurisdiction under Article 226 can direct the CBI established under the Delhi special Act investigate a cognizable offence which take place in the State of West Bengal, without the consent of the State Government.

19 The Judges' Transfer Case, AIR 1982 SC 149.
20 AIR 2010 SC 1476

It was argued by the State referring to entry 80 of list 1 of the Tenth schedule and entry 2 of list II and section 5 and 6 of the special police Act that on these on situational and statutory provisions that there is a complete restriction on Parliament's legislative power in enacting any law permitting the police of one State of investigate an offence committed in another State, without the consent of the State.

On behalf of the Union of India it was argued that the alleged restriction on Parliament's legislative power Entry 80 to list 1 and under 6 of the Special Police Act do not apply to the Supreme Court to exercise their powers under Article 32 and Article 226 of the Constitution as it is the obligation to the Superior Courts to protect the citizens and enforcing fundamental rights. A five Judge constitutional bench of the Court consisting of five judges[21]unanimously held that the argument that the exercise of the Supreme Court and High Courts to order the investigation by the CBI without consent of the State Government would violate the federal structure of the Constitution is also wrong as it overlooks the basic fact that in a federal structure it is the duty of the Courts to up hold the Constitutional values and enforce the Constitutional limitations as the ultimate interpreter of the Constitution. Judicial review is itself a basic feature of the Constitution and no restriction can be imposed on the powers of the Supreme Court and the High Court's with regard to the enforcement of fundamental rights of the citizens which is inherent and cannot be extinguished by constitutional or statutory provision.

4.2.2 Directive Principle of State Policy

Under the Constitution of India, the directive principle of State policy is the reflection of Governance that India is a welfare state. This policy envisaged equal rights to work, equal pay for equal work, adequate means of livelihood to both men and women; these are guaranteed under directive principles

21 K.G. Balakrishnan(CJI), R.V. Raveendran, D.K. Jain, P. Sathasivam, and J.M. Panchal, J.J.

of state policy. Part IV of the Constitution containing Articles 38, 39 (a (d) and (e), 42, 44 and 45 deal with the welfare and development of women.

According to Article 39 (a) the state should direct its policy towards securing that the citizens, men and women equally have the right to an adequate means of livelihood. This Article provides equal right to all citizens, irrespective of sex to adequate means of livelihood. As per Article 39 (d) of the constitution there should be equal pay for equal work for both men and women. According to Article 39 (e) of the constitution the health and strength of workers i.e. men and women and that of the children of underage to be protected equally. They should not be forced to work under inhuman and hazardous condition.

In ***M.C. Mehta Vs. State of Tamil Nadu***[5] it has been held that not in view of Article 39 the employment of children within the match factories directly connected with the manufacturing process of matches and fireworks cannot be allowed as it is hazardous. Children can however, be employed in the process of packing etc. away from the manufacturing process.

4.2.2.1 Equal Justice and Free Legal Aid

Article 39-A of the constitution provides equal justice and free legal aid. On several occasions it has been held by the Apex Court that legal aid and speedy trial have been treated as fundamental rights under Article 21 of the constitution available to all prisoners and enforced by the courts. The state is under a duty to provide lawyer to poor person and it must pay to the lawyer his fee fixed by the court.

4.2.2.2 Political Representations of Women

Article 40 of the Constitution which lay down that the state shall take steps to organize village panchayats and endow them with such powers and authority as may be necessary to enable them to function as units of self government. To realize the Directive the 73rd and 74th Constitutional Amendments had sought to ensure a certain proportion of women as chair persons of panchayats. According to Article 243- D (3) and 243-T (3), not less than one third of the total number of seats to be filled by Directive election in every Panchayat/ Municipality shall be reserved for women (including SCs AND STs). This opportunity of being a part of local level arbitration process has improved the social conditions of women in village areas.

4.2.2.3 Just and Human Conditions of Work and Maternity Relief

Article 42:- Article 42 of constitution of India caste a duty on every employer to ensure just and humane conditions of work and for maternity relief. In reality the position and treatment of women in corporate offices is really bad and in fact they are exploited by their seniors and bosses. In this scenario the provisions of Article 42 are very important and now it is duty of employer to provide good working conditions to all the employees.

4.2.2.4 Uniform Civil Code and Gender Justice

Article 44 of the constitution requires that state shall endeavor to secure a uniform civil code throughout the territory of India. The founding fathers of the constitution were aware of the gender justice and sexual inequality of women and they incorporated Article 44 of the constitution with the aim that it may be exercised in future at appropriate time.

In a landmark judgment of ***Sarla Mudgal Vs. Union of India***[6], the Apex Court has passed direction to the Central Government to take a fresh look at Article 44 of the constitution which enjoins the State to secure a uniform civil code which, according to the Court is imperative for both protection of the oppressed and promotion of national unity and integrity. The above direction was given by the court while dealing with the case where the question for consideration was whether a Hindu Husband married under Hindu law after conversion to Islam, without dissolving first marriage, can solemnize a second marriage. It has been held by the Apex court that such a marriage will be illegal and the husband can be prosecuted for bigamy under section 494 of the Indian Penal Code, 1860.

Article 243 D (3) of the constitution provides that not less than 1/3rd of total number of seats to be filled by direct election in every Panchayat to be reserved for women and such seats to be allowed by rotation to different constituencies in Panchayat. Article 243 T (3) of the Constitution provides that not less than 1/3rd of total number of seats to be filled by direct election in every Municipality to be reserved for women and such seats to be allotted by rotation to different constitution in Municipality. Article 243 T (4) of the constitution provides reservation of offices of Chairperson in Municipalities for SC, ST, Women in such manner as the legislature of a State, may by law provide.

4.2.3 Fundamental Duties

Article-51 (a) deals with the duties and clause (e) relates particularly to women which says: *"it shall be the duty of every citizen of India to promote harmony and the spirit of common brotherhood amongst all the people of India transcend in religious, linguistic and regional and sectional diversities, to renounce practices derogatory to the dignity of women".*

4.2.4 Role of Women's Participation in Politics

Article-40 of the Directive Principles of State Policy, every women represent in the village panchayats. The 73rd and 74th Amendments have passed in 1992 to provide for reservation of seats for women in election to Panchayats and Municipalities in Articles 243-D and 243-T. The Indian constitution provides equal status and opportunity to women in respect of discrimination in one form or the other.

4.3 Protection of Women and Free Legal Aid Service

Article 39a of the Constitution of India talks about the free legal aid and service to poor and weaker sections of the society and thereby ensure justice for all. In order to ensure the constitutional mandate the Legal Service Authority Act 1987 was passed. This Act is an Act to constitute legal services authorities in order to provide free and competent legal services to the weaker sections of our society in order to ensure proper justices for the poor and needy of such right. It is to see that justice are not in any way denied to any citizen because of economic or other disabilities and to organize Lok Adalats in order to provide and promote justice on a basis of equal opportunity. This Act was enacted keeping in mind that no citizen is deprivedfrom justice due to economic or other disabilities.[22]

Article 39A of the constitution of India's main object is to build a welfare State and an egalitarian social order ***Kesavananda Bharati Vs. State of Kerala***[23]. We are living in the 21st century i.e. the modern era. Though, it could be hardly denied that women of our country are the weaker section of our society till date. In order to provide justice Lok Adalats are being established at various places. The Lok Adalats are for disposal, summary way and through the process of arbitration and settlement between the parties. The said Act was enacted to provide total assistance in securing justice to people or citizen who are totally enable to protect their right both fundamental and legal right in a court of law. This Act extends to the whole India except the State of Jammu and Kashmir.

We can refer two important cases here:

1. ***Sukumar Mukherjee Vs. State of West Bengal***[24]

22 Statement of Objects and Resources for enactment of this Act of 1987.
23 (1973) 4 SCC 225
24 1993 Lab IC 2035: AIR 1993 SC 2335

2. ***Ganesh Prasad Seth Kesari Vs. Lakshmi Narayan Gupta***[25]

"Central Authority" means the National Legal Services Authority constituted under Section 3. "Legal Service" includes the rendering of any service in the conduct of any case on other legal proceeding before any court on other authority or tribunal and the giving of advice on any legal matter.

"State authority" means a State Legal Service Authority constituted under Section 6. "State government" includes the administrative of a Union territory appointed by the President under Article 239 of the constitution.

The court cannot re-write, recast or redesign a section but it can only interpret a section ***State of Kerala Vs. Mathal Verghese***[26]

4.3.1 The National Legal Service Authority

The Central Government shall constitute a body to be called the National Legal Services Authority to exercise the powers and perform the functions conferred on or assigned to the Central Authority under this Act.

The Central Authority shall consist of:

- The chief Justice of India who shall be the patron-in-chief.
- A serving on retired judge of the Supreme Court to be nominated by the President, in consultation with the Chief Justice of India, who shall be the executive chairman; and
- Such number of other members, possessing such experience and qualifications, as may be prescribed by the Central Government to be nominated by that Government in consultation with the Chief Justice of India.

25 AIR 1985 SC 964.
26 AIR 1987, SC 33.

4.3.1.1 Function of the Central Authority

The Central Authority shall[27] perform all or any of the following functions, namely:

1. Lay down policies and principles for making legal services available under provisions of this Act.
2. Utilize the funds at its disposal and made appropriate allocations of funds to the State Authorities and District Authorities.
3. Organize a legal aid camps, especially in rural areas, slums or labour colonies with the dual purpose of education the weaker sections of the society as to their rights as well as encouraging the settlement of disputes through Lok Adalats.
4. Make special efforts to enlist the support of voluntary social welfare institutions working at the grass-root level, particularly among the scheduled castes and schedule tribes women and rural and urban labour.
5. Encourage the settlements of disputes by way of consultations, arbitration and conciliation.
6. Undertake and promote research in the field of legal services with special reference to the need for such services among the poor.
7. Take appropriate members for spreading legal literacy and legal awareness amongst the people and in particular, to adequate weaker sections of the society about the rights benefits and privileges guaranteed by social welfare legislations and other enactments as well as administrative programmes and measures.
8. Co-ordinate and monitor the functioning of State Authorities, District Authorities, Supreme Court Legal Service Committee, High Court Legal Service Committees, Taluk Legal Service Committees and voluntary Social Service Committees and other legal

27 Substituted by the Act 59 of 1994

services organizations and give general directions for the proper implementation of the legal services programmes.

Hence, to improve the position of the weaker sections of the women, especially the women laboures of our country, Legal Service Authority Act can play a vital role in our country. But sorry to say that, hundred percent of the said Act is yet to be utilized in our country.

4.3.2 State Legal Service Authority

Constitution of State Legal Services Authority:

Every State Government shall constitute a body to be called the Legal Services Authority for the State to exercise the powers and perform the function conferred on or assigned to a State Authority under this Act.

A State Authority shall consist of:

- The Chief Justice of the High Court, who shall be the Patron-in-chief;
- A serving or retired Judge of the High Court, to be nominated by the Governor, in consultation with the Chief Justice of the High Court, who shall be the Executive Chairman; and
- Such number or the members, possessing such experience and qualifications as may be prescribed by the State Government, to be nominated by that Government in consultation with the Chief Justice of the High Court.

The State Government shall, in consultation with the Chief Justice of the High court, appoint a person belonging the State Higher Judicial Service, not lower in rank than that of a District Judge, as the Member-Secretary of the State Authority, to exercise such powers and perform such duties under the Executive Chairman to him by the Executive Chairman of that Authority.

4.3.2.1 Functions of the State Authority

It shall be the duty of the State Authority to give effect to the policy and directions of the Central Authority.

Without prejudice to the generality of the functions referred to the sub-section (1), the State Authority shall perform all or any of the following functions, namely;

- Give legal service to persons who satisfy the criteria laid down under this Act;
- Conduct[28] [Lok Adalats including Lok Adalats for High Court cases]
- Undertake preventive and strategic legal aid programmes; and
- Perform such other functions as the State Authority may in consultations with the[29] [Central Authority] fix by regulations.
- The Section enumerates the function of the State Authority including the conduct of Lok Adalats.

State Authority to act in co-ordination with other agencies etc. and be subject to directions given by the Central Authority – In the discharge of its functions, the State Authority shall appropriately act in co-ordination with other Governmental agencies, no governmental voluntary service institutions, universities and other bodies engaged in the work of promoting the cause of legal services to the poor and shall be guided by such directions the Central Authority may give to it in writing. (Section 8 of L.S.A. Act 1987)

4.3.2.2 Entitlement to Legal Services: Criteria for Giving Legal Services

According to every person who has to file or defend a case shall be entitled to legal services under this Act if that person is a member of scheduled caste or scheduled tribes. A victim of trafficking in human beings or beggar as referred to in

28 Substituted by the Act 59 of 1994
29 Substituted by the Act of 1996

Act 23 of the constitution and a woman or child. Further a person with disability as defined in clause (i) of section 2 of the Persons with Disabilities (Equal Opportunities, Protection and Rights and full Participations) Act 1995 and a person under circumstances of underserved want such as being a victim of a mass disaster, ethnic violence, caste atrocity, flood, draught, earthquake or industrial disaster. An industrial workman in custody, including custody in protective home within the meaning of clause (g) of Section 2, of the Immoral Trafficking (Prevention) Act 1956 (104 of 1956) or in juvenile home within the meaning of clause (i) of Section 2 of the Juvenile Justice Act, 1986 (53 of 1986) or in a psychiatric hospital or psychiatric nursing home within the meaning of clause (g) of Section 2 of the Mental Health Act, 1987 (14 of 1987). Further those are entitled to get the benefits whose annual income less than rupees nine thousand or such other higher amount as may be prescribed by the State government if the case is before a court, other than the Supreme Court, and less than rupees twelve thousand or such other higher amount as may be prescribed by the Central Government, if the case is before the Supreme Court.This section defines criteria of people who will be entitled to get the benefit of legal services.

From the above, it is clear that Sec. 12 (C) of L.S.A. Act provided specific provision for the free legal aid for woman or child. Thus any woman can move to the proper authority for legal assistance.

Section 20 of the Legal Service Authority Act 1987 vides cognizance of cases by Lok Adalats:

- Where in any case referred to in clause (i) of sub-section (5) of Section 19;
- Parties thereof agree; or
- One of the parties thereof makes an application to the court, for referring the case to the Lok Adalat for settlement and if such court is *prima facie* Satisfied that there are chances of such settlement; or

- The court is satisfied that the matter is an appropriate one to be taken cognizance of by the Lok Adalat.

Provide that no case shall be referred to the Lok Adalat under sub-section (b) of clause (i) or clause (ii) by such court expect giving a reasonable opportunity of being heard to the partied.

Every Lok Adalat shall, while determining any reference before it under this Act, with utmost expenditure to arrive at a compromise or settlement between the parties and shall be guided by the principles of justice, equity, fair play and other legal principles.

This section deals with the matter which are to be taken cognizance or by the Lok Adalats.

The courts are to have an objection approach taking into accounts all the relevant circumstances the need to protect community's one hand and need to preserve the liberty of citizen on the other hand. In constructing statute equity will not relieve against a public statute of general policy is cases admitted to all within the statute and it is the duty of the court to give effect to the legislative intent. In this connection we can refer the case of ***Gauri Shankar Gaur and Others Vs. State of U.P. and Others.***[30] Another case was ***State of U.P. Vs. Hari Thakur.***[31]

4.4 Mother can Act as Natural Guardian During the Life Time of Father

The Court in ***Ms. Githa Hariharan Vs. Reserve Bank of India***[4], held that the father cannot claim that he alone was the natural guardian and his wife could take no decision without his permission. It was held that the mother of a minor was relegated to an inferior position on the ground of sex alone since her right as a natural guardian is made cognizable after the father, which was violation of 14 and 15 of the Constitution on that ground. Hence the mother can

30 AIR 1994, SC 169
31 AIR 1987 SC 2080

act as natural guardian of the minor during the life time of father who would be deemed to be absent.

The Constitution of India prohibits discrimination based on sex but it equally directs and empowers the government to undertake special measures for women. Though the position of women has improved in the last four decades, but still they are struggling to maintain their dignity and freedom. Presently Indian women are facing the toughest time mentally and physically, mainly due to unawareness and lack of knowledge of legal and constitutional rights of a woman. The Constitution provides many protection rights for women such as Protective discrimination in favour of women, Right to freedom of women, Right of women against exploitation, Rights of women under directives and political representations of women.

❑❑❑

CHAPTER

5 Judicial Intervention for Women Rights and Protection

5.1 Introduction

Labour jurisprudence owes its origin to the Pre-independence era, where it existed in a rudimentary form but after independence, it is the Supreme Court that has infused new soul in the legislative skeleton of the welfare State. The role of the judiciary in the growth of industrial jurisprudence can the judged by analyzing its trends in decided labour related issues and thereby giving a clear picture of its contribution towards the evolution of the particular branch of Law in the country. India is a welfare state and has enforced many labour welfare legislations. The meaning of welfare state is that system in which the Government undertakes various welfare programmes for its people such as insurance, old age pension[1] and other social security measures. A social system is characterized by such policies. Justice Bhagwati explained ***Social Justice in Muir Mills Co. Ltd. Vs. Suti Mazdoor Union***[2], According to him social justice is a very vague and indeterminate expression, and added that whatever it meant, the concept of social justice does not emanate from the fanciful notions of any adjudicator but must have a more solid foundation. On the other hand, Chagla C.J. rejected the submission that the Court should not impose its own ideas of social justice in

1 P. Ramanatha Aiyar, Concise Law Dictionary
2 (1955) ISCR 991

interpreting statutory provisions by saying that social justice was an object of the Constitution.[3]The labour welfare is one which lends itself to various interpretations andit has not always the same significance in different countries. State is an important legal institution as it is a source of all the powers and rights. According to Bosanque, "*the state is a working conception of life as a whole.*" In ***Chisholms Vs. Georgia***,[4] the Supreme Court of America held, "*A state is a body, united together for the common benefit, to enjoy peacefully what is their own, and to do justice to other.*"

According to Salmond, "*A state is an association of human beings established for the attainment of certain ends by certain means.*"

The relationship between state and law is inherent. A state maintains peace and administration in a society through law.By the time the role of thestate has been changed. Now the state is a socialwelfarestate. A social welfare state means such a social system whereby the state assumes primary responsibility for the welfare of its citizens, as in matters of health care, education, employment, and social security.[5]A welfare state is a concept of government where thestate plays a key role in the protection and promotion of the economic and social well-being of its citizens. It is based on the principles of equality of opportunity,equitable distributionof wealth, andpublic responsibility for those unable to avail themselves of the minimal provisions for agood life.

Indian laws towards protection of women are young with significant changes in its application and confirmation of a judicial strategy, particularly at highest level of toughening up against dowry bullies and murderers. The Dowry Prohibition Act, 1961 undergone important amendments in 1983, 1984, 1985 and 1986. This close sequence reflects desperate attempts during the 1980s, to counteract the

3 Parkash Cotton Mills Vs. Bombay, 59 Bom. L.R. 836
4 2 Dallas 456.
5 AnuragShyamRastogi, Social Welfare State: New Dimensions of State available at http://www.lawyersclubindia.com/articles/Social-Welfare-State-New-Dimensions-Of-State-3698.asp#_ftnref6

escalation of dowry murders. Since 1986, there has been no further amendment and the emphasis has shifted to the courts, especially the Supreme Court. It appears that Indian Judges have finally accepted their moral and constitutional duty to activate the anti dowry law. Whether this portrayed as human rights protection or a matter of public interest, or pro-women activism does not matter, what counts is that the most judges in the superior courts now take a definite anti-dowry stance and are ready to punish perpetrators of such evils in the harshest possible terms. The Dowry Prohibition Act of 1961 started off, by common consent as a dead letter. There was no reported case until 1975. A trickle of cases on dowry appeared in the Indian Law Reports by 1980s. Some of these are horrible cases; defense lawyers and their clients almost got away with murder.[6]

Time and again the Supreme Court of India has extended the ambit of Art 21 of the Indian Constitution and held that mere existence is not the right to live- it is the right to live with dignity. But unfortunately such has been the social conditions and have been prejudices in the man's society that even personal liberty guaranteed to woman under Art 21 of the Constitution has no meaning to her. Therefore, wherever crimes are committed against women the some should he viewed in the context of violation of her right under Art 21 of the Constitution and not merely as a crime against society[7].

The Supreme Court in the case of ***Bachan Singh Vs. State of Punjab***[8] evolved the 'rarest of rare' principle which means that death sentence should be awarded only in the rarest of rare cases. Of course much was left to the judicial discretion in this case but still the death sentence being the gravest sentence required some criteria to streamline the judicial verdict on this point. Such guidelines ultimately were given by the Supreme Court in the case of ***Machi Singh***

6 Dr Werner Menski, SOAS, University of London, "The Dowry Problem: Progress in Legal Remedies" KLT(1997) 2 at page73

7 Gupta Sadhama " Dowry Death : Law relating of dowry offences", Cr. L.J. 2006 Nov ; 112 (1283) at p. 289

8 A.I.R. 1980 SC 898

Vs. State of Punjab.[9] The Apex Court issued five guidelines for the award of death sentence, which were based on viz. (1) Manner of Commission of murder, (2) Motive for Commission of crime, (3) Anti-social or socially abhorrent nature of the crime, (4) Magnitude of crime, (5) Personality of the victim for the murder. About the third category, while explaining it the Supreme Court has opined as under:

> *"In cases of bride burning and what are known as dowry death or when murder is committed in order to remarry for the sake of extracting dowry once again or to marry another women on account of infatuation"*

Thus, the Supreme Court has also admitted that the crime is of socially abhorrent nature. However, Law Commission of India on October 10, 2007 in its report says

> *"There is no justification for amending section 304B of I.P.C. to provide for death penalty"*

A combined reading together all the provisions occurring under sections 304 B, 498-A of the I.P.C. and sections 113-A and 113-B of the Indian Evidence Act, Section 2 of the Dowry Prohibition Act denote that sincere efforts are still lacking by the legislature in so far as the cases of dowry death have not been made punishable with death sentence. In a case[10] Supreme Court found that on account of not satisfying the demand of certain goods, right from and next day, the wife was repeatedly taunted, maltreated and mentally tortured by calling her ugly etc. There was a quarrel a day before her death. The Supreme Court held that this by itself would constitute to be a willful act to be a cruelty both within the meaning of sections 498-A and 304-B of I.P.C. Even though there was no mention of torture to wife by witnesses, prosecution was not held vitiated.[11]

The Supreme Court held in ***Shanti Vs. State of Haryana***[12] that two sections (304B and 498-A of Indian Penal Code) are not mutually exclusive and in cases of 'dowry death' both

9 1983 Cri LJ (SC) 1457
10 Pawan Kumar Vs. State of Haryana (1998 Cri L.L.1144)
11 ShubhamSundram Vs. State 1997 Cri LJ 499 (Mad)
12 A.I.R. 1991 1226.

from the point of view of practice and procedure and to avoid technical defects, charges under both the sections should be framed. The Supreme Court further held that in the absence of any explanation under section 304-B about the meaning of cruelty, the meaning of cruelty and harassment has to be taken as the same as in the explanation to section 498-A of I.P.C. In ***Baldev Krishnan Vs. State of Punjab***[13] the Supreme Court held that *"taunts to the deceased by the accused saying that better proposals were received for the groom who were willing to give more dowry and making humiliating remarks about the low quality of gifts brought in by her during the marriage amounted to harassment on account of insufficient dowry,"* and that even if there was proof of no physical torture, proof of mental torture was sufficient for conviction.

In the case of ***Kunhiabdhullah Vs. State of Kerala,***[14] the Supreme Court said that menace of dowry cut across caste, religion and geographical location. Both the husband and mother-in-law stood for section 304-B. In ***Joint Women's Programme Vs. State of Rajasthan***[15] a social organization took up a few cases of alleged dowry deaths in Rajasthan and Haryana. The Supreme Court took a path-breaking step directing state Governments to setup special dowry cells at the level to investigate into such unnatural deaths.

In ***Kundalaa Bala Subramanyam Vs. State of A.P.,***[16] dealing with cases of bride burning the Supreme Court has expressed the view that mostly older women in the family are worst perpetrators of crime like bride burning, and urged men to stop being mute spectators.

In the case of ***State of Karnataka Vs. Devaraj***[17], where a young woman was murdered and her in laws misled the authority that it was a suicide. The Karnataka High Court regretted that the quality of police investigation in the dowry death of a poor village womanwas downright shameful and resulted in grave failure of justice.

13 AIR 1997 SC 1666
14 AIR 2004 SC 1731
15 AIR 1987 SC 2060
16 AIR 1993 Cri L J, 1635
17 2002 Cri L J 2299

Allahabad High Court, in ***Dev Prasad Vs. State of UP.***[18] observed-that young girls are killed for dowry as could be seen from large number of FIRs under Sec 303-B, IPC being filed all over the country "*We are surprised that while an ordinary murder can be punished by death sentence under Sec 302, IPC, a dowry death, which is a much worst- offence, has a maximum punishment of life imprisonment. A dowry death is not just an ordinary crime. It is a social crime. It outrages the modern conscience it makes the whole society revert to feudal barbarism. Hence, we recommend to Parliament to amend the law and provide for death sentence in dowry death cases.*" In this case a girl of 23 years was harassed for dowry and burn after three years of marriage. No post mortem examination was done. The husband was convicted under Section 303 B, IPC, hemoved the High Court to quash the FIR.

In ***Sate Vs. Maregowda,***[19] the Karnataka High Court dealt with ahusband who use to come drunk and harass his wife for money. Ultimately she hanged herself; she left a suicide note implicating him. The Session judge acquitted the husband of charges under the Dowry Prohibition Act and under Section 498-A and 304-B of IPC. On appeal, the High Court stated that the suicide note could be treated as dying declaration. It could not be rejected, as the Sessions Judge did, merely because it was written in red ink in the reverse side of the electoral card.

In ***Shaik China Buda Vs. State of Andhra Pradesh,***[20] facts of this case are husband and relatives harassing deceased for additional dowry and the medical evidence proved the deceased died due to consumption of poisonous pesticide. At the same time there is a categorical admission by parents of deceased that accused husband has liking for deceased and evidence of all witness full of inconsistencies. There is no specific evidence against main accused for offence under Sec. 498-A, further all other accused persons were

18 2002 Cri L J 4291
19 2001 Cri L J 4491
20 2002 Cri L J 256

acquitted; therefore court held that appellant also entitled to get benefit of doubt.

In ***Satvir Singh Vs. State of Punjab***, [21]Court held that with regard to demand for dowry the burden of proof is on prosecution. The word dowry in Section 304-B, IPC should be any property or valuable given or agreed to be given in connection with the marriage. The customary payment in connections with birth of child or other ceremonies are not enveloped within the ambit of 'dowry'

However the system of dowry is deeply rooted in the soil of Indian society and can't simply be willed away lightly. It can be said to have reached a stage, of a form of social acceptance. Despite express legislation and statutory provisions to the contrary.

However, it is submitted that the heart of the dowry problem lies in the willingness of people to go to the extent of condemning the bride to death, and pronouncing a death sentence of their own in the event of the dowry demand not being met. This reality is prevalentin India for long, accompanied by subsequent attemptsby the husband and/ or his family members, to try to dress up the incident as an "accident" in most cases.

The present work is an attempt to determine the maximum punishment that should be prescribed for what has popularly been termed as "bride-burning" on account of an unsatisfied dowry demand. The relatively newly envisaged offence to this effect, based on the premise of the Legislature's desire to protect the vulnerable position of women in society;which is close to completing two and half decades since its inception, is that of a deemed "dowry death" under Sec. 304-B of the IPC, which constitutes a special category of offence based on a presumption or a legal fiction. Section 304-B stipulates that a death of a woman within seven years of her marriage by burns or bodily injury or under abnormal circumstances, with evidence of cruelty or by her husband or his relatives in connection with a demand for dowry is a "dowry death". As

21 AIR 2001 SC 2829

a means of extending support to the offence under the IPC, Sections I13A (Presumption as to abetment of suicide of a married woman) and 113B(presumption as to dowry death) were added to the Indian Evidence Act and made invoke able in cases of dowry murder or suicide. Corresponding to this, the Criminal Procedure Code has also been amended in the form of Section 174(3) to provide for a mandatory postmortem when the case involves suicide of a woman within seven years of marriage or a relative has made a request or there is doubt regarding cause of death.

For some in the women's movement, the opposition to death penalty for rape appears to have been a pragmatic position - since it would only make the women more vulnerable if the penalty were so severe. For others, the pragmatic argument was a means of opposing the spread of death penalty into areas where it is not, already. In this regard, recently the Malimath Committee has also recommended that no death penalty needs to be dealt out in rape cases.

However, it is the thrust of the present paper that it is possible to argue for the death penalty to be kept as an option before the judge in a system of graded punishment, for certain heinous offences against women. In this context the failure to challenge the prescription of the death penalty for offences in the Commission of Sati (Prevention) Act, 1987, becomes an indicator of this line of thinking. Further, it has also been suggested that child sexual abuse being of an extraordinary nature, there should be a relaxation of fair trial standards in dealing with it. Thus, in the course of the paper arguments will be presented to uphold this line of argument for tackling the social menace of dowry death.

Capital Punishment is laid down as a penalty in many statutes in India, such as in the IPC and in the penalty provisions of national security and anti-narcotics legislation. Under the IPC eleven offences are punishable by death. A death sentence may also be imposed for a number of offences committed by members of the armed forces under the Army Act, 1950, the Air Force Act, 1950 and the Navy Act 1956.

Against this backdrop, if we look at the offence of causing dowry death within the ambit of section 304-B (2), IPC, we find that the offence is punishable with a minimum term of seven years and a maximum extending up to life imprisonment. Thus, unlike offences such as murder, where a maximum sentence can entail capital punishment, the offence of dowry death carries no such punishment.

According to section 304-B (2), IPC, the punishment prescribed by the Legislature for causing dowry death, carries a minimum sentence of 7 years, which can be stretched to a maximum of a life term in jail.

Before 1983, there were no specific provisions pertaining to violence within the matrimonial home. Husbands could be convicted under the general provisions of murder, abatement to suicide, causing hurt and wrongful confinement. However, these general provisions of criminal law did not take into account the specific situation of a woman facing violence within the home as against assault by a stranger. It was strongly felt that an offence committed within the privacy of home by a person on whom the woman is emotionally dependent needs to be dealt with on a different plane.

But at the same time it was extremely difficult for women to prove violence by husbands and in-laws 'beyond reasonable doubt' as was required by criminal jurisprudence. There would be no witnesses to corroborate their evidence, as the offences are committed behind closed doors and within the four walls of the house. Thus, different criteria had to be evolved to measure injury. For example: generally, complaints can be registered only after an offence has been committed. But in a domestic situation a woman would need protection even before the crime, when she apprehends danger to her life, as she is living with and is dependent on her assaulter. Thus, special concessions have been made in the law dealing with women. In the context of dowry death, a legal fiction of a "deemed" death having been caused by those who had harassed the deceased for dowry has been created.

The apex judiciary in India has played a positive role in developing the law in this area. Decided cases tend to speak for themselves. For instance, in ***Hem Chand Vs. State of Haryana,***[22] the appellant had married the deceased and demanded a sum of Rs.25000/- as dowry for purchasing a plot. The deceased had come to the matrimonial house with Rs.15000/- and a request that her father be allowed to remit the balance within some additional time. Within five years of marriage, the deceased died of strangulation. The trial court held that there was demand for dowry and there was cruelty on the part of the accused and accordingly convicted him under sections 304-B and 498-A of the IPC, awarding a sentence of imprisonment for life.

The Supreme Court held that thepresumption as has been incorporated in section 304-B IPC, is such that irrespective of the fact whether the accused has any direct connection with the death or not, he shall be presumed to have committed the dowry death provided the other requirements mentioned in the section are satisfied. However, it was also added by the court that section 304-B IPC, only raises a presumption and lays down that the minimum sentence should be of 7 years, which may extend to a maximum of imprisonment for life. Therefore, it was reasoned that awarding the extreme punishment of imprisonment for life should be in rare cases and not in every case. Justification for having the capital punishment as a possible option before the judge in cases of dowry death, can be found in the deterrent theory" of punishment. Deterrence, it is submitted, would constitute the principal concern for tackling a wide-spread social evil. In fact, to deter such well-accepted social practices, deterrence might wellbe the only option available.

The Law Commission in its 35th Report (I967) stated that the single thread running through all capital punishment

22 (1994) 6 SCC 727

attracting offences was that the 'sanctity of human life must be protected.' It is the willful exposure of life to peril, it was observed, that it seemed to constitute the basis of a provision for the sentence of death. If this be the accepted criterion, then cases of dowry deaths, where women are condemned to gruesome deaths, after careful planning and machinations, would certainly fall within the category of offences which attract a maximum possible sentence of the death penalty.

Punishment is essential to the law's effectiveness and without it the law would be an empty letter. Punishment has a symbolic significance, i.e., the very physical treatment itself expresses condemnation of the community, and accordingly certain forms of hard treatment have become the conventional symbols of public reprobation. According to Andenaes,[23]

> *"in situations where the probability of detection of criminal behaviour is low, legislatures sometimes are inclined towards compensating by increasing the severity of penalties. This trend has indeed been recurrent in the history of criminal law."*

Andeanes suggests that punishment on the basis of general deterrence is ethically defensible, both in legislature and sentencing, if-

- The penalty is in reasonable proportion to the gravity of the offence,
- The penalty does not violate principles of equality before the law.

It is submitted that on both the counts, having the death penalty as an option in sentencing for dealing with dowry death cases would be justified. Bride burning has been described as the most atrocious and barbarous of offences, because of the motives[24] including greed and avarice, for which such crimes are perpetrated and the, circumstances in which they are committed.[25]

---

23 Johannes Andeanes, The Morality of deterrence, in sentencing 194 (Hyman Gross and Andrew Von Hirscheds, New Work; AUP, 1981)

24 Ashoke Kumar Vs. State of Rajasthan, 1991(1) Crimes 116, it was held that motive for a murder may or may not be there but in dowry death cases it is inherent.

25 A.S. Garg, "Bride Burning: Crime Against Woman 1(Rohtak, the Bright Law House, 1990)

In this regard the ***Bachan Singh***[26] **and** ***Machhi Singh***[27] standard of awarding the capital sentence in the "rarest of the rare cases" may well be adopted. That would be a matter coming within the realm of "sentencing" where the judge can exercise his discretion. In fact, exercise of discretion for determining the appropriate sentence, is what the judge is expected to do in murder cases under section 302 IPC. In dowry death cases, the effect being much the same, the judge should, like in a murder case, be provided with the *option* of imposing death penalty in appropriate cases of dowry death.

According to Rupert Cross, in the case of the more common offences in a society,[28] it is possible to identify five factors capable of affecting the gravity of an offence, based on which the punishment levels are determined by the Legislature. These five factors, which really are self-explanatory, include:

- Social danger,
- Alarm caused in society,
- Social Disapproval in society,
- Harm caused by offence to social morality etc.,
- Wickedness of the offence.

Examining these factors with reference to the offence of causing dowry death, one comes to the irresistible conclusion that the punishment levels to be prescribed for such an offence should be on par with the punishment levels of grave social offences, such as murder. Thus, the gravity of the offence is such that the maximum punishment for the offence should be the capital sentence. However, the implementation of the legislative policy would vary from cases to case. It needs to be remembered that prescription of the maximum possible sentence of capital penalty, would not mean that the punishment would be meted out in every case. But if 'the option is not kept open before the judge at

26 A.I.R. 1980 SC 898
27 AIR 1983 SC 957
28 Dowry deaths certainly are common offence in Indian Society (Statistics available so)

all, then the ends of social deterrence, as has already been pointed out, would not be satisfied.

More recent cases have been driving home an increasingly unambiguous judicial message to dowry murderers and men who drive their wives to suicide: Punishment will be tough and the courts will be unwillingto tolerate prevarications. In ***State (Delhi, Administration) Case,***[29] neighbours had unsuccessfully sought to rescue a burning woman. The Delhi High Court, almost unbelievably, had acquitted the accused but the Supreme Court sentenced the husband and other members of the family to life imprisonment. This was also a landmark decision on the difficult question of law to treat a victim's dying declaration. While in some cases, where a suicide occurred rather than murder, the evidentiary position was less than clear,[30] the Supreme Court has awarded deterrent life sentences in several cases to a murderous mother-in-law,[31] the husband, father-in-law, and sister-in-law, [32]and a husband who prevented neighboursfrom rescuing his burning wife[33]. In this case, the husband appealed against the life sentence imposed by the High Court but it was confirmed. It seems that the other family members were lucky to get away because this husband acted so very obviously to further his evil design.

In ***State of U.P Vs. Dr. Ravindra Prakash Mittal,***[34] a husband had been acquitted of a dowry murder which occurred in 1971, by an unreported High Court decision of 1979. When the case was again taken up after all these years, the Supreme Court brushed aside all suggestions that this old matter should he left alone and awarded life imprisonment. The court clearly expressed its opinion that non-action would have amounted to perpetration of injustice. One cannot emphasize

29 AIR 1986 SC 250

30 In Wazir Chand Case (AIR 1989 SC 378), dowry demands had been made, but it could not be established with certainty that the accused had murdered the woman rather than driven her-to suicide.

31 In Paniben Case[1992] 2 SCC 474, the young woman's dying declarations were fully accepted.

32 State of U.P. Case (1992) 2 SCC 86 where again High Court had acquitted the accused

33 (1992) 3 SCC 106

34 (1992) 3 SCC 300

enough that ten years earlier, this kind of decision would have been unthinkable. The most recent position appears to be, therefore, that the Supreme Court has become extremely alert to issues concerning dowry murder and that the High Courts, too, are now pulling their weight. The Kerala High Court, hardly ever-lacking alertness when it comes to protecting women, has produced an excellent judgment in ***State of Kerala Vs. Jolly Saimon and Others,***[35] considering in detail the appropriate procedures to be followed in cases of suspected dowry deaths. This is a model of procedural structuring, designed to save judicial time and to have maximum effect on the ground.

While dowry murder cases inevitably demand judicial reactions to social practices, most judges have been reluctant to make explicit comments about how, in their view, the menace of dowry may be controlled. In ***Ashok Kumar Vs. State of Rajasthan,***[36] however, R.M. Sahai J. launched into a lecture on the desirability of social ostracism to curtail what he called the 'increasing malady of bride burning'. Significantly, the judge also confirmed, in no uncertain terms, that the poor never resort to that kind of crime. His focus on neighbourhood vigilance and social ostracism echoes very closely the views of the activist, writer MadhuKishwar.[37]

5.2 Judicial Discretion for Anticipatory Bail in Dowry Death Cases

Section 438 of the Code of Criminal Procedure 1973, deals with the direction for grant of bail to a person apprehending arrest. When any person has reason to believe that he may be arrested on an accusation of having committed a non-bailable offence, he may apply to High Court or the Court of Sessions for a direction under this section that in the event of arrest he shall be released on bail. While giving such a direction the Court may impose some conditions.

35 (1994) 4 SCC 1 : 1994 (2) KLT 700
36 AIR1990 SC 2134
37 See the particular Kishwar, Madhu (1990): Women's organisations. The Presence of unrealistic expectations in No. 59 Mnushi, pp 11-14

The concept of Anticipatory Bail has been enshrined under Section 438 of the Code of Criminal Procedure 1973, which is a new concept and term 'Anticipatory Bail' has neither been used by the said Section nor by its marginal notes. The term for the first time was used by the Law Commission of India on its 41st Report. Section 438 reads,

1. When any person has reason to believe that he may be arrested on an action of having committed a non-bailable offence he may apply to the High Court or Court of session for a direction under this section and that, Court may, if it thinks fit direct that in the event of such arrest, he shall be released on bail.
2. When the High Court or the Court of Sessions makes a direction under Sub-Section (1), it may include such conditions in such directions in the light of the facts of the particular case, as it may think fit including:
    - A-condition that the person shall make himself available for interrogation by a Police Officer as and when required;
    - A condition that the person shall not directly or indirectly make any inducement, threat or promise to any person acquainted with the facts of the case so as to dissuade him from disclosing such facts to the court or to any Police Officer;
    - A condition that the person shall not leave India without the previous permission of the court;
    - Such other condition as may be imposed under sub-section 30 of Section 437, as if the bail were granted under the said Section(3) If such person is thereafter arrested without warrant by an Officer In-charge of a Police Station on such accusation, and is prepared either at one time of arrest or any time in the

custody of such officer to give bail, he shall be released on bail, and if a Magistrate taking cognizance of such offences decides that a warrant should be issued in the first instance against the person, he shall issue a bailable warrant in conformity with the direction of the Court under sub-section (1)."

On bare reading of the Section, it is manifestly clear that the legislature has,empowered the High Court or the Court of Sessions to issue direction to the effect that in the event of arrest any person who has reason to believe that he may be arrested on an accusation of having committed a non-bailable offence, shall be released on bail. The provision under, sub-section (I) of Section 438 show that the provision is substantive in nature and provision under sub-section (2) and (3) are procedural.

The necessity for granting anticipatory bail arises mainly because at times influential persons try to implicate their rivals in false cases for the purpose of disgracing them or by getting them detained in jail for some days. Apart from false cases, where there are reasonable grounds for holding that a person accused of an offence is not likely to abscond or otherwise misuse his liberty while on bail, there seems no justification to require him to first submit to custody, remain in prison for some days and then apply for bail.[38]

The main object of anticipatory bail is to relieve a person from unnecessary apprehension, harassment, agony and disgrace. An order of anticipatory bail constitutes an assurance against police custody. So it is a pre-arrest legal process. Although normally, any order of bail can be effective only from the time of arrest because to grant bail means to "set at liberty a person arrested or imprisoned on security being taken for his appearance. But a direction under Section 438 is intended to confer conditional immunity from confinement. So the object and purpose of anticipatory bail

---

38 Government of India, 41st Report of Law Commission of India on Code of Criminal Procedure Code, Vol-I

is to prevent mischief played by false implications, to protect innocent person from unnecessary detention to facilitate the accused to move for regular bail to secure the presence of accused for investigation to frustrate attempts of powerful and influential persons to implicate their rivals in false cases.

The offence relating to cruelty on women, demanding of dowry and offences of dowry deaths are not exception to the law of anticipatory bail.

It is worth noticing that the Supreme Court in ***Samunder Singh Vs. State of Rajasthan,***[39]deprecated the practice of granting anticipatory bail in dowry death cases. It is so that whenever any allegation of dowry death is made against any person, the Court must as a matter of course reject the anticipatory bail application but nowhere the legislature has put a bar on grant of anticipatory bail relating to any offence. The Apex Court observed:

"The widespread belief that dowry deaths are even now treated with some casualness at all levels seems to be well grounded. The High Court has granted anticipatory bail in such a matter. We are of opinion that the High Court should not have exercised its jurisdiction to release the accused on anticipatory bail in disregard of magnitude and seriousness of matter. The matter regarding unnatural death of the daughter-in-law at the house of her father-in-law was still under investigation and the appropriate course to adopt was to allow the concerned magistrate to deal with the same on the basis of material before the court at the time of their arrest in case they were arrested. It was neither prudent nor proper for High Court to have granted anticipatory bail which order was very likely to occasion prejudice by its very nature and timing."

The judgment in ***Satya Parkash Vs. Anand Sarup,***[40]is notable where the Sessions Judge granted the anticipatory

39 AIR 1987 SC 737
40 1999(3) Crimes 300 (H.P.) 301

bail to the respondents and the High Court also upheld the decision of the Sessions Judge. But in ***Rajanna Vs. State***[41]which also relates to dowry death but Court refused to grant the anticipatory bail to the respondents. Again in ***Gianender Kumari Vs. State of Haryana,***[42]Court granted the anticipatory bail for dowry death. The analysis of above judgment all reads that all the cases related to dowry death, the facts and circumstances of the cases are also similar but we find different approach in granting the anticipator bail.

High-Court or the Court of Sessions has been given wider discretionary power to grant anticipatory bail under this Section 438. In ***Gurbakh Singh Vs. State of Punjab,***[43]the Court observed that there is no risk involved in entrusting a wide discretion to the Counts of Sessions or the High Court because:

- these are higher Courts managed by experienced persons,
- their orders are not final but are open to appellate or revisional scrutiny, and
- discretion has always to be exercised by Courts Judicially.

In ***M.P. Lohia Vs. State of West Bengal and Another***[44], appellants have been charged for offences punishable under Sections 304-B, 406 and 498-A read with Section 34 of I.P.C. Their applications for the grant of anticipatory bail have been rejected by the lower Courts. But Supreme Court held that appellants are entitled to be released on bail in event of their arrest on furnishing bail bond of Rupees One lakh. Therefore, Supreme Court granted the anticipatory bail. The analysis of above decisions does not provide any clear guidelines as to what the law of anticipatory bail in Dowry

41 2002(1) H.L.R. (Kar) 550
42 2000(1) H.L.R. (P & H) 282
43 AIR 1980 SC 1632
44 Siddhaaarth Barua, " Supreme Court Views," New era, Law Publication 2005 p. 251

Death cases is? But we know only discretion of the Court in the point of over discussion and nothing more.

5.3 Role of Lower Judiciary in Women Protection

The lower judiciary performs an important function in the prosecution of offences. After the investigations complete, the police is bound to submit a report under Section 173(2) of the Cr.P.C. On receiving the police report the Court may take cognizance of the offence under section 190(1)(b) and 193 of the Cr.P.C. and straightway issue process. The lower judiciary exercises their control over the police in the exercise of their statutory functions, like granting bail. The code has classified all offences into bailable and non-bailable. In bailable offence the accused has a right to be released on bail. In non-bailable offence bail cannot be claimed as matter of right, but at the discretion of the Court. Section 436 of the Cr.P.C. provides that if a person accused of a bailable offence is arrested or detained without warrant he has a right to be released on bail. Section 437 of the Code provides that a person accused of non-boilable offence is arrested or detained without warrant he may be released on bail. But in such a case bail is not a matter of right, but only a privilege to be granted at the discretion of the Court. Section 439 (1) of the Code gives very wide discretion to the High Court and the Court of Session in the matter of granting bail.

5.3.1 Remand

Remand is the custody of an accused given to the police beyond twenty four hours. The police are empowered to keep the accused under custody till the investigation is completed but they cannot detain any person in their custody for more than twenty-four hours. Section 167 of the Cr. P.C lays down that whenever an accused person is arrested and detained in custody by the police and it appears that the investigation cannot be completed within twenty-four hours as fixed by Section 57, the accused person must be forwarded to Judicial Magistrate. The Magistrate to whom the accused in such custody as such Magistrate thinks fit for a term not exceeding 15 days in the whole. However there is no obligation on the part of the Magistrate to grant remand as a matter of course.

5.4 Penal Sanctions and Sentencing in Dowry Related Crimes

Penal sanctions against offenders in dowry related offences are provided in the Indian Penal Code 1860, and the Dowry Prohibition Act, 1961. A study of these statutes indicates that courts are duly armed with the conventional penal sanctions for such crimes. The Indian Penal Code provides the following types of legal sanction: (i) Sentence of death (ii) Sentence of imprisonment for life (iii) Imprisonment for a term which may be rigorous or simple, and (iv) Fine.

The Dowry Prohibition Act provides for only two types of penal sanctions namely:

(i) Imprisonment for a term and (ii) Fine

Both the two laws contain provisions for a minimum sentence of imprisonment in relation to dowry offences. The power of the courts in relation to imposition of penal sanctions is controlled and regulated by various provisions of the Code of Criminal Procedure, 1973. These provisions determine the jurisdiction of the criminal courts, the power to impose various sentences and limitation on such powers. The Cr.P.C also confers power to pass alternative and additional sanctions. It is intended, here, to discuss the nature of sentencing structure and the judicial discretion in sentencing of offenders in dowry related crimes.

5.4.1 Sentencing Structure

The purpose of a criminal trial is to determine the guilty of the offence to the accused to which he is charged. The law confirms a considerably wide discretion on the judge and provides few criteria that should guide him in his sentencing function. The exercise of judicial discretion in sentence determination depends upon several legal factors which include the organization and the hierarchy of the courts, nature of offences, availability of different sentencing measures, mandatory sentences and the age of the offenders. In dowry related offences the sentencing structure is determined by the Indian Penal Code, 1860, and the Dowry Prohibition Act, 1961. Different sentencing structure is provided in penal provisions of these laws. It would be desirable to discuss these provisions at this stage. Section, 302 I.P.C. provides punishment for murder. That Section provides that, whosoever commits murder shall be punished with death or imprisonment for life and shall also be liable to fine. The offence of dowry death is punishment with minimum sentence under section 304-B I.P.C. which provides that a person shall be punishable with imprisonment for a term which shall not be less than seven years but which may extend to imprisonment for life. The offence of abatement of suicide under section 306, I.P.C. is punishable with Imprisonment up to ten year and fine.

Under Section 498 -A I.P.C. the offence of cruelty by the husband or his relatives has been, made punishable with imprisonment up to three years and fine. The offence of dowry death under Section 304-B I.P.C. has been made punishable only with imprisonment and a fine has not been added to this offence.

The Dowry Prohibition Act lays down a number of punitive provisions resting to the dowry offences. Under Section 3 of the Act a minimum of five years imprisonment and a minimum fine of fifteen thousand rupees or the value of dowry whichever is more, is prescribed for giving or taking or abetting the giving or taking of dowry. The Court may however, for adequate and special reasons may impose a sentence of imprisonment less than five years. Under Section 4 of the Act the offence of demanding dowry is punishable with imprisonment for a term not less than six month but which may extend two year and with fine which may extend to ten thousand rupees. The offence of dowry in one form or the other through an advertisement is punishable with six month to five years imprisonment and a fine up to fifteen thousand rupees under Section 4-Aof the Act . Section 6 provides that the dowry received by a person other than the woman in connection with whose marriage it has given, is to be transferred to the woman or her heirs within a period of three months, failing which imprisonment for six months to two years and a fine of five thousand rupees can be imposed upon the offenders.

5.5 Equal Pay for Equal Work

In ***State of West Bengal and Others Vs. Hari Narayan Bhowal and Others***,[45] the Supreme Court has hold that unless a very clear case is made out id satisfied that the scale provided to a group of persons on the basis of the material produced before it amounts to discriminate without there being any justification, the court should not take upon itself the responsibility of fixation of scales of pay, especially when the different scale of pay have been fixed by pay commission or pay Revision Committees, having persons as members who can be held to be experts in the field and after examining all the relevant material. Till the claimants satisfy on material produced, that they have not been treated as equals within the parameters of Article 14, courts should be reluctant to issue any writ or direction to treat them equal.

With a view to give effect to the goal of equal pay for equal work set out in clause (d) of Article 39 of the constitution the President of India promulgated on 26th September, 1975, the Equal Remuneration Ordinance, 1975 so that the above Directive Principles could be implemented in the year which was being celebrated into an Act as Act No. 25 of 1976. The Equal Remuneration Act, 1976 provides for the payment of equal remuneration to men and women workers and for prevention of discrimination, on the ground of sex, against

45 (1995) II L.L.J. 328 (SC)

women in the matter of employment and for matters connected therewith or incidental thereto. The Act ensures against discrimination in recruitment and promotion of men and women. It provides for the setting up of Advisory Committees to promote employment opportunities for women. The Act extends to the whole of the India.

It was held in ***Dharwad District P.W.D. Literate Daily Wage Employees Association and Others Vs. State of Karnataka and Another***,[46] that the Equal Remuneration Act 1976 was enacted for providing equality of pay for equal work between men and women which is a part of the principle 'equal pay for equal work'. The daily rated and monthly rated employees in the State of Karnataka are, therefore entitled to pay like regular employees. Therefore, the Government must pay salary to such workmen of the rates equivalent to the minimum pay in the pay scale of the regularly employed workers.

In the ***State of M.P. and Another Vs. Pramod Bhartiya and Others,***[47] the respondents are lecturers working in High Secondary Schools in the State of Madhya Pradesh. Conditions of their service are governed by Madhya Pradesh Non-gazette class-III Educational Service (Non-Collegiate Branch Service) Recruitment and Promotion rules, 1973. In the State of Madhya Pradesh there is another set of schools Higher Secondary Schools and in these lecturers are categorized as technical lecturers and non-technical lecturers. The conditions of service of lecturers in these schools are governed by M.P. Education Department (Technical) class III (Non-ministerial) Recruitment Rules 1980. It was held that it is not enough to say that the qualifications are the same, nor is it enough to say that the schools are of the same status. It is also not sufficient to say that the service conditions are similar. What is more important is, whether they discharge similar duties, functions and responsibilities. There is no material to show that the duties, functions and responsibilities of both the categories of lecturers are identical

46 (1991), II L.L.J. 318 (SC)
47 (1993), I L.L.J. 490 (SC)

or similar. Though the equal Remuneration Act, 1976 is mainly directed against discrimination against workmen and is not applicable to respondents on establishments to which they belongs, yet relevance of the said definition cannot be denied. It is an enactment made to give statutory shape to the rule of "equal pay for equal work" both for men and women. The Equal Remuneration Act lays stress upon the similarity of the skill, effort and responsibility when performed under similar conditions. Therefore the Equal Remuneration Act would not apply to the respondents.

In ***M.P. Rural Agriculture Extension Officers Association Vs. State of M.P. and Another,***[48] the appellant Association espoused the cause of Village Level Workers who were later on designated as Rural Agriculture Officers who were only matriculates. They complained that they were not paid the same pay scale as was paid to those who were graduates under the rules. The Supreme Court observed that a policy decision had been adopted by the State that the post of Extension Officers should be filled up only by graduates. A different scale was provided by State for the non-graduates with a view to avoid any discrimination between the new recruits and the serving employees who possessed the graduate qualification, the State granted a higher scale of pay also for the existing degree holders. In making such grant the State could not be said to have acted illegally, the Supreme Court said.

It was held in ***Government of West Bengal Vs. Tarun K. Roy,***[49] that the principle of equal pay for equal work would not apply where educational qualifications and other considerations such as source of recruitment and nature of work done vary between two classes of employees, although nature of work done is the same.

In the ***State of Punjab Vs. Talwinder Singh and others,***[50]daily wagers claimed parity of pay scale with those on regular basis. The Supreme Court observed that the claim

48 (2004) II L.L.J. 1114 (S.C.)
49 (2004) I L.L.J. 421 (S.C.)
50 (2004) II L.L.J. 1048 (S.C.)

to the extent of granting minimum in regular pay scale was valid.

Worker means a worker in any establishment on employment in respect of which this Act has come into force.

Words and expression used in this Act and not defined but defined in the Industrial Disputes Act, 1947 (14 of 1947), shall have the meaning respectively assigned to them in that Act.

Act to have overriding effect. The provisions of this Act shall have effect no withstanding anything inconsistent therewith contained in any other law or in the terms of any award, - agreement or contact of service, whether made before or after the commencement of this Act, or in any instrument having effect under any law for the time being in force.

In ***M/s Mackinon Mackenzie & Co. Ltd. Vs. Andery D'Costa & Another,***[51] it was urged on behalf of the management that difference between the remuneration of male stenographers and confidential lady stenographers was on account of a settlement arrived as after proper negotiation. It was held that in view of Section 3 of the Act the provisions of the Act shall have effect not withstanding anything inconsistent therewith contained in any other law or in the terms of any award, agreement or contact of service whether made before or after the commencement of the Act, or in any instrument having effect under any law for the time being in force. Therefore, the settlement must yield to the provisions of the Act.

5.6 Sexual Harassment of Working Women at Work Place

The sexual harassment of women particularly the working women at work place by their male counterparts is one of the known evils of the modern society.The Sexual harassment at a workplace is considered violation of women's right to equality, life and liberty. It creates an insecure and hostile work environment, which discourage women's participation

51 (1987) I L.L.J. 536 (S.C.)

in work, thereby adversely affecting their social and economic empowerment and the goal of inclusive growth.In India there is no one who is capable to combat this evil of the sexual harassment of working place.With this idea the legislature formulated the Sexual Harassment of Women at Workplace (Prevention, Prohibition and Redressal) Act 2013.

5.6.1 Need for Appropriate and Effective Legislation

The need for such legislation was observed first time by the Supreme Court, in ***Vishaka Vs. State of Rajasthan.***[52] In the absence of any law at that time providing measures to check the evil of sexual harassment of working women, the Supreme Court, in exercise of power available under Article 32 of the Constitution, framed guidelines to be followed at all workplaces or institutions, until a legislation is enacted for the purpose. The Supreme Court incorporated basic principles of human rights enshrined in Constitution of India under Article 14, 15, 19(1)(g) and 21, and provisions of Convention on Elimination of All Forms of Discrimination against Women (CEDAW), which has been ratified in 1993 by the Government of India. The guidelines laid down by the Supreme Court were to be treated as the law declared under Article 141 of the Constitution. In this case, the Supreme Court observed that in the absence of enacted law to provide for the effective enforcement of the basic human right of gender equality and guarantee against sexual harassment and abuse, more particularly against sexual harassment and abuse, more particularly against sexual harassment at work places, the court lays down the guidelines and norms for due observance at all work places or other institutions, until a legislation is enacted for the purpose.

5.6.1.1 Duty of the Employer or other Responsible Persons in Work Place and Other Institutions

It shall be the duty of the employer or other responsible persons in work places or other institution to prevent or deter

52 (1997) 6 SCC 241

the commission of acts of sexual harassment and to provide the procedures for the resolution, settlement or prosecution of acts of sexual harassment by taking all steps required.

Definition: For this purpose, sexual harassment included such unwelcome sexually determined behavior (whether directly or by implication) as:

- physical contact and advances;
- a demand or request for sexual favours;
- sexually coloured remarks;
- showing pornography;
- any other unwelcome physical, verbal conduct of sexual nature.

Where any of these acts is committed in circumstances where-under the victim of such conduct has a reasonable apprehension that in relation to the victim's employment or work whether she is drawing salary, or honorarium or voluntary, whether in government, public or private enterprise such conduct can be humiliating and may constitute a health and safety problem.

5.6.1.2 Preventive Steps

All employers or persons in change of work place whether in the public or private sector should take appropriate steps to prevent sexual harassment. Without prejudice to the generally of this obligation they should take the following steps:

1. Express prohibition of sexual harassment as defined above at the work place should be notified, published and circulated in appropriate ways.
2. The Rule/Regulations of Government and Public Sector bodies relating to conduct and disciple should include rule/regulations prohibiting sexual harassment and provide for appropriate penalties in such rules against the offender.

3. As regards private employers steps should be taken to include the aforesaid prohibitions is the standing orders under the Industrial Employment (Standing Orders) Act, 1946.
4. Appropriate work conditions should be provide in respect of work, leisure, health and hygiene to further ensure that there is no hostile environment towards women at work places and no employee women, should have reasonable grounds to believe that she is disadvantaged in connection with her employment.

5.6.1.3 Criminal Proceedings

Where such conduct amounts to a specific offence under Indian Penal Code on under any other law, the employer shall initiate appropriate action in accordance with law by making a complaint with the appropriate authority.

In particular, it should ensure that victims or witnesses are not victimized or discriminated against while dealing with complaints of sexual harassment. The victims of sexual harassment should have the option to seek transfer of the perpetrator or their own transfer.

5.6.1.4 Disciplinary Action

Where such conduct amounts to misconduct in employment as defined by the relevant service rules appropriate disciplinary action should be initiated by the employer in accordance with those rules

5.6.1.5 Complaint Mechanism

Whether or not such conduct constitutes an offence under law or a bench of the service rules, an appropriate complaint should be created in the employer's organization for redress of the complaint made by the victim. Such complaint mechanism should ensure time bound treatment of complaints.

5.6.1.6 Complaints Committee

The complaint mechanism, referred to in (6) above, should be adequate to provide, where necessary, a Complaints Committee, a special counselor of other support service, including the maintenance of confidentiality.

5.6.1.7 Workers Initiative

Employees should be allowed to raise issues of sexual harassment at worker's meeting and in other appropriate forum and it should be affirmatively discussed in Employer Employee Meetings.

5.6.1.8 Awareness

Awareness of the rights of female employees in thisregard shouldbe created in particular by prominently notifying the guidelines (and appropriate legislation when enacted on the subject) in a suitable manner.

5.6.1.9 Third Party Harassment

Where sexual harassment occurs as a result of an act or omission by any third party or outsider, the employer and person in charge will take all necessary and reasonable to assist the affected person in terms of support and preventive action.

The Central/State Governments are requested to consider adopting suitable measure including legislation to ensure that the guidelines laid down by this order are also observed by the employees in Private Sector.

These guidelines will not prejudice any rights available under the Protection of Human Rights Act, 1993.

Accordingly, the Supreme Court directed that the above guidelines and norms would be strictly observed in all work places for the prevention and enforcement of the right to gender equality of the working women. These directions would be binding and enforceable in law until suitable legislation is enacted to occupy the field.

5.6.2 What Amounts to Sexual Harassment

It is true that laws in India do not adequately provide for specific protection of women from sexual harassment at places of work and that enactment of such legislation would take a considerable time. In the absence of relevant legislation in respect of sexual harassment of working women at work place there is no law in India which provides the definition of the term "sexual harassment of working women at work place". However in ***Vishaka's Case***[53] a definition of sexual harassment was suggested by J.S. Verma J. (as the former Chief Justice of India as then was), speaking in the three Judges Bench opined:

Definition: For this purpose sexual harassment includes such unwelcome sexually determined behavior (whether directly or by implication) as:

- physical contact and advances.
- a demand or request for sexual favour.
- Sexually coloured remarks.
- showing pornography.
- any other unwelcome physical, verbal or non-verbal conduct of sexual nature.

5.6.3 Compensation to Victim

In dowry related crimes the victim besides physical harassment and injury also suffer monetarily. Repeated dowry demands some of which are often fulfilled enrich the taker of dowry unlawfully and unjustly. It is just and reasonable that such offender ought not to retain the gains of crime. They must be made to return any monetary gain which they have illegally obtained. The function of a criminal Court is to punish the offender which that of a civil Court is to make

53 AIR 1997 SC 3011

the wrongdoer compensate for the loss or injury censed to the aggrieved party. However, if these two procedures can be combined without affecting the criminal and civil process, it would be just and expedient to do so as it would save time and money in seeking remedies in two different courts. Section 357 of Cr.P.C. 1973 incorporates this idea to an extent and empowers the Court to grant compensation to the victim. This provision can be used liberally by the courts in at least some of the dowry related crimes. The amount of compensation could in no case exceed the amount of fine, and the quantum of fine would again depend upon the limit up to which the fine was awardable by the sentencing court for the particular offence and also upon the extent to which the sentencing Court had power to impose fine. However such compensation can be ordered only if the accused is convicted and sentenced,

The Supreme Court has held that in dowry death cases, no rigid timeframe could be applied under the provisions of Section 304 B of the Indian Penal Code for the purpose of determining cruelty. A Bench of Justice L.S. Panta and Justice AftabAlam said:

"The words 'soon before her death' occurring in Section 304 B of the IPC are to be understood in a relative and flexible sense. Those words cannot be construed as laying down a rigid period of time to be mechanically applied in each case. Whether or not the cruelty or harassment meted out to the victim for or in connection with the demand of dowry was soon before her death and the proximate cause of her death, under abnormal circumstances, would depend upon the facts of each case. There can be no fixed period of time in this regard."

Section 304 B says:

"Where the death of a woman is caused by any burns or bodily injury or occurs otherwise than under normal circumstances within seven years of her marriage and it is shown that soon before her death she was subjected to cruelty or harassment by her husband or any relative of her husband for, or in connection with, any demand for dowry, such death

shall be called 'dowry death' and such husband or relative shall be deemed to have caused her death."[54]

In the instant case, the appellants, DeenDayal, his wife Sukhrani and son Amar Singh were tried for killing Asha Devi, wife of Amar Singh, for not fulfilling the dowry demand, 15 months after the marriage. The trial court acquitted them. On appeal, the Allahabad High Court reversed the order and sentenced them to a 10-year jail term. The present appeal by the three is directed against this judgment. The appellants said there was absolutely no evidence that any demand for dowry was made just prior to her death on September 6, 1998, or that the said demand and the alleged cruelty or harassment meted out to her in connection with it were the proximate cause of her death. Writing the judgment Justice Alam said:

"From the evidence on record we find it fully established that only after 15 months of her marriage and while she was living with the appellants, Asha Devi died under circumstances that were not only far from normal but also plainly indicated homicide. The evidence on record fully establishes that there was a persistent demand of dowry by the appellants and they subjected Asha Devi to cruelty and harassment in connection with the demand and eventually beat her to death due to its non-fulfillment."[55]

Dismissing the appeal, the Bench said:

"We are satisfied that all the ingredients of Section 304 B of the IPC are fully satisfied and on the evidence on record no other view is possible but to hold that the three appellants are guilty of committing dowry death."

In ***Prem Kanwar Vs. State of Rajasthan,***[56] Supreme Court dismissed the appeal filed by PremKanwar against the order of Rajashtan High Court upsetting the order of acquittal by the trial court and directed her conviction. The appeal was filed to the judgment of single judge of Rajashtan

54 Section 304 B of IPC
55 State of Bihar Vs. Deen Dayal AIR PAT 124
56 (2009) 3 SCC 726

High Court at Jodhpur allowing the appeal filed by the State questioning correctness of the judgment of acquittal passed by the learned Sessions Judge, Sriganganagar. The appellant and two others faced trial for alleged commission of offence punishable under sections 306, 304B of IPC and sec. 4 of Dowry Prohibition Act. The Supreme Court followed theprinciples laid down in ***Ajit Savant Majagavai Vs. State of Karnataka,***[57] to regulate the hearing of appeal by the High Court against an order of acquittal passed by the trial court. The Supreme Court took the help of a decision of apex court in ***Ashoke Kumar Vs. State of Rajashtan,***[58] where the Court has held as under,

"While caution is the watchword, in appeal against acquittal as the trial judge has occasion to watch demeanour of witnesses interference should not be made merely because a different conclusion could have been arrived at. Prudence demands restraints on mere probability or possibility but in perversity or misreading, interference is imperative otherwise existence of power shall be rendered meaningless. In the present case the order of the trial court is vitiated as apart from deciding the case on irrelevant consideration the most serious error of which he was guilty and which rendered the order infirm which could be set aside by the High Court was that he misread the evidence and indulged in conjectural inferences and surmises."[59]

The accused Prem Kanwar and others persistently taunted and harassed the deceased Smt. Raju for not having brought sufficient dowry. Therefore, the High Court was justified in upsetting the order of acquittal passed by the trial court and directing her conviction. Appeal has no merit and accordingly dismissed.

Amar Singh Vs. State of Rajasthan,[60] is a case where appellant Amar Singh charged under section 304B and 498-A of IPC read with section 113-B, Evidence Act, 1872.

57 (1997) 7 SCC 110, AIR 1997 SC 3255
58 AIR, 1990 SC 2134
59 State of Bihar Vs. Deen Dayal AIR PAT 124
60 (2010) SCC 64

Prosecution proved that soon before wife's death deceased had been subjected by appellant to taunts in connection with demand for dowry. Once such s fact is established, court has to presume that appellant has committed offence under section 304B of IPC. The fact remains that the appellant was not charged for the offence of murder under section 302 IPC presumable because during investigation no materials were available to establish the offence under section 302 IPC against the appellant. In ***Shanti Vs. State of Haryana,***[61] the Supreme Court has held that where there is no evidence as to the actual part played by the accused, a minimum sentence of 7(seven) years would serve the end of justice. In the present case, since there is no evidence as to the actual role played by the appellant in the death of the deceased (Santosh wife of appellant), a punishment of ten years imprisonment would suffice in the ends of justice. In the result, the appeal is partly allowed and the sentence of life imprisonment imposed on the appellant under section 304-B of IPC is reduced to ten years and the impugned judgement of the High Court is modified accordingly. In case, the appellant has undergone the period of ten years imprisonment, he shall be released forthwith unless he is wanted in any other case.

Research done in the late 1990s by Vimochana, a women's group in the southern city of Bangalore, revealed that many deaths are quickly written off by police. The police record of interview with the dying womanoften taken with her husband and relatives presentis often the sole consideration in determining whether an investigation should proceed or not. As Vimochana was able to demonstrate, what a victim will say in a state of shock and under threat from her husband's relatives will often change markedly in later interviews. Of the 1,133 cases of "unnatural deaths" of women in Bangalore in 1997, only 157 were treated as murder while 546 were categorized as "suicides" and 430 as "accidents". But as in the research of Vimochana an Activist it was explained:

61 (1991) 1 SCC 371

"We found that of 550 cases reported between January and September 1997, 71 percent were closed as 'kitchen/ cooking accidents' and 'stove-bursts' after investigations under section 174 of the Code of Criminal Procedures."[62]

The fact that a large proportion of the victims were daughters-in-law was either ignored or treated as a coincidence by police.

Figures cited in *Frontline* indicate what can be expected in court, even in cases where murder charges are laid. In August 1998, there were 1,600 cases pending in the only special court in Bangalore dealing with allegations of violence against women. In the same year three new courts were set up to deal with the large backlog but cases were still expected to take six to seven years to complete. Prosecution rates are low. *Frontline* reported the results of one court:

"Of the 730 cases pending in his court at the end of 1998, 58 resulted in acquittals and only 11 in convictions, at the end of June 1999, out of 381 cases pending, 51 resulted in acquittals and only eight in convictions."[63]

A number of studies have shown that the lower ranks of the middle class are particularly prone. According to the Institute of Development and Communication,

"The quantum of dowry exchange may still be greater among the middle classes, but 85 percent of dowry death and 80 percent of dowry harassment occurs in the middle and lower stratas."[64]

Statistics produced by Vimochana in Bangalore show that 90 percent of the cases of dowry violence involve women from poorer families, who are unable to meet dowry demands. There is a definite market in India for brides and grooms. Newspapers are filled with pages of women seeking husbands and men advertising their eligibility and social prowess, usually using their caste as a bargaining chip. A "good" marriage is often seen by the wife's family as a means to advance up the social ladder. But the catch is that there is a price to be paid in

62 A research report by Vimochana, a social activist group of Bangalore, in 1990s
63 Report published in Frontline in 1998
64 Report of the Institute of Development and Communication in 1999

the form of a dowry. If for any reason that dowry arrangements cannot be met then it is the young woman who suffers,One critic, Annuppa Caleekal, commented on the rising levels of dowry, particularly during the last decade:

"The price of the Indian groom astronomically increased and was based on his qualifications, profession and income. Doctors, charted accountants and engineers even prior to graduation develop the divine right to expect a 'fat' dowry as they become the most sought after cream of the graduating and educated dowry league."[65]

The other side of the dowry equation is that daughters are inevitably regarded as an unwelcome burden, compounding the already oppressed position of women in Indian society. There is a high incidence of gender-based abortions-almost two million female babies a year. One article noted the particularly crass billboard advertisements in Bombay encouraging pregnant women to spend 500 rupees on a gender test to save a potential 50,000 rupees on dowry in the future. According to the UN Population Fund report for the year 2000, female infanticide has also increased dramatically over the past decade and infant mortality rates are 40 percent higher for girl babies than boys.

Critics of the dowry system point to the fact that the situation has worsened in the 1990s. As the Indian economy has been opened up for international investment, the gulf between rich and poor widened and so did the economic uncertainty facing the majority of people including the relatively well-off. It was a recipe for sharp tensions that have led to the worsening of a number of social problems.

Indian anti-dowry law has now reached a point where almost all possible legal reforms have been made and the highest judiciary is now sensitized. But every day, dowry murders continue as though the law does not exist. Dowry is clearly a social problem, which must be tackled through self controlled action on the part of people as members of society. What is the role of law in this context? In fact, is there a role for law?

65 Annuppa Caleekal in 1999

It is clear from the above discussion that Indian judiciary has played constructive role in interpretation of legal provisions and has directed from time to time for the implementation of these labour welfare laws. Judiciary has given landmark judgments relating to social security, payment of compensation for employment injury and disability etc. The principles contained in Articles 39(a) and 41 must be regarded as equally fundamental in the understanding and interpretation of the meaning and content of fundamental rights. If there is an obligation upon the State to secure to the citizens an adequate means of livelihood and the right to work, it would be sheer pedantry to exclude the right to livelihood from the content of the right to life. The State may not, by affirmative action, be compellable to provide adequate means of livelihood or work to the citizens. The Articles 21, 38, 39, 41, 42, 43, 43-A and 47 of the Constitution of India, are calculated to give an idea of the conditions under which labour can be had for work and also of the responsibility of the Government, both Central and State, towards the labour to secure for them social order and living wages, keeping with the economic and political conditions of the country. While these cases demonstrate the instances in which the Supreme Court stepped in to safeguard the fundamental human rights of workers there are several instances where such rights are brazenly violated. The workers most vulnerable to this are those working in the unorganized sector of the economy like agriculture, forestry, livestock, textile and textile products, construction etc. In these sectors workers, generally, tend to be employed in the lowest paid, most menial tasks using the least technology. Workers often work in labour intensive sectors. They are working different segments of the labour market in unorganized sector getting the lowest wages. There are even instances in some sectors of workers being paid less than work they do for example in the tea plantations, construction, agriculture etc.,as compared to the minimum wages fixed by the state.

CHAPTER

6

Women Rights under Labour Legislations

6.1 Introduction

Nature has created men and women on equal footing with equal authority on earth and it is also a reality that the civilization is moving forward contribution of both men and women and India is not an exception to this reality. It is also undeniable fact that about half of the Indian population is women. History witnesses that women of India have always been discriminated against and have suffered and are suffering discrimination in silence. Self-sacrifice and self-denial are their nobility and fortitude and yet they have been subjected to all equities indignities, inequality and discrimination. Status of women in different societies across the world has been different. No matter whether it is developed, developing or underdeveloped society women have always occupied a special position and also in every present and contemporary societies the position of women have always been discriminatory and they have been one of the weakest sections of the society as nearly all the societies in the world have always been male-dominated. This position of women gave rise to various movements all over the world and there came the concept of 'Feminism'. Feminism is a collection of social theories, political movements, and moral philosophies opposing, varied and confliction views largely motivated by the experience of women, with reference to inequalities in terms of social, political and economic backdrop. In the light of this concept various laws have been enacted for the protection of women and various rights have been given to women so as to uplift them. The constitution makers were also very concerned about this and hence inserted various provisions for women and empowered the pass various laws and amended the existing laws so that women have a better position in the society.

Besides the Constitution of India mandates that women must be treated as equals and prohibits any discrimination against women in all areas, including education, vocational training, skill development and employment. In order to ensure that women get a fair and adequate opportunity of employment, the constitution also mandates reservation for women in educational institutions and in employment in the public sector. Our Constitution also protects the rights of women workers by ensuring that their health and safety is duly protected in the course of employment, particularly those of pregnant women and breast feeding mothers. The Constitution also safeguards the dignity of women workers and ensures that they are provided a safe working environment free of sexual harassment.

In order to fulfill the Constitutional mandate all labour laws contain special provisions regarding the health and safety of women workers by regulating their working hours and by reducing the burden women have to carry. In order to ensure equality the law also mandates that both men and women will be paid the same wages for the same or similar type of work. Recently, a special law has been enacted to protect women against sexual harassment at the workplace. The rights of women under different labour laws are discussed in thissection.

6.2 Principles of Labour Legislation

Industrialisation is the modern trend in almost all developing countries now a days, as industry plays an important role in shaping the economic structure of a society. For the planned, progressive and purposeful development of the society proper regulation of employer - employee relationship is a condition precedent. This relationship is therefore one of the most important factors of success of the industrialisation programme. The workers and employers are two pillars of our national economy. It cannot be denied that labour has a vital role in increasing productivity, and management has to create conditions in which workers can make their maximum contribution towards this objective. In this connection, the social and economic upliftment of the labour is very important for securing industrial peace. With the growth of industrial jurisprudence the concept of master and servant has been abolished and in that place the employer and employee concept came out, where the former may hire the latter but he can no more fire them at his will. The interest of an employee is now in many respects protected by legislations. Democratic ideas have also been grown simultaneously with the growth of industrialisation in our country which have pleaded for and also helped in mass awakening and consciousness for greater power amongst the working class. Therefore labour legislation and industrial jurisprudence are based on certain fundamental principles, like Social Justice, Social Equity, International Uniformity and National Economy, which are discussed below:

Labour legislation in any country should be based on the principles of social justice, social equity, international uniformity, social security and national economy etc.

6.2.1 Social Justice

Social justice is essential to maintaining a sustainable peace as well as encouraging sustainable economic growth. Ensuring gender equality and protection of women's interests in labour law is a key ingredient to improving social justice.

Social justice implies two things. First, equitable distribution of profits and other benefits. Secondly, providing protection to the workers against harmful effects to their health, safety and morality.

According to Justice Bhagwati, Jj,

"The concept of social justice does not emanatefromthe fanciful notions of any particular adjudication but must be founded on a more solid foundation."[1]

In the opinion of the Justice Gajendragadkar:

"The concept of social and economic justice is a living concept of revolutionary import; itgives sustenance to the rule of law and meaning and significance to the idea of welfare safety."[2]

Labour welfare in our country has a special significance for our constitution provides for the promotion of welfare of people, for human conditions of work and securing to all workers full employment of leisure and social and cultural opportunities. The word 'Social Justice' is neither defined in any of the labour legislations nor does it occur in any of them except the Industrial Disputes Act 1947[3]. The Indian Constitution enshrines the concept of social justice as one of the objectives of the State. Article 38 of the Constitution provides that,

"the State shall strive to promote the welfare of the people by securing and protecting as effectively as it may, social order in which justice, social, economic and political, shall inform all the Institutions of the national life".

Article 39 ordains that it shall be the duty of the state to apply certain principles of social justice in making laws.

6.2.2 Social Equity

Any legislation which is based on social justice prescribes a definite standard for adoption in future. Such stand and is fixed after taking into account the past and present circumstances. Once a standard is so fixed by legislation it remains in force until is changed or modified by another legislation passed in conformity with the legislative procedure. No discretion is given to change such law to the authority administering such law. However, where it is fact

1 Muir Mills Co., Ltd Vs. Suti Mills Mazdoor Union, Kanpur, AIR 1955 SC 170: 1955 SCR (1) 991

2 State of Mysore Vs. Workers of Gold Mines AIR 1958 SC 923.

that the law should be flexible and should be changed as the circumstances and conditions change, the law empowers the Government to make such changes. This is generally done by giving the Government rule making power under the provisions of the Act. When power under the act is given to the Government the rules may be modified to suit the changed conditions. Such legislation is said to be based on social equity.

6.2.3 Social Security

The concept of social security has become an integral part of social justice. It is based on ideas of human dignity and social justice. The underlying idea behind social security measures is that a citizen who has contributed or likely to contribute to his country's welfare should be given protection against certain hazards.3 Social security means a guarantee provided by the State through appropriate agencies, against certain risks to which the members of the society may be exposed. Its measures are significant from two view points, i.e. they constitute an important step towards the goal of a welfare state; and secondly, they enable workers to become more efficient and thus reduce wastage arising from industrial disputes. Lack of social security impedes production and prevents formation of stable and efficient labour force.[3]

6.2.4 International Uniformity and National Economy

Freedom from want and security against economic fear is the minimum that has to be secured to the people in the country. Its importance has been expressed by the Universal Declaration of Human Rights in the following order:

"Everyone as a member of the society has the right to social security and is entitled to realization through national efforts and international co-operation and in accordance with the organization and resources of each state of economic, social

3 May - 2017 27 Odisha Review: ISSN 0970-8669

and cultural rights indispensible for his dignity and the free development of his personality."[4]

"Everyone has right to a standard of living adequate for the health and well being of himself and of his family, including food, clothing, housing and medical care and necessary social services and the right to security in the event of unemployment, sickness, disability, widowhood, old age, or other lack of livelihood, or circumstances beyond his control."[5]

The role of International Labour Organisation in certain standards of social insurance has been significant. The social security (Minimum standards) convention adopted in 1952 embodies universally accepted basic principles and common standards of social security. The application of these principles has been guarded developments of this field throughout the world.

6.3 History of Labour Legislations in India

The history of labour legislation in India is naturally interwoven with the history of British colonialism. Considerations of British political economy were naturally paramount in shaping some of these early laws. In the beginning it was difficult to get enough regular Indian workers to run British establishments and hence laws for indenturing workers became necessary. This was obviously labour legislation in order to protect the interests of British employers. Then, came the Factories Act. It is well known that Indian textile goods offered stiff competition to British textiles in the export market and hence in order to make India labour costlier, the Factories Act was first introduced in 1883 because of the pressure brought on the British parliament by the textile magnates of Manchester and Lancashire. Thus we received the first stipulation of 8 hours of work, the abolition of child labour, and the restriction of women in night employment, and theintroduction of overtime wages for work beyond 8 hours. While the impact of this measure

4 Universal Declaration of Human Rights at 70: 30

5 Ibid

was clearly welfarist the real motivation was undoubtedly protectionist.

6.4 Growth of Labour Legislation in India

Labour legislation in India grew with the growth of industry. In the eighteenth century India was not only a great agricultural country but a great manufacturing country too. Asian and European Markets were mainly fed by the looms supplied by India. But the British Government in India as a matter of policy discouraged Indian manufacturers in order to encourage the rising manufacturers of England. Their policy was to make India subservient to the industries of Great Britain and make Indian people grow only raw materials. To obstruct this path of the British the National Movement took a new turn in the twentieth century. There was a common demand for the Indian goods. Nationalism has an obvious economic aspect which in our country was reflected in the urge for economic reforms and for industrialization. All attempts were made to put forward a theory of an economic development and planning suited to conditions of our country. Thus, planned – industrialization became our main goal.

In India, a number of labour legislations have been enacted to promote the condition of the labour keeping in view the development of industry and national economy. But for industrial regeneration it is necessary that the partners of the industry must care their respective defects. Since independence both legislation and public opinion have done a lot to better the conditions of the workers but unfortunately the employers have not responded very appreciably. It is high time that the employers must realise that workers are the dominant partners in the industrial undertakings and without their co-operation and good work, discipline, integrity and character, the industry will not be able to produce effective results or profits. However efficient the machine touch in any industry may be, if the human element refuses to co-operate, the industry will fail to run. Therefore, the profit of the industry must be shared between employers, workers and the community; the workers having a dominant share, being the producers of wealth. The Government and the employers must fully understand the labour psychology and a change in their outlook and attitude is desires to secure the industrial peace. Nothing should be done under threat or coercion but on a clear understanding that whatever is good and is due to the labour must be given. Industry owners should treat the workers as co-partners. Similarly, workers in the country must understand fully that if they desire to secure their due place in the industrial economy of the country, they must think more in terms of responsibilities and duties and not interpret independence for impertinence and liberty for licence. Sabotage and violence of all kinds and bitterness in thought, word and deed must be eschewed. Then alone a Socialist Democracy is possible in this country and industrial relations of a higher order can be maintained for the benefit of the country and the community.

In India, the plantation industry in Assam was the first to attract legislative control. The method of recruitment of workers in the Industry was full of hardships. Workers were employed through professional recruiters. Workers were not allowed by the planters to leave the tea gardens. A number of Acts were passed from 1863 onwards. These legislations protected more the interests of the employers than safeguarding the interest of the workers. The Factories Act was passed in 1881 and the Mines Act in 1901. But the most important of such Acts as were passed to protect the interest of the workers was the worker's compensation Act, 1923. Some other important social security legislations are: the Employees' State Insurance Act 1948, the Employees' Provident funds Act, 1950 and the Maternity Benefit Act, 1961. Labour legislations ensuring labour welfare and minimum standards were also enacted. Some of them are; the Factories Act, 1948, the Minimum Wages Act, 1948, the Payment of Wages Act, 1936 and the Payment of Bonus Act, 1965. In India, a number of labour legislations have been enacted to promote the condition of the labour, keeping in view the development of industry and national economy.

Social and economic justice is ultimate ideal of industrial adjudication[9], and the basis lies in the guiding principles of social welfare, common good and the directive principles of State policy enshrined in the Constitution[10]. The twin objectives of any industrial adjudication are industrial peace and economic justice. According to V.V. Giri, Hon'ble President of India,

"the profit of the industry must be shared between employers, workers and the community; the workers having a dominant share, being the producers of wealth." [11]

6.5 Women and Labour Laws in India

Women constitute a significant part of the workforce in India but they lag behind men in terms of work participation and quality of employment. According to Government sources, out of 407 million total workforce, 90 million are women workers, largely employed (about 87 %) in the agricultural sector as labourers and cultivators. In urban areas, the employment of women in the organised sector in March 2000 constituted 17.6 % of the total organised sector. The situation regarding enforcement of the provisions of this law is regularly monitored by the Central Ministry of Labour and the Central Advisory Committee. In respect of an occupational hazard concerning the safety of women at workplaces, in 1997 the Supreme Court of India announced that sexual harassment of working women amounts to violation of rights of gender equality. As a logical consequence it also amounts to violation of the right to practice any profession, occupation, and trade. The judgement also laid down the definition of sexual harassment, the preventive steps, the complaint mechanism, and the need for creating awareness of the rights of women workers

The Government has provided protective measures especially to women workers in various labour laws like the Factories Act, 1948, the Mines Act, 1952, the Plantation

Labour Act, 1951 and the Maternity Benefit Act, 1961 wherein the aspects of security, safety, health, restriction of hours of employment are provided. The Equal Remuneration Act, 1976 also provides for payment of equal remuneration to men and women workers for same work or work of similar nature. Under Minimum wages Act, 1948, the wages for workers in the scheduled employments fixed by the appropriate Governments are equally applicable to both men and women. The Act does not discriminate on the basis of gender and the female workers are entitled for same wages as fixed by the appropriate Governments for their male counterparts engaged in the scheduled employments. Further, the Government has enacted the Sexual Harassment of Women at Workplace (Prevention, Prohibition and Redressal) Act, 2013 which mandates to constitute Internal Complaint Committee (ICC) for complaints of sexual harassment. The Government has prepared a preliminary draft of Labour Code on Occupation Safety, Health and Working Conditions, 2018 by simplifying, amalgamating and rationalizing the relevant provisions of the 13 Central Labour Laws relating to safety and health standards, working conditions, welfare provisions for employees, leave & working hours. The comments of stakeholders including general public have been invited on the said draft Code.

6.6 Development of Industrial Justice

Lasting peace in any industry is possible only when an attempt is made to eliminate the real causes of conflict. Therefore, restoration of peace with justice is necessary. Both social and economic justices are essential for obtaining whole hearted co-operation of labour in the task of production for labour co-operation equitable distribution of the gains in necessary.

The principle of equality should also be taken into consideration. Social justice requires equal work and equal pay for men and women and equality of opportunity, etc. Equality in economic life, that sets the process of social inequality, political weakness and evolution of community with superior and inferior classes. Justice requires acceptance of the principle of equality.

Justice also lays adjustment of rival claims in a fair and just manner. In the case of industrial adjudication the claims for the employer based on the freedom of contract have to be adjusted with the claims of industrial employees for social justice. The task of making a reasonable adjustment is not always easy, and so, in reaching conclusions in such a matter it is essential not to decide more than is necessary. If industrial adjudication purports to lay down broad general principles it is likely to make its approach in future cases inflexible and that must always be avoided. In ***State of Mysore Vs. Workers of Gold Mines***, the Supreme Court also observed that:

"In its attempt to do social justice industrial adjudication has to adjust rival claims of the employer and his workmen in a fair and just manner and this object can best be achieved by dealing with each problem as it arises on its own facts and circumstances."[6]

During post constitutional period, the planners of the country to fulfill the goals of welfare state and to provide justice to women have made various legislations and amendments therein to equalize women with their counterparts of men. To provide an idea about those legislations in general and dowry related laws in particular is need to analyze the whole province of the working of Government to avert dowry deaths in Indian sub-continent.

6.7 Labour Laws and Women

Women constitute a significant part of the workforce in India but they lag behind men in terms of work participation and quality of employment. According to Government sources, out of 407 million total workforce, 90 million are women workers, largely employed (about 87 %) in the agricultural

6 AIR 1958 SC 923

sector as labourers and cultivators. In urban areas, the employment of women in the organised sector in March 2000 constituted 17.6 % of the total organised sector.The situation regarding enforcement of the provisions of this law is regularly monitored by the Central Ministry of Labour and the Central Advisory Committee. In respect of an occupational hazard concerning the safety of women at workplaces, in 1997 the Supreme Court of India announced that sexual harassment of working women amounts to violation of rights of gender equality. As a logical consequence it also amounts to violation of the right to practice any profession, occupation, and trade. The judgement also laid down the definition of sexual harassment, the preventive steps, the complaint mechanism, and the need for creating awareness of the rights of women workers.

6.8 Legislative Support for Women

India has witnessed many social changes post-independence. Today, women have come out of homes and established an identity of their own in different areas of work. Though most Indian adult women make an economic contribution in one form or another (including housework, working in family land etc.), much of their work is not documented. This is because majority of women workforce is employed in the unorganized sector and working for family is considered as responsibility which should not be counted. The Economic survey data for 2007-08 reveals that the overall percentage share of female participation in work was comparatively low as compared to that of male.

Owing to cultural restrictions and family responsibility, women participation in the formal economy is limited. Some other concerns that affect working women relate to gender discrimination, quantum of payment, safety at work place, working hours and conditions of employment that are sensitive to cultural and religious bondages as well as family responsibilities. Indian legislature has been active on this front. Its main focus is on reducing inequality of any sort, and thereby promoting a fair, non-discriminatory and safe work environment. Indian political and administrative structure is multi-layered. At the apex is the central government, under which there are states and local self-bodies. Responsibilities for legislation are also divided accordingly, so that autonomy of states is protected. In labour legislation, both center and states have powers to enact suitable legislations. The government has given greater focus to issues relating to women through creation of an independent Ministry of Women and Child Development, initiation of legislation that has taken the country closer to complete legal equality for women, gender budgeting and initiation of programs for greater inclusion of women in all walks of life. There are over 45 labour legislations from the Central Government and the number of legislations enacted by the State Governments is close to four times that of the Central Act. The government has so far passed/amended 5 women specific legislations. However, effectiveness of the laws can be seen/felt if women's are politically and socially empowered. Important labour legislations are discussed below:

6.8.1 Protection under Equal Remuneration Act, 1976

The exploitation and discrimination of women have been multifaceted, all round and pervading. The worst exploitation is located in wages and remuneration. There are hardly any jobs, employment or engagement in which women were not giving wages less than the men, even when they have been engaged in the same type of work, and for the same duration. Despite the constitutional mandate, the women will not be discriminated to any sphere, discrimination is being continued. The social justice enshrined in the constitution, enjoins the state that exploitation of weaker section of the society should be ceased.

The principle of equal pay for equal work is contained in clause (d) of Article 39 of the Indian Constitution which envisages that the state shall, in particular, direct its policy towards securing that there is equal pay for equal work for both men and women. This principle implies that where all things are equal, that is, where all relevant considerations are the same, persons holding identical posts may not be treated differently in the matter of their pay merely because they belong to different departments. Of course, if officers of the same rank perform dissimilar functions and the persons duties and responsibilities of the posts held by them vary, such officers may not be heard to complain of dissimilar pay merely because the posts are of the same rank and the nomenclature is the same.[1] In ***Randhir Singh Vs. Union of India***, the Supreme Court held that the principle of equal pay for equal work though nor a fundamental right is certainly a constitutional goal and therefore capable of enforcement through constitutional remedies under Article 32 of the constitution. The doctrine of equal pay for equal work is applicable to persons employed on a daily wage basis. Daily wagers are entitled to the same wages as other permanent employees in the department employed to do the identical work.[2]

Equal pay for equal work finds its place in the Directive principles of State policy and it is an accompaniment of equality clause enshrined in Article 14 and 16 of the constitution of India. Nevertheless the abstract doctrine of equal pay for equal work cannot be read in Article 14. Reasonable classification based on intelligible criteria, having nexus to the object sought to be achieved, is permissible.[7] Accordingly it has been held in ***State of A. P. and Others Vs. G. Sreenivasa Rao and Others,***[8] that equal pay for equal work does not mean that all the members of a cadre must receive the same pay packet, irrespective of their seniority, source of recruitment, educational qualifications and various other incidents of service. It was further held that ordinarily grant of higher pay to a junior would ex-facie be arbitrary, but the equality doctrine cannot be invoked where there are justifiable grounds in doing so. For example, when persons recruited from different sources are given pay protection,

7 Article 14 of the Constitution of India
8 (2013) 12 SCC 680

when a promote from a lower cadre or a transferee from another cadre is given pay protection, when a promote from a lower cadre or transferee from another cadre is given pay protection, when a senior is stopped at efficiency bar, when advance increments are given for experience, passing a test, acquiring higher qualification of the even qualities when a junior may be drawing higher pay than this senior without violating the mandate of equal pay for equal work.

6.8.2 Protection under the Maternity Benefit Act, 1961

This Act was enacted to regulate the employment of women in certain establishments for certain periods before and after child birth and to provide for maternity benefit and certain other benefits. This Acts extends to the whole except the State of Jammu and Kashmir. It shall come into force on such date as may be notified in this behalf in the official Gazette (a) in relation to mines and to any other establishment wherein persons are employed for the exhibition of equestrian, acrobatic and other performance, by the Central Government and (b) in relation to other establishments in a state by the State Government (Section-1 of the Act).

Section 2: It applies in the first instance:

- to every establishment which is a factory, mine or plantation, including any such establishment belonging to Government and to every establishment wherein persons are employed for the exhibition of equestrian, acrobatic and other performances.
- to every shop or establishment within the meaning of any law for the time being in force in relation to shops and establishments in a state, in which ten or more persons are employed, or were employed, on any day of the preceding twelve months.

Section 3: Save as otherwise provided in Section 5-A and 5-B nothing contained in this Act shall apply to any factory or other establishment to which the provisions of Employees' State Insurance Act, 1948 apply. Proviso in section 2(1) empowers the State Government to extend all or any of the provisions of this Act to any other establishment or class of establishments whether the establishments are industrial, commercial, agricultural or otherwise. The State Government can do so after giving two months notice by notification in the Official Gazette of its intention to do so and shall also take the approval of the Central Government.Now it will be nice if we discuss some other important sections for the purpose.

Section 4: Provides employment of, or work by woman prohibited during certain period-Under this section, the employer is prohibited from knowingly employing any woman in any establishment during the six weeks immediately following the day of her delivery, miscarriage or medical termination of pregnancy.

No woman shall work, in any establishment during the six weeks immediately following the day of her delivery, miscarriage or medical termination of pregnancy.

Without prejudice to the provisions of Section 6, no pregnant woman shall, on a request being made by her, be required by her employer to do any work of the following nature during the period of one month immediately preceding the period of six weeks before the date of her expected delivery and during the said period of six weeks for which the pregnant woman does not avail of the leave of absence under Section 6:

- any work which is arduous nature;
- any work which involves long hours of standing;
- anywork which in any way is likely to interfere with her pregnancy of the normal development of foetus or likely to cause her miscarriage or otherwise adversely affect her health.

In ***Punjab National Bank by Chairman and Another Vs. Astamija Dash,***[9] it was held that as per provisions of the Maternity Benefit Act 1961 (amended in the year 1988), a woman can avail leave during the period of six weeks

9 (2008) 14 SCC 370: 2008 III L.L.J. 584 (S.C.)

from the day immediately following the day of her delivery, miscarriage or medical termination of pregnancy. If request is made by herself she would not be asked to work for the period specified as per Section 4(4). She would be entitled to the benefits of Section 6 and 9 of the Act.

In ***Tata Tea Ltd. Vs. Inspector Plantations***[10]**,** the question for consideration was whether an employee entitled to the benefit of Maternity Benefit Act, 1961, is eligible to claim the benefit under Section 5(1) of the Kerala Industrial Establishments (National and Festival Holidays) Act 1958. Under Section 4-A of the National and Festival Act, on employer could require any employee to work on any holidays and any such employee was under Section 5(2) entitled to twice the wages for working on that day. Under Section 4 of the Maternity Benefit Act an employee is entitled to certain benefits including maternity leave during the period mentioned in that Section. It was held during the period mentioned in sub-section (1) and (2) of Section 4 of the said Act, the employer cannot in exercise of his right under Section 4-A of the National and Festival Holidays Act call upon a woman employee to come and do work on the aforesaid holidays allowed under Section 3 of the said Act. The said right of the employer as regards the period made mention of in Section 4 of the Maternity Benefit Act however is subject to the restrictions imposed by sub-section (3) thereof. Considered in this background the claim of the employees for the wages under the National and Festival Holidays Act is not sustainable.

Section 5: Right to Payment of Maternity Benefit (Section 5), provides that the maternity benefit to which every woman shall be entitled and her employer shall be liable for, is a payment to a worker at the rate of average daily wages for the period of her actual absence immediately preceding and including the day of her delivery and for six weeks immediately following that day.

10 (1992) ILLJ 603 Ker

Section 5 (2):Provides that no woman shall be entitled to maternity benefit unless she has actually worked in an establishment of the employer from whom she claims maternity benefit for a period not less than one hundred and sixty days in the twelve months immediately preceding the date of her expected delivery. The qualifying period of one hundred and sixty days as stated above shall not apply to a woman who has immigrated into the State of Assam and was pregnant at the time of immigration.

For the purpose of calculation the days on which a woman has actually worked in the establishment, the days for which she has been laid off during the period of twelve months immediately preceding the date of her expected delivery, shall be taken into account.

Section 5(3): Provides that a woman shall be entitled to maternity benefit for a minimum period of twelve weeks that six weeks upto and including the day of her delivery and six weeks immediately following that day:

Provided that where a woman dies during this period, the maternity benefits shall be payable only for the days upto and including the day of her death. Where a woman having been delivered of child, dies during her delivery or during the period of six weeks immediately following the date of her delivery, leaving behind in either case the child, the employer shall be liable for the maternity benefit for the entire period of six weeks immediately following the day of her delivery but if the child dies during the said period, then, for the days upto and including the day of the death of the child.

A woman worker who expects a child is entitled to maternity benefit for a maximum period of twelve weeks which is split up into two periods; namely Pre-natal and Post-natal. In ***B. Shah Vs. Labour Court, Coimbatore***[11] question arose, whether Sunday is to be countered in calculating the amount of maternity benefit. It was held that in the context of sub-sections (1) and (3) of Section 5, the terms week has to be taken to signify a cycle of seven days including Sundays. The

11 1978 AIR 12 1978 SCR (1) 701 1977 SCC (4) 334

legislature intended that computation of maternity benefit is to be made for the entire period of the woman workers' actual absence, i.e. for all the days, including Sundays, which may be wage-less holidays falling within that period. This computation ensures that the woman worker gets for the said period not only the amount equaling 100 percent of the wages which she was previously earning in terms of Section 3 (X) of the Act but also the benefit of the wages for all Sundays and rest days failing within the aforesaid two periods which would ultimately be conducive to the interest of both the woman and her employer.

In ***Ram Bahadur Thakur (P.) Ltd. Vs. Chief Inspector of Plantation***[12], the point for determination by Court was whether in calculating, 160 days period which will entitle a woman employee to get maternity benefit, the work on half days can be included or not. It was held that according to explanation to section 5 (2) of the Maternity Benefit Act, the period during which a woman worker was laid off should also be taken into consideration for ascertaining the eligibility. During the lay-off period a woman worker cannot be expected to have actually worked in the establishment. So, actual work for 160 days cannot be insisted as a condition precedent for claiming the maternity benefit.

Continuance of payment of maternity benefit in certain cases (Section-5A). Every woman entitled to the payment of maternity benefit under this Act shall not withstanding the application of the employees' State Insurance Act 1948, to the factory or other establishment in which she employed, continued to be so be entitled until she becomes qualified to claim maternity benefit under Section 50 of the Act.

Payment of maternity benefit in certain cases (Section-5B). Every woman-

- Who is employed in a factory or other establishment to which the provisions of the Employees' State Insurance Act 1948, apply;

12 AIR 1978 S.C. 12; Malayalam Plantations Vs. Inspector of Plantation, AIR 1975 Kerala, 86, overruled.

- Whose wages (including remuneration for over-time work) for a month exceed the amount specified in sub-clause 9b) of clause (9) of Section 2 of that Act; and
- Who fulfills the conditions specified in sub-section (2) of Section 5, shall be entitled to the payment of maternity benefit under this Act.

Section 6: Provides the notice of claim for maternity benefit and employed in an establishment and entitled to maternity benefit under the provisions of the Act may give notice in writing in such from as may be prescribed to her employer, stating that her maternity benefit and any other amount to which she may be entitled under this Act may be paid to her or to such person as she may nominate in the notice and that she will not work in any establishment during the period for which she receives maternity benefit.

In the case of a pregnant woman, such notice shall state the date from which she will be absent from work, not being a date earlier than six weeks from the date of her expected delivery. Any woman has not given the notice when she was pregnant may give such notice as soon as possible after delivery. On receipt of the notice, the employer shall permit such woman to absent herself from the establishment until the expiry of six weeks after the day of her delivery.

Further, the amount of maternity benefit for the period preceding the date of her expected delivery shall be paid in advance by the employer to the woman on production of such proof as may be prescribed that the woman is pregnant and the amount due for the sub-sequent period shall be paid by the employer to the woman within forty-eight hours of production of such proof as may be prescribed that the woman has been delivered of a child.

Section 7: Provides the payment of maternity benefit in case of death of woman.

If a woman entitled to maternity benefit or any other amount under this Act, dies before receiving such benefit or amount, the employer shall pay such benefit or amount to the person nominated by the woman in the notice given under Section 6 and in case there is no such nominee, to her legal representative.

Section 8: Payment of Medical Bonus (1)Every woman shall also be entitled to receive from her employer a medical bonus of one thousand rupees, if no pre-natal confinement and post natal care is provided for by the employer free of charge. (2) The Central government may before every three years, by notification in the Official Gazette, increase the amount of medical bonus subject to the maximum of twenty thousand rupees.

Section 9: Leave for Miscarriage: In case of miscarriage of medical termination of pregnancy, a woman shall, on production of such proof as may be prescribed, be entitled to leave with wages at the rate of maternity benefit for a period of six weeks immediately following the days of her miscarriage or, as the case may be, her medical termination of pregnancy.

Section 10: Other Leaves: A woman suffering from illness arising of pregnancy out of pregnancy, delivery, premature birth of child, miscarriage shall, on production of such proof, as may be prescribed, be entitled in addition to the period of absence allowed to her under Section 6, or as the case may be, under Section 9 to leave with wages at the rate of maternity benefit for a maximum period of one month.

Section 11: Nursing Breaks: After giving birth of a child, a woman worker is entitled to get two breaks of the prescribed duration for nursing until the child attains of fifteen months, in addition to the interval for the rest allowed to her in the course of her daily work.

Section 12: Dismissal during Absence of Pregnancy: When a woman absents herself from work in accordance with the provisions of this Act, it shall be unlawful for her employer to discharge or dismiss her during or on account of such absence or to give notice of discharge or dismissal on such a day that the notice will expire during such absence, or vary her disadvantage any of the conditions of her service.

The discharge or dismissal of a woman at any time, during pregnancy, if the woman but for such discharge or dismissal would have been entitled to maternity benefit or medical bonus referred to Section 8 shall not have the effect of depriving her of the maternity benefit or medical bonus.

Provided that, where the dismissal is for any prescribed gross misconduct, the employer may be order in writing communicated to the woman, deprive her of the maternity benefit or medical bonus or both.

Any woman deprived of maternity benefit or medical bonus both, may, within sixty days from the date of which the order of such deprivation is communicated to her, appeal to such authority as may be prescribed and the decision of that authority on such appeal, whether the woman should or should not be deprived of maternity benefit or medical bonus or both, shall be final.

The maternity benefit Act is intended to achieve the object of doing social justice to woman workers. Therefore in interpreting the provisions of this Act beneficent rule of construction, which would enable the woman worker not only to subsist but also to make up her dissipated energy, nurse her child, preserve her efficiency as a worker and maintain the level of her previous efficiency and output, has to be adopted by the Court.[13]

6.8.3 Protection under the Payment of Gratuity Act, 1972

We know the right of Industrial Workers to receive gratuity has long been recognized by the Tribunals, yet the law relating to payment of gratuity was very vague and uncertain before passing of the present Act. There was a good deal of disparity in the various schemes for the payment of gratuity. The Supreme Court had made efforts to regulate through judicial

13 B. Shah Vs. Labour Court, Coimbatore, AIR 1978 S.C. 12

decisions by laying down principles for grant of gratuity. Still controversies with regard to the rules and principles were continuing. Ultimately all controversies were set at rest by passing of the Payment of Gratuity Act in the year 1972.

We know that the preamble of the Act suggests, this Act aims to provide for a scheme for the payment of gratuity to employees engaged in factories, mines, oil fields, plantations, ports, railway companies, shops or other establishments and for matter connected therewith or incidental thereto. It was pointed out in ***Delhi Cloth and General Mills Co. Ltd. Vs. Their Workmen***,[14] that the object of providing a gratuity scheme is to provide a retiring benefit to the workmen who have rendered long and unblemished service to the employer and thereby contributed to the prosperity of the employer.

In ***Indian Ex-Services League and Others Vs. Union of India and Others,***[15] writ petitions were filed by some commissioned and non-commissioned ex-servicemen. Gratuity was payable at enhanced rate to persons retiring on a later date. Therefore, those who had retired earlier to the specified date also claimed enhancement and payment of gratuity at rates payable to retires after the specified date on the ground of one rank one person rule. It was held that the claim for gratuity can be made only on the date of retirement on the basis of salary drawn on the date of retirement and being already paid on that footing; the transaction was completed and closed. It could then not be reopened as a result of enhancement made at a later date for persons retiring subsequently. The concept of gratuity is different from pension. The conclusion of the Court in ***D.S. Nakara Vs. Union of India***[16] was that the benefits of liberalization of the pension scheme have to be given equally to all retires irrespective of their dates of retirement and those benefits cannot be confined only to the persons who retired on or after the specified date because for the purpose of grant of

---

14 1967 AIR 469 1967 SCR
15 (1992) I L.L.J. 765 (S.C.)
16 (1983) I L.L.J. 104 (S.C.)

the benefits of liberalization in pension, all retires constitute one class irrespective of their date of retirement.

In ***Krishna Kumar and Others Vs. Union of India and Others***,[17] also the Supreme Court held that Provident Fund retires and pension retirees constitute different classes and it was never held in Nakara case that pension retirees alone did constitute a homogeneous class, even though pension retirees alone did constitute a homogeneous class within which any further classification for the purposes of liberalized pension scheme was impermissible.

Thus from these decisions it is clear that the concept of pension, provident fund and gratuity are different from each other.

6.8.3.1 Scope and Application

The Payment of Gratuity Act 1972 was passed as Act No. 30 of 1972 and received the assent of the President of India on August 21, 1972. This Act extends to the whole of India except the State of Jammu and Kashmir.According to sub-section (3) of Section 1, this Act shall apply to:

- Every factory, mine oil-field plantation, port and railway company;
- Every shop or establishment within the meaning of any law for the time being in force in relation to shops and establishments in a State in which ten or more persons are employed, or were employed, or any day of the preceding twelve months;
- Such other establishments or class of establishments in which ten or more employees are employed or were employed, on any day of the preceding twelve months, as the Central Government may, by notification specify in this behalf.

Section 3 A:A shop or establishment to which this Act has become applicable shall continue to be governed by this Act not withstanding that the member of persons employed

17 4 (1991) I L.L.J. 191 (S.C.)

therein at any time after it has become so applicable falls below ten.

Thus, it is clear from the above provisions that the Act is wide enough to bring within its scope, the entire organized section of industry and commerce. In relation to its application to shop or establishment, in view of clause (b) of Section 1 (3) it applies to every shop or establishment within the meaning of any law for the time being in force. It has been held in ***B.N. Sarda (Pvt.) Ltd. Vs. Kishan K. Borade***[18], that there is no justification whatsoever to qualify the words 'any law' by introducing a qualification that the law should be either a central law or a state law.

It was held in ***Nagar Palika, Muradabad Vs. App. Authority and Addl. Labour Commr. U.P., Kanpur & Others***,[19] that Municipal Board is an 'establishment' governed by the payment of Gratuity Act, 1972. It is not necessary for a legal heir of an employee to first obtain a succession Certificate and then apply for payment of Gratuity amount. It will depend upon the facts of the case as to whether such certificate would be necessary or not.

In ***Laxmi D.V. Vs. A.P. Agricultural University Another***,[20] the high Court held that the educational institutions such as University carrying on systematic activity by employing more than ten persons was 'establishment' within the meaning of 'Payment of Gratuity Act 1972. It was observed that the definition of establishment under Section 1 (3) (b) of the said Act – was comprehensive to include 'establishment' within the meaning of any law, not only law relating to shops and establishments, for the time being in force in a State.

We can refer here an interesting case. In the ***Management of S.I.E.T. Women's College, Madras Vs. Mohamed Ibrahim and Others***,[21] the question was whether the provisions of

18 1981 LabIC 911
19 Muir Mills Ltd. Vs. Suti Mill Mazdoor Union (1955) I LLJ 1 (SC)
20 2001 (6) ALD 694, 2002 (92) FLR 57
21 2004 (101) FLR 386: (2004) IILLJ 398 Mad (2004)

the payment of Gratuity Act, 1972 are applicable to the petitioner's educational Institution? According to Section 1 (3) (b) of the payment of Gratuity Act, the Act applies to every shop or establishment within to meaning of any law for the time being in force in relation to shops and establishments in the State. It was held in ***State of Punjab Vs. Labour Court, Julluder and Others***,[22] that Section 1 (3) (b) of the Payment of Gratuity Act applied to every establishment within the meaning of any law for the time being in force in relation to an establishment in a State and it was held that Employees' Provident Fund and Miscellaneous Provisions Act, 1952 is applicable to educational institutions, therefore S.I.E.T. Women's College is an establishment within the meaning of law for the time being in force. It is necessary that the law referred in Section 1 (3) (b) of the Payment of Gratuity Act should be a law already in force in the concerned State and not any law which comes into force subsequently. It further held that S.I.E.T. Women's College is also an establishment as defined in Section 2 (c) of the Tamil Nadu Payment of Subsistence Allowance Act. Educational institution is an industry within the meaning of Industrial Disputes Act. Therefore, the S.I.E.T. Women's College in an establishment falling within the preview of Section 1 (3) (b) of the payment of Gratuity Act 1972.

6.8.4 The Factories Act, 1948

The Factories Act is a welfare legislation enacted with an intention to regulate working conditions in the factories and to provide health, safety and welfare measures.[1] Besides, the Act envisages to regulate the working hours leave holidays, overtimes, employment of children, women and young persons etc.[2] The Act was drastically amended in 1987 whereby safeguards against use and handling of hazardous Substances and procedures for setting up hazardous industries were laid down.

22 1980 SCR (1) 953

6.8.4.1 Special Provisions Relating to Women

6.8.4.1.1 Latrine and Urinal Facilities

Separate conservancy facilities are provided to women workers in Factories Act, 1948.[3] The Factories Act, 1948 makes it obligatory for every factory to maintain an adequate number of latrines and urinals of the prescribed type separately for men and women workers. Such facilities are to be conveniently situated and accessible to workers at all times while they are in factory. Every latrines is required to be under cover and so partitioned off as to secure privacy and have a proper door and fastenings. Sweepers are required to be employed to keep latrines, urinals and washing places clean. Standard of construction and the scale of the latrine accommodation to be provided for men and women workers are contained in the rules framed by the concerned stategovernment.[4]

6.8.4.1.2 Prohibition of work in Hazardous Occupations

The Factories Act, 1948 prohibits employment of women in dangerous occupations. Section 22(2) of the Factories Act, 1948 provides that no women shall be allowed to clean, lubricate or adjust any part of a prime mover or of any transmission machinery while the prime mover or transmission machinery is in motion, or to clean, lubricate or adjust any part of any machine if the cleaning, lubrication or adjustment thereof would expose the women to risk of injury from any moving part either of that machine or of any adjacent machinery.

In an English case, the question was whether stationary parts of a machine can be cleaned by woman if the machine as a whole is in motion. It was held by the Court that if the machinery as a whole is in motion even stationary parts of the machine cannot be cleaned by woman. But in ***Richard***

Thomas and Baldwins Ltd. Vs. Cummings,[23] the Court observed that there would be no breach of statutory duty if an injury occurs while the machinery is unfenced, if the power is cut off and the machinery is under repairs and the parts are not in motion but are moved by hand for purposes of repairs.

The Factories also prohibit the employment of women in pressing cotton where a cotton opener is at work.[7] There is a proviso that if the feed end of a cotton opener is in a room separated from the delivery end by a partition to the roof or to such height as the inspector may in any particular case specify in writing, women may be employed on the side of the partition where the feed end is situated.[8] In ***B.N. Gamadia Vs. Emperor***[24] the Bombay High Court observed that the provisions of the Section are not complied with if there is a door made in a partition between the two portions of the room and if it can be opened by a woman employed although the door is shut, yet it is not locked nor other effective means are taken to prevent its being opened by a woman. This shows that both legislature and judiciary have shown concern about the security of women workers and every precaution is being taken to protect them against the risks of employment.

Again Section 87 of the Factories Act, 1948 empowers the State Government to prohibit employment of women in dangerous operations. According to this Section where the State Government is of the opinion that any manufacturing process or operation carried on in any factory exposes any persons employed in it to a serious risk of bodily injury, poisoning or disease, it may make rules applicable to any factory or class or description of factories in which manufacturing processor operation is carried on specifying the manufacturing process, or operation and declaring it to be dangerous and prohibiting or restricting the employment of women in the manufacturing process or operation.

23 [1955] A.C. 321. 59
24 (1925) 27 BOMLR 1405

6.8.4.1.3 Washing and Bathing Facilities

Separate facilities washing and bathing are provided for women workers under the Factories Act. According to Section 42 (1)(b) of the Act, separate and adequately screened washing facilities shall be provided for the use of male and female workers. Such facilities shall be conveniently accessible and shall be kept clean.[10] However, the State Government is empowered to prescribe standards of adequate and suitable facilities for washing.[11]

6.8.4.1.4 Crèches

A crèche is a nursery.[12] It is a place where babies of working mothers are taken care of while the mothers are at work. Section 48 of the Factories Act, 1948 provides that in every factory wherein more than 30 women workers[13]are ordinarily employed there shall be provided and maintained a suitable room for the use of children under the age of 6 years of such women. Such rooms shall provide adequate accommodation, and shall be adequately lighted and ventilated. Such rooms shall be maintained in a clean and sanitary condition and shall be under the charge of women trained in the care of children and infants. The State Government is authorised to makerules:

1. Prescribing the location and the standards in respect of construction, accommodation, furniture and other equipment of rooms to be provided to be used ascrèches,
2. Requiring the provision in factories of additional factories for the care of children belonging to women workers, including suitable provision of facilities for washing and changing their clothing,
3. Requiring the provision in any factory of free milk or refreshment or both for such children.
4. Requiring that facilities shall be given in any factory of free milk or refreshment or both for such children.

5. Requiring that facilities shall be given in any factory for the mothers of such children to feed them at the necessary intervals.
6. The State Governments have been given wide powers to make rules for the benefit and welfare of children of working mothers and to provide facilities to mothers in this regard.

6.8.4.1.5 Hours of Work

Under the Factories Act, 1948, the daily hours of work of adult workers have been fixed at 9.[14] Though the Act permits men under certain circumstances to work for more than 9 hours on any day it does not permit women to work beyond this limit.[15] Also in case of women workers there shall be no change of shifts except after a weekly holiday or any other holiday.

The maximum permissible hours of work for men and women are 48 per week in factories.[16] The daily spread over of working hours has been limited to 10½ hours in factories. The Act provides that no adult worker whether man or woman employed in factories shall be allowed to work for more than 5 hours at a stretch without a rest pause of atleast half an hour.

Maximum Permissible Load: To safeguard women against the dangers arising out of lifting to heavy weight, the Factories Act authorise the appropriate Governments to fix the maximum load that may be lifted by women. Rules framed by all the State Governments (Except U.P.) have fixed the following maximum weights for women employed infactories.

Adult females	: 65 lbs
Adolescent females	: 55 lbs

Prohibition of Night Work: The Factories Act, 1948 prohibit the employment of women during night hours. It is under special circumstances and in certain industries that this restriction may be relaxed.

According to Section 66(1)(b) of the Factories Act 1948, no woman shall be required or allowed to work in any factory between the hours of 6a.m.and 7p.m. However, the State Government may by notification in the official gazette, in respect of any factory or group or class or description of factories, vary the limits pertaining to night duties but no such variation shall authorise the employment of any woman between the hours of 10 p.m. and 5 p.m.[17] Section 66(2) further empowers the State Government to make rules providing for exemption from the restriction set out in Sub-Section (1) of the Section 66 concerning restrictions on employment of women to such an extent and Subject to such conditions as it may prescribe of women working in fish curing or fish canning factories, where the employment of women beyond the hours specified in the said restrictions is necessary to prevent damage to or deterioration in any raw material. However, such rules made by the Government shall remain in force for not more than three years at atime.[18]

In ***Triveni K.S. and Others Vs. Union of India and Others***,[25] the Constitutionality of Section 66 (1) (b) was challenged being discriminatory on the basis of sex. The High Court held that women should not be employed during night for their own safety and welfare was a philosophy of a bygone age out of tune with modern claims of equality, especially between sexes. With regard to exception given to fish currying and canning industry, it was observed that it looked an absurd argument that women would be safe in such industries but not safe in the textile industry. Consequently Section 66(1)(b) of the Act was struck down an declared unconstitutional by the High Court and declared that the same safeguard as provided women in fish industry should be given to women workers in others industries during nighttime.

In ***Haldia Refinery Canteen Employees Union and Another Vs. Indian Oil Corporation Ltd. and Others***,[26] settling a lingering debate, the Supreme Court has ruled that even if management of an organisation exercises control over

25 2002 (5) ALT 223 : (2002) IIILLJ 320 AP
26 Appeal (civil) 658 of 2002: Date of Judgment: 29/04/2005

the types of workers to be engaged in its canteen run by a contractor, they do not become employees of the office

Factories Act, 1948 only and not for any other purpose, the Supreme Court pointed out.The Supreme Court referred also to certain facts which rendered the claim of the appellants not tenable. First, the management was not reimbursing to the contractor the wages of the workmen. Second, two settlements had been made between the contractor and the canteen workmen. The respondent was not a party to either of them. So the appeal was dismissed.

This ruling assumes significance since the Apex Court had, in its earlier judgments held that the workers in a canteen attached to an office would be treated as employees of that office if the management exercised control over the selection of the canteen workers and payment of their salaries, even if they were being engaged by a contractor.

Rest rooms/shelters and lunch rooms with provision for drinking water (when ordinarily 150 or more workers are employed in the factory).

Annual Leave with Wages: A workers who works for 240 days is allowed an annual leave with wages at the rate of one day for every 20 days of work. Annual leave can be accumulated up to 30 days for adults and 40 days for children. The annual leave pay is to be paid at the rate average to the daily wage immediately preceding the leave. This will include basic and other allowances except boxes and overtime.

It is now clear that there are various provision in Factories Act which provide health safety and welfare for women workers. Unfortunately, all of these provisions are applicable to the organised sector which employ barley 10 percent of the total female labour force. So there is urgent need to extent these provisions to unorganised sector where majority of womenwork.

In factories Act the hours of work for men and women working in perennial factories are the same at present. It is, therefore, necessary to reduce the hours of work from 9 to 6 for women because they have to work both inside their homes as well as outside. A woman worker is both a domestic drudge as well as wage earner. It is in the interest of working women and her family to set special limit to her hours of work.

6.8.5 The Mines Act, 1952

The Act has been enacted to amend and consolidate the law relating to the regulation of labour and safety in mines. It seeks to regulate the working conditions in mines by providing for measures required to be taken for the safety and security of workers employed therein and certain amenities for them. The Act contains detailed provision relating to the health and safety, hours and limitation of employment, leave with wages. The Act extends to the whole of India and applies to all mines as defined in the Act. The Act came into force w.e.f. 01.07.1952.

The Act applies to all 'mines' which means[47] any excavation where any operation for the purpose of searching for or obtaining minerals has been or is being carried on and includes (i) All borings, bore holes, oil wells and accessory crude conditioning plants including the pipeline within the oilfield, (ii) all shafts belonging to a mine, (iii) all levels and inclined planes, (iv) all open cast workings, (v) conveyors or aerial ropeways used for the removal of minerals or refuse from the mine, (vi) workshops and stores within the precincts of a mine, (vii) railways, tramways and sidings belonging to a mine, and (viii) the power station supplying electricity for the purpose of working the mine.

6.8.5.1. Special Provisions Relating to Women

6.8.5.1.1 Prohibition of Night Work

The Mines Act, 1952 prohibits employment of women during night hours. According to Section 46(1)(b) of this Act no women shall, notwithstanding anything contained in any other law be employed in any mine above ground except between the hours 6 a.m. and 7 p.m. Every women employed in a mine above ground shall be allowed an interval of not less than eleven hours between the termination of employment on any one day and the commencement of the next period of employment.[48] However, notwithstanding anything contained in Sub- Section (1), the Central Government may, by notification in the official gazette, vary the hours of employment above ground of mine or class or description of mines, so that no employment of any women workmen between the hours of 10p.m. and 5 a.m. is permitted thereby.[49]

6.8.5.1.2 Prohibition of Work in Hazardous Occupation

The Mines Act, 1952 also prohibits employment of women in any part of a mine which is below ground.[50] Section 57(j) of the Mines Act, 1952 empowers the Central Government to make regulations for prohibiting, restricting or regulating the employment of women in mines or in any class of mines or on particular kinds of labour which are attended by danger to the life, safety or health of such persons.

Also, the Indian Merchant Shipping Act puts a ban on recruitment of women except as nurses, to take employment on board sea-going ships.

6.8.5.1.3 Creches

Under the Mines Act, 1952 the Central Government is authorised to make rules requiring the mines to maintain crèches if women workers are or were employed at one day of the preceding 12 months.[51] Thus the Mines Creche Rules 1966 make it obligatory for the owner, agent or manager of every mine, wherein women are employed or were employed on any day of the preceding 12 months, to provide a crèche at his colliery to look after the children of such workers. Each crèche is required to have a trained nurse and the prescribed set of equipment. Supply of food to the children attending crèche is also obligatory in the part of the management.

6.8.5.1.4 Latrine and Urinal Facilities

Section 20 says that there shall be provided, separately for males and females in every mine, a sufficient number of latrines and urinals of prescribed types so situated as to be convenient and accessible to persons employed in the mine at all times. It also provides that the latrines and urinals shall be adequately lighted, ventilated and maintained in a clean and sanitary condition. It also empowers Central Government to specify the number of latrines and urinals to be provided in any mine, in proportion to the number of males and females and provide other matters relating to sanitation.

6.8.6 The Plantation Labour Act,1951

This Act regulates, for the first time, the condition of work of plantation workers and provides for their welfare. Though, in the first instance, it applies only to tea, coffee, rubber and cinnamon plantations, the State Governments have been empowered to extend the provisions of the Act to other plantations with the approval of the Central Government.

For the purpose of this Act the plantation means any plantation to which this Act applies and includes offices, hospitals, dispensaries, schools, and any other premises used for any purpose connected with such plantation, but does not include any factory covered under the Factories Act,1948.

Under the Plantation Labout Act 1951 the definition of worker is provided as a person employed in a plantation for hire or reward, whether directly or through any agency, to do any work skilled, unskilled, manual or clerical but does not include (a) medical officer employed in plantation, (b) any person employed in plantation including any member of medical staff whose monthly wages exceed Rs. 750 (c) any person employed in the plantation primarily in a managerial capacity, notwithstanding that his monthly wages do not exceed Rs. 750 and (d) any person temporarily employed in the plantation in any work relating to the construction,

development or maintenance of buildings, roads, bridges, drains or canals.

6.8.6.1 Special Provisions Relating to Women

6.8.6.1.1 Prohibition of Night Work

The Plantation Labour Act, 1951 also contains provisions for prohibition of employment of women during night. Section 25 of the Act provides that except with the permission of the State Government no woman worker shall be employed in any plantation otherwise than between the hours of 6 a.m. and 7 p.m. However, this prohibition does not apply to midwives and nurses employed as such in any plantation.

6.8.6.1.2 Crèches

Under the Plantation Labour Act, 1951, every plantation wherein fifty or more women workers (including women workers employed by any contractor) are employed or were employed on any day of the preceding twelve months, or wherethe number of children of women workers (including women workers employed by any contractor) is twenty or more, there shall be provided and maintained by the employer suitable rooms for the use of children of such women workers.[63] If, in respect of any plantation wherein less than fifty women workers including women workers employed by any contractor are employed or were employed on any day of the preceding twelve months, or where the number of children of such women workers is less than twenty, the State Government, having regard to the number of children of such women workers deems it necessary that suitable rooms for the use of such children should be provided and maintained by the employer, it may, by order, direct the employer to provide and maintain such rooms and thereupon the employer shall be bound to comply with such directions. The rooms shall provide adequate accommodation, be adequately lighted and ventilated, be maintained in a clear and sanitary condition

and be under the charge of a woman trained in the care of children and infants.[64]

6.8.6.1.3 Latrine and Urinal Facilities

Section 9(1) of the Plantations Labour Act, 1951 also provides that in every plantation a sufficient number of latrines and urinals of prescribed types so situated as to be convenient and accessible to workers employed shall be provided. These latrines and urinals shall be maintained in a clean and sanitary condition.[65]

6.8.7 Building and Other Construction Workers' (Regulation of Employment and Conditions of Service) Act,1996

The purpose of this Act to regulate the employment and conditions of service of construction workers and to provide for their safety, health and welfare measures. The Act applies to every establishment which employs/had employed on any day of preceding 12 months, 10 or more building workers in building or construction work. It covers all Central and State Government establishments. The special feature of the Act is that it covers all private residential buildings if the cost of construction is more than rupees tenlakhs.For the purpose of this Act, the building and other construction work is defined as construction, repair etc. of buildings, roads etc. The definition does not include any building or other construction work to which Factories Act or Mines Act applies.

6.8.7.1 Special Provisions Relating to Women

6.8.7.1.1 Latrines and Urinals[78]

In every place where building or other construction work is carried on, the employer shall provide sufficient latrine and urinal accommodation of such type as may be prescribed and they shall be so conveniently situated as may be accessible

to the building workers at all times while they are in such place.

Provided that it shall not be necessary to provide separate urinals in any place where less than fifty persons are employed or where the latrines are connected to a water - borne sewage system.

6.8.7.1.2 Creches

In every place wherein, more than fifty female building workers areordinarily employed, there shall be provided and maintained a suitable room or rooms for the use of children under the age of six years of such femaleworkers.

Such rooms shall:

- provide adequateaccommodation,
- be adequately lighted andventilated,
- be maintained in a clean and sanitarycondition,
- be under the chare of women trained in the care of children andinfants.

6.8.8 The Beedi and Cigar Workers (Conditions of Employment) Act,1966

Beedi manufacturing is one of the traditional and largely home-based industries in India. It is largely labour intensive and engages 45 million workers and nearly two thirds of them are women.[86]

The Beedi and Cigar workers (Conditions of Employment) Act, 1966 is the only labour enactment, which deals with, home workers in a detailed manner. The enactment is particularly relevant, as bulks of the home workers in beedi rolling are women. The very existence of this law has encouraged the formation of trade unions among workers in beedi rolling industry and this has led to demand for similar laws for home-workers in other occupations andindustries.

The purpose of this Act is to provide for the welfare of workers in beedi and cigar establishments self-employed and regulation of work conditions. The Act applies to all employees in beedi and cigar establishments except self employed persons working in their ownhouses.

6.8.8.1 Special Provisions Relating to Women

6.8.8.1.1 Prohibition of Nightwork

Section 25 of the Beedi and Cigar Workers (Conditions of Employment) Act, 1966 prohibits employment of women in any industrial premises except between 6 a.m. and 7 p.m.

6.8.8.1.2 Creches

The Act provide for crèche facility. According to Section 14 of the Act in every industrial premises wherein more than fifty (now thirty after the Amendment of 1993)[87] female employees are ordinarily employed, there shall be provided and maintained a suitable room or rooms for the use of children under the age of six years of such female employees. Such rooms shall be provided with adequate accommodation, be adequately lighted and ventilated, be maintained in a clean and sanitary condition and be under the charge of women trained in the care of children and infants. The State Government is also empowered to make rules with respect to the same matters as are provided under the Factories Act.[88]

6.8.9 The Contract Labour (Regulation and Abolition) Act,1970

Contract Labour (Regulation and Abolition) Act, 1970 was enacted not only to regulate the contract labour but also to abolish it. To lessen their burden and to avoid liability towards regular employees, employer devised a Scheme of getting their work done through contract workers. Contract labour which forms a unorganised sector of employment were Subjected to lot of discriminations and expenses. Contract

Labour Act came to mitigate their sufferings and to regulate theiremployment.[102]

For the purpose of this Act a person is said to be employed as contract labour, in or in connection with the work of an establishment, when he is hired for such work by or through a contractor, with or without the knowledge of the principal employer.

The Act extends to the whole of India. It applies to:

- every establishment wherein 20 or more workmen are or were employed on any day of the preceding 12 months as contract labour,and
- every contractor who employs or employed on any day of the preceding 12 months, 20 or moreworkmen.[103]
- The Act does not apply to establishments where only intermittent / casual work isperformed.

The Act empowers the Appropriate Government to prohibit employment of contract labour in any process, operation or other work in any establishment keeping in view (i) the condition of work and benefits provided for the contract labour in that establishment, (ii) whether the process, operation or other work in incidental to or necessary for the work of that establishment and (iii) whether it is of perennial nature.[104]

After the commencement of *the Contract Labour (Regulation and Abolition) Act, 1970,* ***Air India Case***[105] of 1997 is the landmark judgment given by the Apex Court. In this case the Court noted that there is no express provision under Section 10 of the Contract Labour (Regulation and Abolition) Act for absorption of contract labour on abolition of the contract labour system. In the absence of such a provision the Supreme Court has played a creative role by bridging the gap left open by the legislature. Thus, in above, in the majority judgment Ramaswamy, J. observed:

Though there is no express provision in the Contract Labour (Regulation and Abolition) Act for absorption of the contract labour when engagement of contract labour stood prohibited on publication of the notification under Section

10(1) of the Act, from that moment the principal employer cannot continue contract labour and direct relationship gets established between the workmen and the principal employer;

The Act did not intend to denude the contract labour of their source of livelihood and means of development throwing them out from employed;and

In a proper case the Court as sentinel on the *qui vive* is required to direct the appropriate authority to Submit are port and if the finding is that the workmen were engaged in violation of the provisions of the Act or were continued as contract labour despite prohibition of the contract labour under Section 10(1), the High Court has Constitutional duty to enforce the law and grant them appropriate relief of absorption in the employment of the principal employer.

In Secretary State of ***Karnataka and Ors. Vs. Uma Devi and Ors.***[113]. In this case it was held that under the appointment is in terms of the relevant rules and after a proper competition among qualified persons, the same would not confer any right on the appointee. If it is a contractual appointment, the appointment comes to an end at the end of the contract, if it were an engagement or appointment on daily wages or casual basis, the same would come to an end when it is discontinued. Similarly, a temporary employee could not claim to be made permanent on the expiry of his term of appointment. It has also to be clarified that merely because a temporary employee or a casual wage worker is continued for a time beyond the term of his appointment he would not be entitled to be absorbed in regular service or made permanent, merely on the strength of such continuance, if the original appointment was not made by following a due process of selection as envisaged by the relevant rules. It is not open to the Court to prevent regular recruitment at the instance of temporary employees whose period of employment has come to an end or of ad hoc employees who by the very nature of their appointment, do not acquire any light. High Courts acting under Article 226 of the Constitution of the India, should not ordinarily issue directions for absorption, regularisation, or permanent continuance unless the recruitment itself was made regularly and in terms of the ConstitutionalScheme. The judgment in ***Uma Devi's Case***[114] was followed in ***Surinder Prasad Tiwari Vs. U.P. Rajya Krishi Utpadan Mandi Parishad***,[115] wherein it was held that where appointments were made without following the procedure laid down under Articles 14, 16 and 309 of the Constitution, they cannot be directed to be regularised in service.

Hence, apart from discrimination, Article 14 of the Constitution will also be violated on the ground of arbitrariness and unreasonableness if employees who have but in such a long service are denied the benefit of regularisation and are made to face the same. Selection which fresh recruits have to face. In view of such a categorical observation made by the Honourable Apex Court, the petitioners are working for the last 25 years or so without any benefit when compared to other similarly situated persons, the prayer of the applicants to regularize their services deserves to be allowed. The respondents are directed to regularise the service of the applicants within a period of eight weeks from the date of receipt of a copy of this order.

6.8.9.1 Special Provisions Relating to Women

6.8.9.1.1 Creches

Creches are extended to the contract workers by the Contract Labour (Regulation and Abolition) Central Rules, 1971, Construction and Maintenance of Creches. It provides that in every establishment where twenty or more women are ordinarily employed as contract labour there must be provided a crèche located within 50 meters of establishments. While the crèche should beconveniently accessible to the mothers of the children accommodated therein, it shall not be situated in close proximity to establishment where obnoxious fumes, dust or ordour are given off or in which excessively noisy processes are carriedon.[122]

6.8.9.1.2 Washing and Bathing Facilities

Under the Contract Labour (Regulation and Abolition) Central Rules, 1971 separate and adequately screened washing facilities be provided for the use of male and female workers.[123] Such facilities shall be conveniently accessible and shall be kept in clean and hygienic conditions.[124]

6.8.9.1.3 Latrines and Urinal Facilities

Contract labour (Regulation and Abolition) Central Rules, 1971 also provides provision for separate latrine and urinal facilities for male and female workers. It also provides that there shall be atleast one latrine for every 25 femalesif number of female workers is 100 and one for every 50 if the number exceeds100.[125] Every latrine shall be under cover and so partitioned off as to secure privacy and shall have a proper door and fastenings. Outside these latrines and urinals a notice providing "for men only" or "for women only" as the case may be should be displayed. The notice should also bear the figure of a woman or of a man as the case may be.[126] It is suggested that the same provision should be incorporated in other enactment also.

6.8.9.1.4 Rest Rooms and Canteens

Rule 41(3) of the Contract Labour (Regulation and Abolition) Central Rules, 1971 provides that separate rest rooms shall be provided for women employees. These rooms should be properly ventilated and maintained. Rules 44 of the same provides that in a canteen a portion of dining hall and service counter shall be partitioned off and reserved for women workers, in proportion to their number. There are a number of provisions in the Act for the welfare and safety of contract labour.[127] There shall be provided and maintained by the contractor so as to be readily accessible during all working hours a first aid box equipped with the prescribed contents at every place where contract labour is employed by him.[128]Section 20(1) provides that if any amenity required to be provided under Section 16, Section 17, Section 18 and Section 19 for the benefit of the contract labour employed in an establishment is not provided by the contractor within the time prescribed therefore, such amenity shall be provided by the principal employer within such time as may be prescribed.

In ***People's Union for Democratic Rights Vs. Union of India***[27] is very interesting leading case on contract labour. There was a writ petition brought by way of public interest litigation in order to ensure observance of the provisions of various labour laws including Contract Labour (Regulation of Employment and Conditions of Service) Act, 1979 in relation to workmen employed in the construction work of various projects connected with the Asian Games.

It was observed that the workmen whose cause has been championed by the petitioners are employees of the contractors but the Union of India, the Delhi Administration and the Delhi Development Authority which have entrusted the construction work of Asiad projects to the contractors cannot escape their obligation for observance of various labour laws by the contractor. So far as the Contract Labour (Regulation and Abolition) Act, 1970 is concerned, it is clear that under Section 20, if any amenity required to be provided under Section 16, 17, 18 or 19 for the benefit of the workmen employed in any establishment is not provided by the contractor, the obligation to provide such amenity rests of principal employer and, therefore, if in the construction work of Asiad projects the contractors do not carry out the obligations imposed upon them by any of these Sections, Union of India, the Delhi Administration, and the Delhi Development Authority as principal employers would be liable and these obligations would be enforceable againstthem.

In ***Salal Hydro Electric Project Case,***[28] judicial intervention by means of Public Interest Litigation has yielded positive results for the benefit of the workmen employed in the Salal Hydro Electric Project. The litigation started on

27 AIR 1982 SC 1473
28 (1984) 3 SCC 538

the basis of a news in Indian Express dated 26 August, 1982 that a large number of workmen from different States including the State of Orissa were working on the Salal Hydro Electric Project in difficult conditions and they were denied the benefits of various labour laws and were Subjected to exploitation by the contractors to whom different portions of the work were entrusted by the Central Government. The People's Union for Democratic Right there upon addressed a letter to Mr.Justice D.A. Desai enclosing a copy of the news report and requested him to treat the letter as a writ petition so that justice may be done to the poor labourers working in Salal Hydro Electric Project. The letter was treated as a writ petition and the Court directed Labour Commissioner, Jammu to visit the site of the project and thereupon Submitted a report to the Court. Pursuant to the order of the Court, the Labour Commissioner, Jammu visited the site of the project and made an interim report on October 11, 1982 followed by a final report dated October 15, 1982.

6.8.10 Inter-State Migrant Workmen (Regulation of Employment and Conditions of Service) Act,1979

The vast majority of migrant workers fall in the unorganised sector. Workers are recruited from various parts of a State through contractors or agents commonly known as 'Sardars', generally for work outside the State wherever construction projects are available. This system leads itself to various abuses. The promises that contractors make at the time of recruitment about higher wages and regular and timely payments are not usually kept. No working hours are fixed for these workers and they have to work all days in the week under extremely bad, often intolerable working conditions in hospitable environments. The provisions of various labour laws are not observed and migrant workers are often Subjected to various forms of malpractices.

The Inter-State Migrant Workmen (Regulation of Employment and Conditions of Service) Act, 1979 was enacted to regulate the employment and conditions of service of inter-state migrant workers.

The Act extends to the whole of India and applies to:

- Every establishment in which five or more inter-state migrant workmen (whether or not in addition to other workmen) are employed or were employed on any day of the preceding 12 months,and
- Every contractor who employs or employed five or more inter-state migrant workmen (whether or not in addition to other workmen) on any day of the preceding 12 months.[131]

6.8.10.1 Special Provisions Relating to Women

6.8.10.1.1 Prohibition of Night Work

The Inter-State Migrant Workmen (Regulation of Employment and Conditions of Service) Central Rules, 1980 also apply in the area to which the Inter-State Migrant Workmen (Regulation of Employment and Conditions of Service) Act, 1979 applies. Rule 11 of the Inter-State Migrant Workmen (Regulations of Employment and Conditions of Service) Central Rules, 1980 provides that no female migrant worker shall be employed by any contractor before 6 a.m. or after 7 p.m. But this shall not apply to the employment of female migrant workmen in pit head baths, crèches and canteens and midwives and nurses in hospital anddispensaries.[132]

6.8.10.1.2 Creches

The Inter-State Migrant Workers (Regulation of Employment and Conditions of Service) Central Rules, 1980 provide crèche facility. Rule 44 says that in every establishment where twenty or more women are ordinarily employed as migrant workmen and in which employment of migrant workmen is likely to continue for three months or more, the contractor shall provide and maintain two rooms of accessible dimensions for the use of their children under the age of 6 years. One of such rooms shall be used as play room for the children and the other as bedroom for them.

6.8.10.1.3 Rest Rooms and Canteens

Rule 40 of the Inter-State, Migrant Workmen (Regulation of Employment and Conditions of Service) Central Rules, 1980 provides that separate rest rooms shall be provided for female migrant workmen. The rooms should be effective, suitable and adequately ventilated and should be at convenient distance from the establishment. Rule 41 of the same provides that a portion of the dining hall and service counter shall be partitioned off and reserved for women migrant workmen in proportion to their number. Washing places in the dining hall shall be separate and screened to secure privacy.

6.9 Social Security Measures for Women through Labour Legislations

Social Security is a basic need of all women regardless of employment in which they work and live. It is an important form of social protection. In a general sense social security refers to protection extended by the society and State to its members to enable them to overcome various contingencies of life. Women have to face various contingencies when they involved in employment such as sickness, maternity, disablement, employment insecurities and risks. There is a greatest need to provide security and protection to women workers against various contingencies. Thus, social security measures have a two-fold significance. They constitute an important step towards the goal of a welfare state, by improving living and working conditions and affording the women protection against the uncertainties of the future.

The various legislative measures adopted by the Government and which provide protection to the women workers in certain contingencies have been given as follows:

6.9.1 The Maternity Benefit Act, 1961

The Act was passed with a view to reduce disparities under the existing Maternity Benefit Acts and bring uniformity with regard to rates, qualifying conditions and duration of maternity benefits. The Act, repeals the Mines Maternity Benefit Act, 1941, the Bombay Maternity Benefit Act, 1929, the provisions of maternity protection under the Plantations Labour Act, 1951 and all other provincial enactments covering the same field. However, the Act does not apply to factory or establishment to which the provisions of Employee's State Insurance Act 1948 applies,[138] except as otherwise provided in Section 5A and 5B of the Act.

The Act was amended from time to time. The Amendment of 1972 provides that in the event of the application of the Employees' State Insurance Act, 1948 to any factory or establishment, maternity benefit under the Maternity Benefit Act would continue to be available to women workers, until they become qualified to claim similar benefit under Employees' State Insurance Act. Again in 1973 the Act was amended so as to bring within its ambit establishments in the circus industry. The 1976 Amendment, further extends the scope of the Act to the women employed in factories or establishments covered by the Employees'StateInsurance Act, 1948 and in receipt of wages exceeding entitlement specified in that Act.

The Act was again amended in 1988 to incorporate the recommendations of a working group of Economic Administration Reforms Commission. The Act has been extended to shops or establishments employing 10 or more persons. The rate of maternity has been enhanced and some other changes have been introduced.[144] The Amendment of 1995 further expands the coverage of the Act and legalises the medical termination of pregnancy and provides incentives for family planning programme. The Act was amended again in 2007. By which medical Bonus to be increased from Rs. 250 to Rs. 2500/- for working women.

6.9.1.1 Meaning of Maternity Benefit

Prior to the amendment of 1989, if a woman employee could not avail of the six weeks' leave preceding the date of her delivery, she was entitled to only six weeks leave following the day of her delivery. However, by the above Amendment, the position has changed. Now, in case a woman employee does not avail six weeks' leave preceding the date of her delivery, she can avail of that leave following her delivery, provided the total leave period, i.e., preceding and following the day of her delivery, does not exceed 12weeks.[145]

A woman employee is entitled to maternity benefits under the Act irrespective of the number of children she has. This matter was considered in a high level Committee set up by the Central Government. The Committee thought that though it is contrary to the family planning norms being advocated by the Government, it is also not appropriate to deny a woman employee the benefits under the law, once she gave birth to a child.

6.9.1.2 Restriction on Employment of Pregnant Woman

No employer should knowingly employ woman during the period of 6 weeks immediately following the day of her delivery or miscarriage or medical termination of pregnancy. Besides, no woman should work in any establishment during the said period of 6 weeks. Further, the employer should not require a pregnant woman employees to do an arduous work involving long hours of standing or any work which is likely to interfere with her pregnancy or cause miscarriage or adversely affect her health, during the period of 1 month preceding the period of 6 weeks before the date of her expected delivery, and any period during the said period of 6 weeks for which she does not avail of the leave as provided for in Section 6 of theAct.[146]

6.9.1.3 Right to Payment of Maternity Benefit

Section 5(1) of the Act provides that the maternity benefit to which every woman shall be entitled to and her employer shall be liable for, is a payment to a worker at the rate of average daily wages for the period of her actual absence immediately preceding and including the day of her delivery and for six weeks immediately following that day.

For the purposes of payment of the maternity benefit to a woman worker, the average daily wage means the average of woman's wages payable to her for the days on which she has worked during the period of three calendar months immediately preceding the date from which she absents herself on account of maternity, the minimum rate of wage fixed, or revised under the Minimum Wages Act, 1948 or ten rupees,[147] whichever is thehighest.

Section 5(2) provides that no woman shall be entitled to maternity benefit unless she has actually worked in an establishment of the employer from whom she claims maternity benefit for a period of not less than eight days[148] in the twelve months immediately the date of expected delivery. The qualifying period of eight days shall not apply to a women what has migrated into the state of Assam and was pregnant at the time ofimmigration.

For the purpose of calculating the days on which a woman has actually worked in the establishment, the days for which she has been laid off or was on holidays declared under any law for the time being in force to be holiday with wages during the period of twelve months immediately preceding the date of her expected delivery shall be taken into account.[149]

Section 5(3) provides that a woman shall be entitled to maternity benefit for a maximum period of twelve weeks of which not more than six weeks shall precede the date of her expecteddelivery.

Provided that where a woman dies during this period, the maternity benefits shall be payable only for the days upto and including the day of herdeath.

Only a few cases have come up before the Courts, so far in the area of maternity benefit. In ***Malayalam Plantations Ltd. Vs. Inspector of Plantations***,[29] the Full Bench of Court

29 AIR 1975 KER 86

while linking the maternity benefit with the average daily wages of a women worker indicated that such benefit was to be calculated with reference to the working days only. The Court, accordingly held, that there was nothing in the Maternity Benefit Act to show that the duration of maternity benefit covers non-working wage-less days in the week. Therefore, in calculating the benefit the number of weeks for which a women worker is entitled to the benefit must be multiplied by six and not by seven. This view, however did not find the approval of Supreme Court in ***B. Shah Vs. Labour Court Coimbatore***,[30] the Supreme Court referred to various dictionary meanings of the word "week" and observed:

"In the context of Sub-Sections (1) and (3) of Section 5 of the Act, the term "week" has to be taken to signify a cycle of seven days including Sundays."

The Court further held, that,

"the computation of maternity benefit has to be made for all the days including Sundays and rest days which may be wage-less holidays comprised in the actual period of absence of the women extending up to six week preceding and including the delivery as also for the days falling within the six weeks immediately followings the day of delivery thereby ensuring that the woman worker gets for the said period not only amount equally 100 percent of the wages, which she was previously earning in terms of Section 3(n) of the Act, but also the benefit of the wages for all the Sundays and rest days falling within the aforesaid two periods which would ultimately be conducive to the interest of both the woman worker and her employer."[31]

6.9.1.4 Protection against Discrimination

According to Section 12(1) when a woman absents herself from work, in accordance with the provisions of the Act, it shall be unlawful for her employer to discharge or dismiss her during or on account of such absence or to give notice of discharge or dismissal on such a day that notice will expire

30 AIR 1978 SC 12
31 Ibid

during such absence or to vary to her disadvantage any of the condition of her service.

Section 12(2)(a) guarantees that a working woman who is discharged at any time during her pregnancy but who would otherwise have been eligible for benefits will still a right to maternity benefits and medical bonus. The only exception to this is if she is discharged for 'gross misconduct' as prescribed under rules. In such a case the employer must notify her in writing that her benefits and bonus will be denied. Women who are not eligible for benefits because they have worked less than the required period of time are also not protected against dismissal or discrimination.

6.9.1.5 Leave for miscarriage etc. and illness

In case of miscarriage or medical termination of pregnancy, a woman shall, on production of the prescribed proof, be entitled to leave with wages at the rate of maternity benefit, for a period of 6 weeks immediately following the day of her miscarriage or medical termination of pregnancy.

6.9.1.6 Leave for Tubectomy Operation

In case of tubectomy operation, a woman shall, on production of prescribed proof be entitled to leave with wages at the rate of maternity benefit for a period of two weeks immediately following the day of operation

6.9.1.7 Leave for illness

Leave for a maximum period of one month with wages at the rate of maternity benefit are allowable in case of illness arising out of pregnancy, delivery, premature birth of child, miscarriage or medical termination of pregnancy or tubectomy operation.

6.9.2 The Employees' State Insurance Act, 1948

The Employees' State Insurance Act, 1948 provides for health care and cash benefit payments in the case of sickness, maternity and employment injury. The Act is applicable to non-seasonal factories using power and employing 10 or more employees and non-power using factories and certain other establishments employing 20 or more employees. Seasonal factories, mines and plantations have not been covered under the Act. It also does not cover the unorganized labour or self-employed workers. It is applicable to employees drawing wages not exceeding Rs. 10,000 per month.

The Employees' State Insurance (Amendment) Bill, 2009 has been introduced to amend the Employees' State Insurance Act, 1948. Some of salient features of the Bill are: (i) it enhances the age limit from the existing eighteen years to twenty-one years for the purpose of giving benefits to dependents. (ii) It provides benefits to worker for the accidents happening while commuting to the place of work and vice versa. (iii) it provides for a new definition of "factory" to provide that when ten or more persons are employed or were employed in the preceding twelve months irrespective of the use of power.

6.9.2.1 Objective

The main objective of the Employees' State Insurance Act, 1948, is to provide to the workers medical relief, sickness cash benefits, maternity benefits to women workers pension to the dependents of deceased workers and compensation for fatal and other employment injuries including occupational diseases, in an integrated form through a contributory fund. Where a workman is covered under Employees' State Insurance Scheme, no compensation could be claimed from his employer under the Workmen's Compensation Act in respect of employment injury sustained by him.

6.9.3 Funding and Operation of Scheme

The Employees' State Insurance Scheme is mainly financed by contributions from the employers and employees. The rates of the employers' and employees' share of contribution are 4.75% and 1.75% respectively. Employees earning less than and upto Rs. 75 per day are exempted from payment of contribution.[180] The State Governments' share of the expenditure on the provision of medical care is to the extent of 12.5% (1/8th within the per capita ceiling). The corporation has prescribed a ceiling on the shareable expenditure on medical care. From 1st April 2005, the ceiling on expenditure per insured person family unit has been raised to Rs. 900/- per annum. All capital expenditure on construction of ESI hospitals, and other buildings including their maintenance is borne exclusively by the corporation.

6.9.4 Benefits

Sickness Benefit

Every insured Employee is entitled to the cash benefit for the period of sickness occurring during any benefit period and certified by a duly appointed medical practitioner if the contributions in respect of him were payable for not less than (78 days) the corresponding contribution period. However, in the case of a newly appointed employee, eligible for the first time who has got shorter contribution period of less than 156 days, he shall be entitled to claim sickness benefit if he pays contribution for not less than half the number of days available for working in such contribution period. The benefit is payable at the 120 percent of the standard benefit rate against the existing 100 percent, corresponding to his daily average wages. The benefit is, however not payable for any day on which the employees works, remains on leave, holiday or strike, in respect of which he receives wages.

Disablement Benefit

Disablement benefit[185] is payable in the form of cash in installments, to an employee who is injured in the course of his employment and is, permanently or temporarily, disabled, or contacts any occupational disease. It is sufficient if it is proved that the injury was caused by an accident arising out of, and in the course of employment, no matter when it occurred, and where it occurred. However, the place or time of accident should not be totally unrelated to the employment.

The benefit is payable at the following rates:

(a)	For temporary disablement of not less than 3 days and permanent total disablement.	At the rate of 50% more than the standard benefit rate.
(b)	For permanent partial disablement.	At such percentage of the benefit payable in case (a) above as is proportionate to the percentage of the loss of earning capacity.

Dependent's Benefit

If an employee dies as a result of any injury sustained in the course of his employment or an occupational disease, his dependents[189] shall be entitled to a benefit in the form of pension. The dependent's benefit is payable at 40% more than the standard benefit rate.

Medical Benefit

An insured employee and his family members, who require medical treatment and attendance, is entitled to receive medical benefit in the form of treatment and attendance at an E.S.I. Hospital, dispensary or clinic. A person is entitled to medical benefit during any period for which contributions are payable in respect of him, or in which he is qualified to claim sickness benefit or maternity benefit, or he is in receipt of such disablement benefit as does not disentitle him to medical benefit under the regulations. If in respect of a person contribution ceases to be payable, he may be allowed medical benefit for such period and at such conditions as the regulations may specify.

Provided further that and insured person who ceases to be in insurable employment on account of permanent disablement shall continue, Subject to payment of contribution and such other conditions as may be prescribed by the Central Government, to receive medical benefit till the date on which he would have vacated the employment on attaining the age of superannuation had he not sustained such permanent disablement.

Employees' State Insurance (Amendment) Bill 2009

In Section 56 of the Principal Act, in Sub-Section (3), for the third proviso the following proviso shall substituted, namely:

"Provided also that an insured person who has attained the age of superannuation, a person who retires under a Voluntary Retirement Scheme or takes premature retirement, and his spouse shall be eligible to receive medicalbenefits Subject to payment of contribution and such other conditions as may be prescribed by the Central Government".[32]

Funeral Expenses

If an insured employee dies the eldest surviving member of his family or the person who incurs the expenditure on funeral of the deceased employee, is entitled to reimbursement of such expenditure Subject to a maximum of Rs. 3000. The claim for the payment of funeral expenses should be submitted in form 22 along with prescribed documents within 3 months of the death of the insured employee.

Maternity Benefit

Maternity benefit is provided to women workers who are covered under the Employees' State Insurance Act, 1948. The Act provides for periodical payment to an insured woman at the prescribed rate and for a prescribed period in case of confinement, miscarriage, sickness arising out of pregnancy or premature birth of a child. The term confinement means "labour resulting in the issue of a living child or labour after 26 weeks of pregnancy resulting in the issue of a child whether alive or dead" and the expression miscarriage as defined in the Act means "expulsion of the contents of a pregnant uterus at any period prior to or during twenty six weeks of pregnancy, but does not include any miscarriage the causing of which is punishable under the Indian Penal Code.

32 Section 56 the Employees' State Insurance Act, 1948

6.9.5 The Employees' Provident Funds and Miscellaneous Provisions Act, 1952

The Employees' Provident Funds and Miscellaneous Provision Act, 1952 is a welfare legislation enacted for the purpose of instituting a Provident Fund for employees working in factories and other establishments. The Act aims at providing social security and timely monetary assistance to industrial employees and their families when they are in distress and/or unable to meet family and social obligations and to protect them in old age, disablement, early death of the bread winner and in some other contingencies. Presently, the following three Schemes are in operation under the Act through the EPFO:

- Employees' Provident Funds Scheme, 1952 this Scheme is amended in 2007 and 2008
- Employees' Deposit Linked Insurance Scheme, 1976 this Scheme is amended in 2008
- Employees' Pension Scheme, 1995 this Scheme is amended in 2008 and 2009

6.9.5.1 Coverage of Establishments and Members

The Employees Provident Fund and Miscellaneous Provisions Act, 1952 extends to whole of India, excluding the State of Jammu and Kashmir. The Act is applicable to factories and other classes of establishments engaged in specific industries, classes of establishments employing 20 or more persons. The Act, however, does not apply to cooperative societies employing less than 50 persons and working without the aid of power. The Act also does not apply to employees of the Central Government or State Government or local authority. The Central Government is empowered to apply the provisions of this Act to any establishment employing less than 20 persons after giving not less than two months notice of its intent to do so by a notification in the official gazette. Once the Act has been made applicable, it does not cease to be applicable even if the number of employees falls below 20.

An establishment/factory, which is not otherwise coverable under the Act, can be covered voluntarily with mutual consent of the employers and the majority of the employees under Section 1(4) of the Act. Thus membership of the fund is compulsory for employees drawing a pay not exceeding Rs. 6500 per month (at the time of joining). Every employee employed in or in connection with the work of a factory or establishment shall be entitled and required to become a member of the fund from the date of joining the factory or establishment. The employees drawing more than Rs. 6500/- per month at the time of joining may become member on a joint option of employer and employee. The Act is currently applicable to factories and other establishment engaged in about 182 specified industries, class of establishment employing 20 or more persons (Industries are specified in Schedule 1 of the Act). As on 31st March 2006, there were 4,44,464 establishment and factories covered under the Act with membership of 429.53 lakh both in the exempted and unexemptedsectors.

6.9.6 Employees' Provident Fund Schemes,1952

(1) The Central Government may, by notification in the Official Gazette, frame a Scheme to be called the Employees' Provident Fund Scheme for the establishment of provident funds under this Act for employees or for any class of employees and specify the (establishments) or class of establishments to which the said Scheme shall apply and (there shall be established, as soon as may be after the framing of the Scheme, a Fund in accordance with the provisions of this Act and the Scheme).

[(1A) The Fund shall vest in, and be administered by, the Central Board constituted under Section5A.

(1B) Subject to the provisions of this Act, a Scheme framed under Sub-Section

(1) may provide for all or any of the matters specified in Schedule II]

[(2) A Scheme framed under Sub-Section (1) may provide that any of its provisions shall take effect either prospectively or retrospectively on such date as may be specified in this behalf in the Scheme.] This Scheme is amended from time to time.

6.9.7 Employees' Provident Funds (Amendment) Scheme 2007

In exercise of the powers conferred by Sub-Section (1) of Section 7 of the Employees' Provident Funds and Miscellaneous Provisions Act, 1952, the Central Government hereby makes the following Scheme further to amend the Employees' Provident Funds Scheme, 1952 namely:

(i) The Scheme may be called the Employees' Provident Funds (Amendment) Scheme, 2007.

In the Employees' Provident Funds Scheme, 1952 in paragraph 60, after the second proviso to clause (b) of Sub-paragraph (2), the following proviso shall be added, namely:

"Provided also that the rate of interest to be allowed on claims for refund for the broken currency period shall be the last declared rate on Employees' Provident Fund and if the rate declared for any current year happens to be less than the previous year's declared rate, then it would accrue as bonus to the outgoing members and it shall be incorporated into calculation for deriving the current year's rate of interest at the end of the year and the claims settled under this proviso shall be final."[33]

6.9.8 Employees' Provident Fund (Amendment) Scheme, 2008

In exercise of the powers conferred by Section 5, read with Sub-Section (1)of Section 7 of the Employees' Provident Funds and Miscellaneous Provisions Act, 1952 (19 of 1952), the Central Government hereby makes the following Scheme further to amend the Employees' Provident Funds Scheme,

33 Paragraph Employees' Provident Funds Scheme, 1952

1952, namely: 1(1) This Scheme may be called the Employees' Provident Funds (Amendment) Scheme, 2008. It shall come into force on the 1st day of April, 2008.

In the Employees' Provident Funds Scheme, 1952, after Paragraph 81, the following paragraph shall be inserted, namely:

"*82 Special provisions in respect of certain employees*: The Scheme shall, in its application to an employee who is a person with disability under the Persons with Disabilities (Equal Opportunities, Protection of Right and Full Participation) Act, 1995 (1 of 1996) and under the National Trust for Welfare of Persons with Autism, Cerebral Palsy, Mental Retardation and Multiple Disabilities Act, 1999 (44 of 1999) respectively, be Subject to the following modifications, namely:

For clause (1) of Paragraph 2, the following clause shall be Substituted, namely:

'(1) "excluded employee" means,

a person with disability, who having been a member of the Fund has withdrawn the full amount of his accumulations in the Fund under clause (a) or clause (c) of Sub-paragraph (1) of Paragraph 69;

a person with disability, whose pay at the time he is otherwise entitled to become a member of the Fund, exceeds twenty-five thousand rupees permonth.

An apprentice."

In Paragraph 30, after Sub-paragraph (3), the following proviso shall be inserted, namely:

"Provided that the Central Government shall contribute the employer's share of contribution up to a maximum period of three years from the date of commencement of membership of the Fund, in respect of an employee who is a person with disability, employed directly by the principal employer or through a contractor.",[34]

34 Paragraph 30

In Paragraph 34, after the first proviso, the following proviso shall be inserted, namely:

"Provided further that in the case of any such employee who is a person with disability, the aforesaid Declaration form shall further contain such particulars as are necessary for such employees."[35]

In Paragraph 36, after Sub-paragraph (1), the following Sub-paragraph shall be inserted, namely:

"(1-A) Every employer shall send to the Commissioner, within fifteen days of every month commencing from the 1st day of April, 2008, in such form as the Commissioner may specify, the particulars as are necessary, of an employee who is a person with disability and is a member on or entitled to become a member after the 1st day of April, 2008".

In Paragraph 38, in Sub-paragraph (1), after the second proviso, the following proviso shall be inserted, namely:

"Provided also that the Central Government shall pay the employer's share of contribution in respect of an employee who is a person with disability, up to a maximum period of three years from the date of commencement of the Fund."[36]

6.9.9 Employees' Provident Funds (Second Amendment) Scheme, 2008[209]

In exercise of the powers conferred by Section 5 read with Sub-Section (1) of Section 7 and Section 14-B of the Employees' Provident Funds and Miscellaneous Provisions Act, 1952 (19 of 1952), the Central Government hereby makes the following Scheme further to amend the Employees' Provident Funds Scheme, 1952, namely:

1.(1) This Scheme may be called the Employees' Provident Funds (Second Amendment) Scheme, 2008.

(2) It shall come into force on the date of its publication in the Official Gazette.

35 Paragraph 34
36 Paragraph 38

2. In the Employees' Provident Funds Scheme, 1952, for Sub-paragraph (1) of Paragraph 32-A, the following Sub-paragraph shall be Substituted, namely:

"(1) Where a employer makes default in the payment of any contribution to the Fund, or in the transfer of accumulations required to be transferred by him under Sub-Section (2) of Section 15 or Sub-Section (15) of Section 17 of the Act or in the payment of any charges payable under any other provisions of the Act or the Scheme or under any of the conditions specified under Section 17 of the Act, the Central Provident Fund Commissioner or such officer as may be authorised by the Central Government by notification in the Official Gazette in this behalf, may recover from the employer by way of penalty, damages at the rates given in the table below:

Sl. No.	***Period of default***	***Rate of damages (percentage of arrears per annum)***
(a)	*Less than 2 months*	*Five*
(b)	*Two months and above but less than four months*	*Ten*
(c)	*Four months and above but less than six months*	*Fifteen*
(d)	*Six months and above*	*Twenty Five*

6.9.10 Employees' Provident Funds (Third Amendment) Scheme, 2008

In exercise of the powers conferred by Section 5, read with Sub-Section (I) of Section 7 of the Employees' Provident Funds and Miscellaneous ProvisionsAct, 1952 (19 of 1952), the Central Government hereby makes the following Scheme further to amend the Employees' Provident Funds Scheme, 1952, namely:1.(1) This, Scheme may be called the Employees' Provident Funds (Third Amendment) Scheme, 2008. (2) It shall come into force on the date of its publication in the Official Gazette. In the Employees' Provident Funds

Scheme, 1952, after Paragraph 82, the following paragraph shall be inserted, namely:

83 Special provision in respect of International Workers: The Scheme shall, in its application to International Workers as defined in clause (ff) of Paragraph 2 of this Scheme be Subject to the following modifications, namely:

For clause (f) of Paragraph 2, the following clauses shall be Substituted, namely:

(f) "excluded employee" means an International Worker, who is contributing to a social security programme of his/her country of origin, either as a citizen or resident, with whom India has entered into a social security agreement on reciprocity basis and enjoying the status of detached worker for the period and terms, as specified in such an agreement.

(ff) "International Worker" means:

an Indian employee having worked or going to work in a foreign country with which India has entered into a social security agreement and being eligible to avail the benefits under a social security programme of that country, by virtue of the eligibility gained or going to gain, under the said agreement;

an employee other than an Indian employee, holding other than an Indian passport, working for an establishment in India to which the Act applies.

For the Paragraph 26, 26-A and 26-B, the following paragraphs shall be Substituted, namely:

26. Class of employees of International Workers entitled and required to join the fund: (1) (a) Every International Worker of an establishment to whom this Scheme applies, other than an excluded employee, shall be entitled and required to become a member of the Fund from the beginning of the month following that in which this paragraph comes into force.(b) Every International Worker employed to do any work, in or in relation to any establishment to which this Scheme applies, other than an excluded employee, shall be entitled and required to become a member of the Fund from the beginning of the month following that in which this paragraph comes into force, if on the date of such coming into force, such employee is a Subscriber to a provident fund maintained in respect of that establishment in India.

Where the Scheme applies to an establishment on the expiry or cancellation of an order of exemption under Section 17 of the Act, every International Worker who, but for the exemption would have become and continued as a member of the Fund shall become a member of the Fund forthwith.

After this paragraph comes into force in an establishment, every International Worker thereof, other than an excluded employee, who has not become a member already shall also be entitled and required to become a member from the beginning of the month.

An excluded employee of an establishment to which this Scheme applies shall, once asing to be such an employee been titled and required to become a member of the Fund from the beginning of the month following that on which he ceases to be such employee.

One re-election of a class of International Workers exempted under Paragraph 27-A to join the fund or on the expiry or cancellation of an order under that paragraph, every International Worker, who but for such exemption would have become and continued as a member of the Fund, shall forthwith become a member thereof.

Every International Worker who is member of a private provident fund maintained in respect of an exempted establishment and who, but for the exemption, would have become and continued as a member of the Fund shall, or joining an establishment to which the Scheme applies, become a member of the Fund forthwith.

26-A. Retention of membership: A member of the Fund shall continue to be a member until he withdraws under Paragraph the amount standing to his credit in the Fund or is covered by a notification of exemption under Section 17 of the Act or an order of exemption under Paragraph 27 or 27-A or the benefits are settled in terms of the relevant provisions under the social security agreement entered into between India and his country of origin.

Explanation: In the case of a claim for refund by a member under Sub- paragraph (2) of Paragraph 69, the membership of the Fund shall be deemed to have been terminated from the date the payment is authorised to him by the authority specified in this behalf by the Commissioner irrespective of the date of claim.

26-B. Resolution of doubts: If any question arises as to whether an International Worker is entitled or required to become or continue as member, or as to the date from which he is entitled or required to become a member, the decision thereon of the Regional Commissioner shall be final:

Provided that no decision shall be given unless both the employer and the International Worker have been given an opportunity of being heard. (3) For Paragraph 36, the following paragraphs shall be substituted, namely:

36. Duties of employers: (1) Every employer shall send to the Commissioner within fifteen days of the commencement of this Scheme, a consolidated return in such form as the Commissioner may specify, of the International Workers (indicating distinctly the nationality of each and every International Worker) required or entitled to become members of the Fund showing the basic wage, retaining allowance (if any) and dearness allowance including the cash value of any food concession paid to each of such International Worker.

Provided that if there is no International Worker who is required or entitled to become a member of the Fund, the employer shall send a 'NIL' return.

Wages Protection for Women in Form 5, of the International Workers qualifying to become members of the Fund for the first time during the preceding month together with the declarations in Form 2 furnished by such qualifying International Worker (indicating distinctly the nationality of each and every International Worker) and in such form as the Commissioner may specify, of the International Workers (indicating distinctly the nationality of each and every International Worker) leaving service of the employer during the preceding month:

"Provided that if there is no International Worker qualifying to become a member of the Fund for the first time or there is no International Worker leaving service of the employer during the preceding month, the employer shall send a 'NIL' return".

Though labour welfare enactment's have provided various protections, safeguard and benefits to working women in our country, there was an emergent need to give more protection to women workers who are discriminated as regards employment and wages. The wages of women workers in India are extremely low. They are generally not paid the minimum wages for the kind of work they do. The wages paid below the minimum wages is a form of gender discrimination at workplace. There are several unfair labour practices pertaining to the payment of wages. The employers did not make payment of wages in definite form, that is sometimes they made payment of wages in cash and sometimes in kind. The wages were paid after much delay which resulted into poverty and growing indebtedness. In an economy where even minimum wages are not paid to the women workers, the need to protect the wages earned by them has greatest significance. In this regard the most relevant and important pieces of legislations for the women workers are discussed below.

6.10 The Minimum Wages Act, 1948

Even though there is no uniform and comprehensive wage policy for all sectors of the economy in India, mechanism exists for determination of wages in the organised and organised sectors and their enforcement. Wages in the organised sector are determined through negotiations and settlements between employer and employees. In unorganised sector, where labour is vulnerable to exploitation due to illiteracy and lack of effective bargaining power, minimum rates of wages are fixed both of Central and State Governments in the Scheduled employments falling within their respective jurisdictions under the provisions of the Minimum Wages Act,1948.

The Minimum Wages Act, 1948 is also very relevant for women workers because it is primarily designed for the protection of workers in the unorganised sector, where majority of women work.

6.10.1 Objective

The Minimum Wages Act 1948 envisages to provide minimum statutory wages for scheduled employments with a view to obviate the chances of exploitation of labour through payment of very low and sweating wages. The Act also provides for the maximum daily working hours, weekly rest day and overtime. Rates fixed under Minimum Wages Act prevail over the rates fixed underaward/agreement.[223]

In ***Madhya Pradesh Mineral Industry Association Vs. The Regional Labour Commissioner (Central Jabalpur and Others)***,[37] has held that it is true that the provisions of the Minimum Wages Act are intended to achieve the object of doing social justice to workmen employed in the scheduled employments by prescribing minimum rates of wages for them, and so in construing the said provisions, the Court should adopt what is sometimes described as a beneficent rule of construction.

The Constitutional Bench of the Apex Court in ***M/s Bhipusa Yamasa Kshatriya and Another Vs. Sangamner Akola Taluka Bidi Kamgar Union and Others***[38] has held that the object of the Act is to prevent exploitation of the workers, and for that purpose it aims at fixation of minimum wages which the employers must pay. The Legislature undoubtedly intended to apply the Act to those industries or

37 AIR 1960 SC 1068: (1960) 62 BOMLR 903: 1960 (1) FLR 18
38 AIR 1963 SC 806

localities in which by reason of causes such as unorganised labour or absence of machinery for regulation of wages the wages paid to workers were, in the light of the general level of wages, and Subsistence level, inadequate.

Further power to fix minimum rates of wages does not by itself invest the Appropriate Government with authority to make unlawful discrimination between employers in different industries.

The Apex Court in ***Airfreight Ltd. Vs. State of Act Karnataka and Others***,[39] has held that what the Act purports to achieve is to prevent exploitation of labour and for that purpose authorises the appropriate government to take steps to prescribe minimum rates of wages in the scheduled industries. So, in prescribing the minimum wage rates the capacity of the employer need not be considered. What is being prescribed is minimum wage rates which a welfare state assumes every employer must pay before he employs labour. Since the capacity of the employer to pay is treated as irrelevant it is but right that no addition should be made to the components of the minimum wage which would take the minimum wage near the lower level of the fair wage, but the contents of this concept must ensure for the employee not only his sustenance and that of his family but must also preserve his efficiency as a worker. The Act contemplates that minimum wage rates should be fixed in the scheduled industries with the dual object of providing sustenance and maintenance of the worker and his family and preserving his efficiency as a worker.

6.10.1.1 Fixation of Minimum Rates of Wages

The State Government is empowered to fix minimum rates of wages for different classes of employees – skilled, unskilled, clerical, supervisory, etc., employed in any scheduled employment and to review and revise the same from time to time, the interval between two revisions not

39 AIR 1999 SC 2459: JT 1999 (5) SC 320

exceeding five years, considering the change in price index and dearness allowance.

In ***Workmen of Reptakos Brett and Co. Ltd. Vs. The Management of Reptakos Brett and Co. Ltd.***[40] The Tripartite Committee of the Indian Labour Conference accepted five norms for the fixation of 'minimum wage' in 1957:

- In calculating the minimum wage, the standard working class family should be taken to consist of 3 consumption units for one earner; the earning of women, children and adolescents should bed is regarded.
- Minimum food requirement should be calculated on the basis of a net intake of calories, as recommended by Dr. Aykroyd for an average Indian adult of moderate activity.
- Clothing requirements should be estimated at per capita consumption of 18 yards per annum which would give for the average worker's family of four, a total of 72 yards.
- In respect of housing, the rent corresponding to the minimum areaprovided for under Government's industrial housing Scheme should be taken into consideration in fixing the minimum wage.
- Fuel, lighting and other 'miscellaneous' items of expenditure should constitute 20% of the total minimum wage."
- The concept of the minimum wage is not the same as it was in 1936. Keeping in view of the socio-economic aspect of the wage structure one more additional component viz., 'children's education, medical requirement, minimum recreation and provision for old age, marriage etc. should constitute 25% of the total minimum wage' should be added.

40 AIR 1992 SC 504

6.10.1.2 Fixation of Working Hours etc.

In regard to any scheduled employment in respect of which minimum rates of wages have been fixed, the Government may:

- Fix the number of working hours constituting a normal working day, inclusive of one or moreintervals.
- Provide for a rest day with wages, in every period of 7 daysand
- provide for payment for work on a rest day at a rate not less than the overtime rate.[229]

6.10.1.3 Wages for Two or more Classes of Work

Where an employee does two or more classes of work, to each of which a different minimum rate of wages is applicable, the employer shall pay to such employee in respect of the time respectively occupied in each such class of work, wages at not less than the minimum rate in force in respect of each class.

6.10.1.4 Payment of Minimum Wages

The employer is bound to pay to every employee engaged in a scheduled employment under his wages, at a rate not less than the minimum rates of wages fixed for that class of employees in that employment, without making any deduction there from except those permitted under the Payment of Wages Act.[231]

The employees are entitled to the minimum wages at all times and under all circumstances. An employer who cannot pay the minimum wage has no right to engage labour and no justification to run theindustry.[232]

Where an employee works on any day for a period less than the requisite number of hours constituting a normal working day, he shall still be entitled to receive wages for t he full normal working day except:

- Where his failure to work is caused by his unwillingness to work and not by the omission of the employer to provide him with work, and
- In such other cases and circumstances as may be prescribed.

If an employee is employed on piece-work basis, the employer shall pay to him, wages at not less than the minimum time rate.[234] The linkage of minimum wages with performance or output, if it falls short of such wages, shall be illegal.

In ***People's Union for Democratic Rights and Others Vs. Union of India and Others***.[41] the Apex Court has held that the casual labourers/ workers temporarily employed by the contractors in connection with construction work were entitled for benefit of relevant labour and industrial laws, including Minimum Wages Act. While dealing with the issue of maintainability of the petition under Article 32 of the Constitution of India with regard to enforceability of relevant labour/industrial laws the Court held asunder:

"The essential requirement for maintaining the petition under Article 32 for breach of any fundamental right may be provided by the breach of the statutory laws. Non-enforcement of Equal Remuneration Act amounts to denial of equality under Article 14. So also the non-observance of the Contract Labour (Regulation of Employment and Conditions of Service) Act, 1970 amounts to violation of Article 21 in as much as these Acts are clearly intended to ensure basic human dignity to the workmen and the State cannot deprive anyone of this previous and invaluable right because no procedure by which such deprivation may be effected can ever be regarded as reasonable, fair and just. The non-payment of minimum wage is a breach of the fundamental right under Article 23."[42]

In ***Sanjit Roy Vs. State of Rajasthan***,[43] the Apex Court held that every person who provides labour or service

41 AIR 1982 SC 1473: 1983 SCR (1) 456
42 Ibid
43 AIR 1983 SC 328: 1983 SCR (2) 271

to another is entitled at least to the minimum wage and if anything less than the minimum wage is paid to him, he can complain of violation of his fundamental right under Article 23 and ask the Court to direct payment of the minimum wage to him so that the breach of Article 23 may be abated.

The Apex Court in ***Mukesh Advani Vs. State of M.P.***[44] directed the release of benefits to the bonded labour in Raisen Mine in Madhya Pradesh as envisaged in Minimum Wages Act. Where the temporary daily waged employees were claiming parity and equal pay scale with regularly employed employees, the Apex Court in ***Ghaziabad Development Authority and Others Vs. Vikram Chaudhary and Others***[45] held that even though the petitioners were not entitled for the parityin pay scale with regularly appointed employees, but however, a direction was issued that the temporary daily waged employees be given minimum wages fixed under the Minimum Wages Act, 1948 as would be prevalent in the locality.

Even later on in ***State of Orissa and Others Vs. Balaram Sahu and Others***,[46] the Apex Court directed payment under the Minimum Wages Act to daily waged employees who were seeking parity with regularly appointed employees.

In ***Smt. Kala Devi Vs. State of H.P. and Ors***[47] In this case the petitioner was employed as "school mother" with the respondent. It is her grievance that even though she was employed on temporary basis, she was entitled to the wages payable to class-IV employees of the State.

Undisputedly the State of Himachal Pradesh has issued various circulars/notifications under the Minimum Wages Act fixing the wages payable to the workers employed by the State. The petitioner is admitted to have worked on part time basis for at least 3 to 4 hours in a day. Even though the petitioner was working for the same time / duration as the regularly appointed employees, but however she was not

44 AIR 1985 SC1363
45 1995 AIR 2325: 1995 SCC (5) 210
46 (1996)11 SCC 77
47 1992 Cri.L.J. 2164

given the same scale of salary for which she was working. Keeping in view the various circulars issued by the State her wages ought to have been enhanced with the passage of time.

The petitioner could not have sustained herself on meagre payment of Rs. 110/- per month. The employee is definitely entitled to minimum wages or wages which are fair, just and reasonable. It is not the petitioner's fundamental right to have periodical revision of wages but definitely it is petitioner's legal right to have such wages which are considered to be minimum wage as fixed by the respondents in terms of its various circulars. Rs. 110/- per month is too inadequate for a person to live life with human dignity. Petitioner said that is conscious of the fact that fixation of pay scale / salary depends upon various factors and attending circumstances and it is solely the prerogative of the Government but however the present case is a rare exception in which judicial interference is warranted due to lackadaisical approach adopted by the respondent/State. The State may not have adopted unfair labour practice but definitely has not shown concern for enhancing the wages so as to make a person sustain herself. The apathy on the part of the State is appalling. Comparison and empathy ought to have been shown in this regard.

This Court has not gone into the question of applicability of the Minimum Wages Act but has only applied the principles and the benefits under the Act.

Under these circumstances it is directed that the respondents shall pay to the petitioner wages in proportion to the hours of her service rates fixed under the notification / circulars issued by the Government under the Minimum Wages Act, for such period she rendered her services with the respondent / State. The petitioner has retired. The arrears shall be disbursed within a period of three months from today, failing which, thereafter she shall be entitled to interest at the rate of 9%.

6.10.1.5 Wages in cash/kind

As a rule, the wages payable under the Act should be paid in cash. The appropriate government may, however, permit the payment of wages wholly or partly in kind, keeping in view the prevailing custom and also allow the supply of essentials commodities at concessional rates.[241] The cash value of wages in kind and of concession in respect of supply of essential commodities at concessional rates shall be estimated in the prescribed manner.[242]

6.10.1.6 Overtime wages

If an employee works on any day in excess of the normal working hours, the employer shall pay to him overtime wages for every hour or for part of an hour, so worked in excess at the rate prescribed under this Act or under any other law, whichever ishigher. As per Factories Act, overtime wages are to be paid at twice the normal rate ofwages.

While the Act provides a mechanism for fixing and revising minimum rates of wages, it does not give any guidelines as to the basis on which the minimum wages are to be fixed or revised. This has been the Subject of considerable criticism and discussion over the years. It has been recommended that in fixing minimum wages, the basic minimum needs of workers and his/her family for sustenance should be kept in view so that the wage prescribed is a just wage.

In some notifications of the wages under the Act, there is a tendency to classify work as *"light work usually done by women" and "heavy work usually done by men."* Such notifications are highly objectionable and have been criticised as a device to circumvent the law and perpetuate the practice where women workers' wages are fixed at lower levels than those of men workers. It has been recommended that specific occupations must be listed out and minimum rates of wages notified against these so that it is possible to verify whether women-related occupations are ranked lower in the matter of wages.

6.10.2 The Payment of Wages Act, 1936

The Payment of Wages Act, 1936 was enacted to regulate payment of wages to workers employed in industries and to ensure a speedy and effective remedy to them against illegal deductions and/or unjustified delay caused in paying wages to them. The wage ceiling under Payment of Wages Act, 1936 was fixed at Rs. 1600/- pm. in 1982. With a view to enhance the wage ceiling to 6500/-.

p.m. for applicability of the Act, to empower the Central Government to further increase the ceiling in future by way of notification and to enhance the penal provision etc. the Payment of Wages (Amendment) Act, 2005, which was passed by both houses of Parliament, has been notified on 06.09.2005 as an Act 41 of 2005 by the Ministry of Law and Justice. Subsequently, the Ministry of Labour and Employment has issued the Notification S.O. 1577 (E) to make the Payment of Wages (Amendment) Act, 2005 effective from the 9th November 2005.[244]Recently the Labour Law Notification S.O. 1380 (E) has been issued which enhance the wage limit from 6500/- to 10000/- p.m.[245] The Payment of Wages Act applies to person employed in any factory, railway-directly or through a 'Sub- contractor', any industrial/other establishment like mine, dock, plantation etc. can be extended by Government.

For the purpose of this Act the 'wages' means all emoluments expressible in terms of money and payable to the employee including any sum payable for termination of service, wages in lieu of holidays or leave, overtime wages and bonus payable under the Bonus Act or under the terms of employment. However, 'wages' does not include value of any house accommodation, supply of light, water, medical attendance or any other amenity, contribution to any pension or provident fund, traveling allowance, reimbursement of any special expense and gratuity. Nor does it include suspension/ Subsistence allowance given during suspension period of an employee.[246]

6.10.2.1 Fixation of Wage-periods

Every employer or the person responsible for payment of wages, should fix the wage period, which may be per day, per week or per month, etc. But in no case it should exceed one month.[247]

6.10.2.2 Time of Payment

Every employer/manager should make timely payment of wages. If the number of persons employed in an establishment is less than 1000, then wages must be paid within 7 days of the expiry of the wage period, and in other cases within 10 days of the expiry of the wage period and is other cases within 10 days of the expiry of the wageperiod.[248]

Where the employment of any person is being terminated, his wages should be paid within 2 days of the date oftermination.

Besides, all payments of wages should be made only on a working day.

6.10.2.3 Mode of Payment

The employer should pay the wages in cash, i.e. in current coins or currency notes. However, wages may be paid either by cheque or by crediting in employee's bank account, after obtaining his written consent.

6.10.2.4 Not to make Unauthorised Deductions

The employer should not make any deduction from wages other than, the following:

- Fines
- Deduction for absence from duty
- Deduction for damage or loss of goods or money, expressly entrusted to the employee's custody, not exceeding the amount of actual damage or loss caused due to his neglect or default.
- Deduction for house accommodation and other amenities or services as notified by the Government, provided by the employer.
- Deduction for recovery of advances.
- Deduction for recovery of loans made from any labour welfare fund.

- Deduction for income-tax payable by the employee
- Deduction required to be made by order of a Court or other competent authority.
- Deduction for Subscription to provident fund and repayment of advances from provident fund.
- Deduction for payment to co-operative societies approved by the Government or an insurance Scheme of post office.
- Deductions can be made, with the written authorisation of the employee for payment of any life insurance premium etc.
- Deductions for payment of insurance premia on Fidelity Guarantee Bonds and Contribution to any insurance Scheme framed by the Central Government.

From the provisions of the Act, it is clear the Act is not applicable to self employed/home-based workers, as they are not persons employed in the category of establishments mentioned in the Act. It does not, therefore protect a large number of workers in the unorganised sector.

6.10.3 The Equal Remuneration Act,1976

In Part IV relating to the Directive Principles of State Policy Article 39 of the Constitution envisages that the state shall direct its policy, among other things, towards securing that there is equal pay for equal work for both men and women. In order to give effect to this provision, in the year which was being celebrated as the International Women's Year, President of India promulgated the Equal Remuneration Ordinance, 1975 on 26th September, 1975 to provide for the payment of equal remuneration to men and women workers and for the prevention of discrimination on the ground of sex, against women in the matter of employment.[251] The ordinance was replaced by the Equal Remuneration Act, 1976 which received the assent of the President of India on 11th February, 1976.

6.10.3.1 Objectives

The Equal Remuneration Act provides for payment of equal remuneration to men and women workers, for same work or work of a similar nature and for the prevention of discrimination, on grounds of sex, against women in the matter of employment.

Though the Equal Remuneration Act was passed in 1976, it is one of the least invoked legislations by the intended beneficiaries. There have been a few cases where women have challenged the lower salaries paid to them. In ***Air India Vs. Nargesh Meerza and Others***,[252] the Central Government had made a declaration by virtue of a notification that the differences in the remuneration of air hostesses and flights stewards were not based on sex because Section 16[253] clearly authorises restrictions regarding remuneration to be paid by the employer if a declaration under it is made by the appropriate government. An air hostess challenged the discriminatory employment conditions for air hostesses and stewards along with other thing. The Supreme Court held that the benefit conferred on the female under the Act is not absolute and unconditional. From a comparison of the mode of recruitment, the classification, promotional avenues and other matters, it is clear that air hostesses form an absolutely separate category from the Assistant pursers in many respects such as different grades, different promotional avenues and different service conditions. No hostile discrimination is therefore, involved. The declaration made by the Government of India is presumptive proof of the fact that in matter of allowances, conditions of service and other types of remuneration, no discrimination has been made only on the ground of sex.

Thus equal pay for equal work has been denied to the air hostesses which resulted as tremendous set back to the working women. Secondly, this case has also shown that even during their period in service, discrimination against women was practiced. This situation was remedied by the passing of Equal Remuneration (Amendment) Act 1987, which specifically mentions that there should not be discrimination during employment between men and women.

Thirdly, it also proved beyond doubt in this case that Section 16 is defective and can work against the interests of women employees. Under this Section government can declare that difference in wages in a particular post is not based on sex and the Courts have to accept it without any inquiry. This rule could be used arbitrarily not only in public sector undertakings but also in private employment to shut out an enquiry by the Courts. Therefore, Section 16 needs amendment so that equal pay for equal work cannot be denied.

However, after the ***Air India Case***[254] the judiciary has played an active role in enforcing and strengthening the Constitutional goal of *"equal pay for equal work."*

A milestone in the area of implementation of Equal Remuneration Act was reached with the pronouncement of the Supreme Court decision in ***People's Union for Democratic Rights Vs. Union of India***[48] in this case the Supreme Court ruled:

"It is the principle of equality embodied in Article 14 of the Constitution which finds expression in provision of the Equal Remuneration Act".[49]

In other words if the provisions of the Act are not observed the principle of equality before the law enshrined in Article 14 is violated. In ***Randhir Singh Vs. Union of India***[50]while construing Article 14 and 16 in the light of the preamble and Article 39(d), the Supreme Court held that the principle of "equal pay for equal work" is deducible from them and may be properly applied to cases of unequals scales of pay based on no classification or irrational classification though those drawing different scales pay do identical work under the same employer. This case is a harbinger of a new judicial trend of reading directive principles into fundamental rights. The Supreme Court in this case further observed:

48 AIR 1982 SC 1473
49 Ibid
50 AIR 1982 SC 879: 1982 SCR (3) 298

"Equal pay for equal work is not a mere demagogic slogan. It is a Constitutional goal capable of attainment through Constitutional remedies by the enforcement of Constitutional rights."

In ***Sanjit Roy Vs. State of Rajasthan***,[51] the Supreme Court directed the State Government not only to pay minimum wages but also to pay wages in accordance with the principle of equal pay for equal work to men and women worker engaged in famine relief work.

Again in ***Bhagwan Das Vs. State of Haryana***,[52] the Supreme Court was of the view that (i) person doing similar work cannot be denied equal pay on the ground that mode of recruitment was different, and (ii) a temporary or casual employee performing the same or similar duties and functions is entitled to the same pay as that of a regular or permanent employee.

The Supreme Court again in a recent case namely ***Food Corporation of India Vs. Shyamal K Chatterjee***,[53] held that equal wages will be payable even to casual workers engaged through contractor when they are doing the same work.

However, in one case the Division Bench of Kerala High Court has held that unless it is shown that there is discrimination amongst the same set of employees by the same master in the same establishment doing the same job and similarly situated, the principle of equal work cannot be enforced.

The applicability of the Act does not depend upon the financial viability of the employer to pay equal remuneration as provided by it

6.10.3.2 Scope and Coverage

The Act extends to whole of India and applies to the establishments or employments notified by the Central

51 AIR 1983 SC 328
52 W P A No. 12311 of 1985: Judgment dated 31/07/1987
53 AIR 2000 SC 3554: 2000 (87) FLR 677

Government.[264] (The Act is now applicable to almost every kind of establishments).

According to Section 3 the provisions of the Act shall have an effect notwithstanding anything inconsistent therewith contained in any other law or in the terms of any award, agreement or contract of service, whether made before or after the commencement of this Act, or in any instrument having effect under any law for the time being in force.

However, nothing in this Act shall apply:[265]

- to cases affecting the terms and conditions of a woman's employment in complying with the requirements of any law giving special treatment to women,or
- to any special treatment accorded to women in connectionwith:
- the birth or expected birth of a child,or
- the terms and conditions relating to retirement, marriage or death or to any provision made in connection with the retirement, marriage or death.

The Act was amended in 1987. According to this Amendment, Courts can take cognisance on the basis of complaints made by recognized organisations notified by the Central or State Governments. The Amendment removed certain loop holes and made it mandatory for the employer to pay equal wages to men and women workers and prohibit discrimination of women on the ground of sex in matter of recruitment, training, promotion and transfer. The Amending Act also provides for stricter punishment for the violation of this statute.

6.10.3.3 Salient Features of the Act

6.10.3.3.1 Duty to Pay Equal Remuneration

Section 14 of the Act imposes a duty on the employer to pay equal remuneration to men and women workers for the same work or for work of a similar nature.

For the purpose of this Act *"same work or work of a similar nature"* means work in respect of which the skill, effort and responsibility required are the same, when performed under similar working conditions, by a man or a woman and the differences, if any, between the skill, effort and responsibility required of a man and those required of a woman are not of practical importance in relation to the terms and conditions of employment.

No employer can pay to any worker, employed by him in an establishment or employment, remuneration, whether payable in cash or kind, at rates less favourable than those at which remuneration is paid by him to the workers of the other sex in such establishment or employment performing the same work or work of a similar nature. With a view to implement this duty, no employer should reduce the rate of remuneration of any worker. It has further laid down that where in an establishment or employment, the rates of remuneration payable before the commencement of the Act for men and women workers for the same work or work of a similar nature are different only on the ground of sex, then the higher (in cases where there are only two rates), or as the case may be, the highest (in cases where there are more than two rates), of such rates are to bepaid.

With a view to further strengthen this principle, Section 5 lays down that after the coming into force of the Act, no employer while making recruitment for the same work or work of a similar nature, (of in any condition of service Subsequent to recruitment such as promotions, training or transfer)[267] make any discrimination against women except where the employment of women in such work is prohibited or restricted by or under any law for the time being in force. However, this provision will not effect any priority or reservation for scheduled castes or scheduled tribes, ex-servicemen, retrenched employees or any other class or category of persons in the matter of recruitment to the posts is an establishment.

In ***Air India Cabin Crew Assn. Vs. Yeshaswince Merchant and Others***[54] with ***Air India Officers Assn. and Another Vs. Air India Ltd.***[55] *and* tagged cases, where appeals were filed against the Division Bench Judgment of the Bombay High Court. In a batch of petitions filed by the respondents Air India Air Hostesses Association and its members, the High Court held that the age of retirement from flying duties of our hostesses at the age of 50 years with option to them to accept post for ground duties after 50 and upto the age of 58 years is discrimination against them based on sex which is violative of Articles 14, 15 and 16 of the Constitution of India as also Section 5 of the Equal Remuneration Act, 1976 and contrary to the mandatory directions issued by the Central Government under Section 34 of the Air India Corporation Act, 1953.

The Supreme Court negatived the grievance that service conditions providing lower age of retirement to air hostesses is unfavourable as compared to flight persers, who are the male members of the crew on board and are allowed the age of retirement 55 to 58 years The argument claiming parity on retirement age by females with male members of the crew wasnegativated.

It was held that there is no discrimination against air hostesses based only on sex. It further held that the service condition is neither unconstitutional under Articles 15 and 16 of the Constitution nor violative of Section 4 of the Equal Remuneration Act. The Court quoted notification issued by the Central Government under Section 16 of the Equal Remuneration Act. It upheld the stand of the employer that the different ages of retirement and salary structure for male and female employees in Air India are based on their different conditions of service and not on sex alone.

Section 4 of the Equal Remuneration Act prohibits the employer from paying unequal remuneration to male and female workers for same work or work of similar nature. Section 5 of the Act prohibits discrimination by the employer

54 (2003) 6 SCC 277
55 2014 (141) FLR 654: 2014 (1) LLN 364 (BOM)

while recruiting men and women workers for same work or work of similar nature. By amendment introduced to Section 5 by Amendment Act 49 of 1987, the employer has been prohibited from discriminating men and women after their recruitment in the matter of their conditions of service for the same work or work of similar nature.

6.10.3.3.2 Maintenance of Register

Every employer should maintain an up-to-date register in relation to the workers employed by him, in the prescribed form. This register contains particulars such as category of workers, nature of work, number of menand woman employed, rate of remuneration paidetc.[271]

The major problem with the Act is the definition of *"same work or work of a similar nature."* The definition leaves much to be desired and can defeat the object of the Act. It leaves the door wide open for employers to continue mainly with the practice of paying less to women workers as men and women seldom do the same work. It has therefore, been suggested that the term *"same work or work of a similar nature"* is to be replaced by *"same work or comparable worth."* It is not the similarity or identity of work alone that will entitle women to equal pay but also work which is comparable in terms of skill required and its value to the employer that will entitle them to equalvalue.

It has also been found that Section 16 of the Equal Remuneration Act is defective and can work against the interests of women employees. Under this Section government can declare that the difference in wages in a particular post is not based on sex and the Courts have to accept it without any inquiry. This rule could be used arbitrarily not only in public sector undertakings but also in private employment to shut out an inquiry by the Courts. Therefore, Section 16 needs amendment so that equal pay for equal work cannot be denied.

From the foregoing discussion, it is clear that to provide security against various risks, peculiar to their nature, women workers have been given various rights, benefits, concessions, protection and safeguard under different labour legislations. The main objective for enactment of labour laws was to prohibit the violation of rights of women workers and to provide them security and protection. But despite this all, much remains to be achieved. Women workers are still made to suffer discrimination in social and economic spheres and continue to be the most exploited lot. Most of the labour legislations apply to the organised sector only, leaving unorganised sector, where a majority of the women work, unattended. Even in organised sector, where these legislations apply, the statutory provisions are not strictly complied with. In many cases it has been found that protective measures such as crèches, maternity benefits, separate toilet and washing facilities etc. are neither provided nor properly maintained. The Penal provisions of these enactments are not deterrent enough to prevent the employer from violating then. The machinery for inspection and enforcement is inadequate andineffective.

It is true that laws are made for the welfare and benefit of people but laws and Constitution do not by themselves solve all the problems. It is the sincere and strict implementation which matters. Although, the need for more and more laws is always felt in a welfare state like ours, yet the existing labour laws,with necessary modifications and amendments are sufficient, for the time being to take care of the women workers in the organised sector leaving unorganised sector of employment unattended. Therefore, these laws should be extended to unorganised sector also where women workers are in a large number. Let us try to be honest in the implementation of these labour laws. The employers should be made to change their attitude towards women labour by strengthening the enforcing agencies and by imposing stringent punishment on the guilty. Women workers should be treated as partners in industry and not as products.

Moreover, much also depends upon the women workers themselves. Their ignorance and lack of awareness about their right is also responsible for the evasion of these beneficial legislations. Therefore, the need of hour is that women should get fully conscious about their rights and should get courageous enough to fight for their rights by participating in the various activities of tradeunions.

6.10.4 The Way Forward

It can be seen from the multiple special provisions created for the welfare of women that both at the national and international levels, there has been a movement towards the empowerment of women in labor law. There has been a transparent move towards creating equal pay, equal access to opportunity, bar, and redressal of harassment and provision of maternity benefits a reality in Republic of India. in fact, a majority of laws in respect to the special provisions for women are modeled after the International Labour Organization conventions. India being a founding member of the International Labour Organization has tried terribly onerous to stick to the standards provided by the International Labour Organization : The special rights provided to women in various labour laws like The Factories Act, 1948, The Mines Act, 1952, The Plantation Labour Act, 1951, The Building and Other Construction Workers' (Regulation of Employment and Conditions of Service) Act, 1996, The Beedi and Cigar Workers (Conditions of Employment) Act, 1966, The Contract Labour (Regulation and Abolition) Act, 1970, The Inter-State Migrant Workmen (Regulation of Employment and Conditions of Service) Act, 1979, The Maternity Benefit Act, 1961, The Employees' State Insurance Act, 1948, The Employees' Provident Funds and Miscellaneous Provisions Act, 1952, The Payment of Gratuity Act, 1972, and The Workmen's Compensation Act, 1923, Minimum Wages Act, 1948, Payment of Wages Act, 1936 and Equal Remuneration Act, 1976) are proof of this.

However, it is important to note that some of these protective legislations have backfired and proved to be counterproductive in nature. The only way to solve such issues in socially rather than legally, i.e. by making the work environment safer through social intervention, legal rules that are paternalistic i*n nature can be relaxed. The next level of effort that India needs to make is to develop effective implementation and redressal mechanisms. The best way to ensure effective implementation of these provisions and redressal of any complaints is to begin implementation at a grassroots level, i.e. at the level of individual enterprises, and employers. This will ensure that the actions are more specific in nature and will bring about more concrete outcomes.[56]

❑❑❑

56 Jaiswa, Kabir, Women's Rights and Labour Law Statutes in India, available on https://blog.ipleaders.in/ womens-rights-labour-law-statutes-india, February, 2019

CHAPTER

7

Women Rights under Specialized Protective Mechanisms

"We all know that women are half the world and hold up half the sky but where are they when it comes to equality?"

– Leela Seth

7.1 Introduction

The concept of equality, however, requires equity. The history of social development is also the history of inequality. Inequality between nations, religions, ethnicity, class, caste, race and sexuality. However, the question of women's rights looms large, cutting through all the layers of social stratification. German philosopher and social scientist Friedrich Engels in his classical writing *"Origin of the Family, Private Property and the State"* states that, "*Woman was the first human being that tasted bondage. Woman was a slave before slavery existed*". The feminist struggle for equal rights has been paved through legislation, be it the Suffragette movement and the right to vote, to employment rights, property rights, rights governing divorce and marriage to child-care and medicine – legislation based on equal rights affects the very values of society, impacting not just the way we vote, but the way we work, live and function as a family, the way we access education, healthcare and justice.

In India, the constitutionally guaranteed equality for women is often contradictory to the harsh societal reality of the land and its cultural norms. The struggle for women's equality began in India in the 20th century, during the struggle for Independence. In the fight against the British, western educated leaders like B.R.Ambedkar, Mahatma Gandhi, Raja Ram Mohan Roy and Savitribai Phule encouraged women to step away from their homes and hearths and enter the public sphere in the fight for Independence. Indian values, nationalism and cultural heritage were glorified through the symbolism of 'Mother India'. Perhaps for the first time in India, the idea that a woman is part of the larger Indian tapestry as a legal citizen, took root. The inclusion of the female citizen into the public sphere necessitated citizenship rights and changes in the law such as right to education, inheritance rights, abolition of sati and polygamy as well as allowance for widow- remarriage.

While a struggle for nationalism changed the legal landscape of women's rights through the colonial era, the post-colonial era in India has been marked by sweeping changes such as globalization, neo-liberal policies and the leaps and bounds in technological development. This has expanded women's participation in the public sphere. More Indian women than ever are engaged in business enterprises, international platforms, multi-national careers like advertising and fashion, and have better opportunities because of the free movement of goods, capital and ideas. Has our legal system kept up with social change? Does our constitution have provisions for equality or equity? Do rights guarantee justice? Is citizenship gendered? The following article gives a brief overview of the current spate of women centric legal reform in India and concludes with a discussion on its socio-cultural impact on the very fabric of Indian citizenship. However, a portrait of the position of women can be draw, after going through the specialised mechanism established for the protection, protection and participation of women in all social-political activities.

7.2 The National Commission for Women (1990)

7.2.1 Importance of Commission

Women in India, as is well known, have never been treated well even at home or while at work. The matter has all along been agitated inside and outside the Parliament by Parliamentarians, by common men, by organizations and societies for the welfare of the women. Several Commissions had been set up by the Government to look into the matter of status of women in Indian society. Successive Commissions on women had noted in their repots the unequal status of women obtaining in every sphere of life and had suggested me setting up of an agency to fulfill the surveillance functions as well as to facilitate redressal of the grievances of women. Several women activities and voluntary action groups had also been making persistent demands for setting up of a commission for women. Keeping in view the desirability of women at the national level the National Commission for Women Bill, 1990 was introduced in the LokSabha on 22nd May, 1990. Later on this Bill became an Act to be known as the National Commission for Women Act, 1990 *w.e.f.* 30-8-1990.

7.2.2 Constitution of the National Commission for Women

According to Section 3(2) of the National Commission for Women Act, 1990 the Commission shall consist of:

- Chairperson, committed to the cause of women, to be nominated by the Central Government;
- Five members to be nominated by the Central Government from amongst persons of ability, integrity and standing who have had experience in law or legislation, trade unionism, management of an industry or organization committed to increasing the employment potential of women, women's voluntary organizations (including women activities),

administration, economic development, health, education or social welfare.

- Provided that at least one member each shall be from amongst persons belonging to the Scheduled Castes and Scheduled Tribes, respectively;
- Member Secretary to be nominated by the Central Government who shall be
- an expert in the field of management, organizational structure or sociological movement; or
- an officer who is a member of a civil service of the Union or of an India service or holds a civil post under the Union with appropriate experience.

7.2.3 Term of Office and Conditions of Service of Chairperson and Members (Section 4)

The Chairperson and every member of the National Commission for Women shall hold officer for such period, not exceeding three years as may be specified by the Central Government.

The chairperson or a Member (other than the Member-Secretary who is a member of a civil service of the Union or of an all India service or holds a civil post under the Union) may be, by writing and addressed to the Central Government, resign from the office of Chairperson or Member as the case may be, at any time.

7.2.3.1 Disqualification: Chairperson/Member

As provided under Section 4(3) of the National commission for Women Act, 1990 the Central government shall remove a person from the office of Chairperson or a member, if that person:

- becomes an un-discharged insolvent;
- gets convicted and sentenced to imprisonment for an offence which in the opinion of the Central Government involves moral turpitude;

- becomes of unsound mind and stands so declared by a competent Court;
- refuses to act or becomes incapable to act;
- is, without obtaining leave of absence from the Commission absent from three consecutive meetings of the Commission; or
- in the opinion of the Central Government has so abused the position of Chairperson or Member as to render that person's continuance in office detrimental to the public interest.

However, no person shall be removed from his office until that person has been given a reasonable opportunity of being heard in the matter.

7.2.4 Functions of the National Commission for Women

According to Section 10 of the National Commission for Women Act, 1990 the National Commission for Women shall perform, all or any of the following functions namely:-

- Investigation and Examination: investigate and examine all matters relating to the safeguards provided for women under-the Constitution of India, 1950 and other laws;
- Presentation of Reports: present reports to the Central Government, annually and at such other times as the Commission may deem fit, reporting upon the working of those safeguards;
- Recommendations: make in such reports recommendations for the effective-implementation of those safeguards for improving the conditions of women by the Union or any State;
- Review: review, from time to time, the existing provisions of the Constitution of India, 1950 and other laws affecting women and recommend amendments thereto as to suggest remedial legislative measures to

meet any lacunae, inadequacies or shortcomings in such legislation;

- Taking up of cases of Violation: take up the cases of violation of the provisions of the Constitution of India, 1950 and of other laws relating to women with the appropriate authorities;

Suo Moto Notice: looks into complaints, and take *suomoto* notice of matters relating to:

- Women's rights: deprivation of women's rights;
- Protection of Women:non-implementation of laws enacted to provide protection to women and also to achieve the objectives of equality and development;
- Policy Decision:non-compliance of policy decisions, guidelines or instructions aimed at mitigating hardships and ensuring welfare and providing relief to women; and take up the issues arising out of such matters with appropriate authorities;
- Special Studies and Investigation: call for special studies or investigation into specific problems or situation arising out of discrimination and atrocities against women and identify the constraints so as to recommend strategies for their removal;
- Promotional Research: undertake promotional research so as to suggest ways of ensuring due representation of women in all spheres and identify factors responsible for impeding their advancement;
- Participation in Planning: participate and advise on the planning process of socio-economic development of women;
- Evaluation: evaluate the progress of the development of women under the Union and any State;
- Inspection: inspect or cause to be inspected a jail, remand home women's institution or other place of custody where women are kept as prisoners;

- Funding: fund litigation, involving issues affective a large body of women;
- Reporting: make reports on any matter pertaining to women and in particular various difficulties under which women toil.

7.2.5 Power of Women's Commission

According to Section 10(4) of the National Commission for Women Act, 1990 the national Commission for Women shall have all the powers of a civil court trying a suit, in respect of the following matters, namely :

- Summoning and enforcing the attendance of any person from any part of India and examining him on oath;
- requiring the discovery and production of any document;
- receiving evidence on affidavits;
- requisitioning any public or copy thereof, any court or office;
- issuing commissions for the examination of witnesses and documents; and
- any other matter which may be prescribe.

7.2.6 Grants by the Central Government

As provided under Section 11 of the National Commission for Women Act, 1990 the Central Government is empowered to grant such sum of money to the National Commission for Women, however, with prior approval of the Parliament. The Commission may spend such sum of money for the purpose of performing such functions as laid down under the said Act.

In the light of the above Act, rules & regulations it is clear that the National Commission for Women enjoys huge power for taking action in favour of the distressed women of our country. Some lacunae are found at the time of application of those aforesaid laws/rules etc. hence, we have to discuss in detail, the Act and its applicability for the protection of distressed women of our country.

Since women's empowerment is a global issue, U.N.O. has also expressed concern in the matter.

The Charter of the United Nations declares equal dignity and worth of human person – all types of human rights, civil, political, economic, social and cultural. In 1993, the Vienna Declaration and Programme of Action proclaimed the rights of women and girl child as – *"Inalienable, integral and indivisible part-Priority objective of the international community."*

The National Commission for Women made a number of recommendations for changes and removal of lacunae in 34 laws and 8 bills. It also mode recommendations on Older persons Maintenance, care and protection Bill 2005. The compulsory Registration of Marriage Bill 2005, Protection of Women from Domestic Violence Rules, 2005, laws relating to rape / sexual assault etc.

Gender discrimination is the violation of the very right to life of women and deprives them of the civil, political and economic liberty both within the family and the society. In the modern era, it is astonishing enough that the women are not allowed equal access to the freedom of faith and religion, freedom of movement and residence. Right to equality of opportunity either *de-jure or de-facto* is missing for them. The principle of equal wages for equal work, does not apply to them. They are underrepresented in the parliament and public life as well as the top incorporate world. Gender based violence, including wife battering, dowry, murders, incest, marital rape, foeticide, infanticide, rapeand sexual harassment, sexual slavery and exploitation and violence resulting from superstitions and cultural prejudices, racialism, terrorism, mal-nutrition, poor health lack of education etc are absolutely in- compatible with the dignity of a human person specially women. Social democracy is still a mirage to the women. Despite all the safeguards, the women in our country continue to suffer.

It is true that gender justice is possible only through womens' empowerment which involves economic and political opportunities, social equality and personal rights. Besides a lot needs to be done to elevate the status of women and put an end to discriminatory, humiliating and torturous practices in the society.

Some of them are:

- Promotion of education and awareness among men and women.
- Addressing the capacity building needs of women, both for skill development and enterprise management to facilitate their economic empowerment.
- Transferring the technologies to women both in farm and non-farm activities.
- Strict implementation of legal changes in inheritance property, divorce, maintenance and domestic violence and other concerned laws.
- Providing project opportunity guidance to enterprising women.
- Promotion of women specific clusters, self-Help Groups and area programmes for women.
- Wide dissemination and replication of successful model on women development.
- Promote involvement of women in decision making through consensus building developing system for power sharing and active participation in socio political system.
- 40% of women should be given work.
- Strict implementation of gender budgeting by all the ministries in Central and State Governments. Poverty eradication programme should also be specifically addressed to the needs and problems of women

- Special attention for Reproductive Rights of Women needs to be given as per the needs of women and girl at all the stages of life cycle by providing quality health care and reducing malnutrition, reduction of maternal Mortality, Female feticide, Infant Mortality, Death Rate etc; these spheres need be accorded priority to achieve the goal.

We know the National Commission for women (NCW) is a statutory body set up in the year 1992, safeguards the rights and interests of women. It continues to pursue its mandated role and activities; i.e. safeguarding women rights through investigations into the individual complaints of atrocities, sexual harassment of women at work place; conducting Paravarik / Mahila Lok Adalats, legal awareness programmes/ camps; review of both women-specific and women related legislations; investigates into individual complaints, atrocities, harassment, denial of rights etc. and takes *suo moto* remedial action to restore their legitimate rights NCW, since its inception, investigated several complaints wherein dowry deaths and dowry harassments accounted for the maximum number.

Open Adalats (public hearing) is the most innovative and informal style adopted by the Commission to ear the individual grievances. Out of the 41 legislations having direct bearing on women, the Commission reviewed and suggested remedial legislative measures in 32 Acts and forwarded the same to the government for necessary action, besides drafting a Bill on Sexual Harassment at the Work Places and a Bill on SAARC Regional Convention for Prevention and combating Trafficking in Women and Children.

Amongst it s success stories, the Commission requested the State Governments to reserve a certain percentage of resources for women even at the village level for programmes such as water supply, health services, nutrition, sanitation etc. and reviewed the functioning of womens' cells in governmental organisations and issued fresh guidelines to reactivate the cells.

It has also organised many seminars/ workshops on important emerging problems of women, e.g. impact of globalization on women, prevention of atrocities against women, economic empowerment of tribal women, girl child abuse, child marriages, empowerment of dalit women, women in prostitution, images of women in the electronic media, rehabilitation of devadasis, beside conducting legal awareness camps in states like Haryana, Punjab, Rajasthan, Bihar, Uttar Pradesh, etc. where the status of women is comparatively lower. The commission has also been very successfully documenting information on many important social problems like rape, devadasis , sexual harassment, etc. besides sponsoring studies on various subjects to women.

On 8th March 1996, on the occasion of International Womens' Day, the Parliament passed resolution to set up a Standing committee for the 'improvement of the status of women' in India, and the Committee on Empowerment of women was constituted in April 1997. The functions of the Committee, included examining the recommendations of the National Commission for Women, the measures taken by the Union Government to ' to secure for women equality, status and dignity in all matters' including the steps taken for securing 'Comprehensive education and adequate representation of women in legislative bodies/services and other fields, 'to report on the working of the welfare programmes for the women' and to report on the action taken by the Union Government and Administration of the Union Territories on the measure proposed by the Committee.

Despite of those measures taken by the Union Government, some women also find that there is no space for them to perform effectively as decision makers because men dominate debate, make assessment, determine promotions and sexist stereotypes. Necessary changes in the attitudes of the people in the society are to be instilled. Orientation programmes need to be organized for women to handle different situations in different fields.

Further, there is need to coordinate gender balance in government, administration, private sectors and other spheres. Women and men together must then negotiate a new institutional setting that provides space for both of the groups.

The remedy for protecting the women lies in a strong will power and a gender just reform in the whole system covering the major interrelated issues of economic welfare, social justice, education, health, and traditions / spirituality. It requires involvement of every segment of society, Women as well as men; Government, laws, judiciary, political parties as well as social reformers, religious leaders, journalists and media.

7.2.7 Achievements of the Commission

The following chapter will, very briefly, summarize the achievement, highlights and successes of the Commission since its inception in 1992.

The complaints and counseling cell of the Commission is perhaps the most successful organ of the organization,. Besides these achievements, the Legal Cell of the Commission has proposed amendments to a number of Acts and has proposed a number of new bills. The Commission has proposed amendments to the Hindu Marriage Act, 1955, Medical Termination of Pregnancy Act, 1971 and the Indian Penal Code, 1960. The Commission has also proposed bills such as the Marriage Bill of 1994, the Domestic Violence to Women (Prevention) Bill of 1994 and the Prevention of Barbarous and Beastly cruelty against Women Bill, 1995 amongst others.

Some of these bills, such as the Domestic Violence to Women (Prevention) Bill, have recently been passed. The Commission has also intervened in a number of court cases and these have been mentioned in the chapter dealing with the functions of the Commission.The Research Cell of the Commission has carried out a number of studies pertaining to topics such as social mobilisation, maintenance and divorcee women, women labour under contract, gender bias in judicial decisions, family courts, violence against women, women access to health and education in slums and similar topics.

A number of inquiry commissions have also been established by the Commission, under Section 8 (1) of the Act of 1990, to look into matters such as Law and legislation, Political empowerment, Custodial justice for women, Social security, Panchayati Raj, Women and media, Development of Scheduled Tribe Women, Development of women of weaker sections, Development of women of minority communities, Transfer of technology in agriculture for development of women. Among other highlights are included the anti child marriage agitations in Rajasthan, Madhya Pradesh, Andhra Pradesh and Uttar Pradesh. Public hearings on problems of Muslim women, impact of globalization on women, on land related problems, economic empowerment of tribal women have been successfully organized by the have been organized by the Commission all over the country.

Within the short span of fourteen years, the Commission has fulfilled managed to fulfill most of the responsibilities laid down in its mandate. The different public hearings, out reach programs, counseling and legal function have definitely improved conditions of the Indian woman.

7.2.8 Analysis and Shortcomings

Analysis: From the previous chapters, it may be said that in the short period of fourteen years the Commission has managed to fulfill the mandate, if not completely then to a great extent. The achievements mentioned in the prior chapter are only a few of many similar achievements and they are proof of the popularity and support the Commission is gaining from the Indian woman. There is no doubt about the effectiveness of the Commission and about the good work which it is doing for the women of India, however, there are certain shortcomings in the working of the Commission, which, if rectified, would lead to a more efficient and productive Commission. The following are the shortcomings

7.2.8.1 Shortcomings

- The Commission has no concrete legislative powers. It only has the powers to recommend amendments and submit reports which are not binding on state or Union Governments.
- The Commission does not have the power to select its own members. This power is vested with the Union Government and in India's volatile political scenario the Commission may be politicized.
- The Commission is dependent on grants from the Union Government for its financial functioning and this could compromise the independence of the Commission.
- The Commission's jurisdiction is not operative in Jammu and Kashmir and considering the present political unrest and human rights violations in the region, the Commission's presence there is vital.

7.2.9 Recommendations for Betterment

The above mentioned causes have itspositives and negatives both, but every shortcomings has its own way out. To overcome the aforementioned shortcomings, it may be useful to incorporate the following suggestion:

The Commission suggested that the chairperson of NCW be given the status of the Union Cabinet Minister and the Members that of Minister of State. This will put more power in the Commission's hands and thus its recommendations will have a greater degree of force.

The Commission must be granted the power to select its own members. If needed a separate body, selected from within the Commission, should be constituted in order to carry these functions.

The Commission must be given allocated funds in the Union as well as the State Budgets in order facilitate smooth functioning. Currently funds are only allocated at the Central level and not the state level.

The atrocities in Jammu and Kashmir are common knowledge. Taking these acts into account the Commission's presence in the region is quite vital and should be allowed.

7.3 Human Rights Commissions

The Protection of Human Rights Act, 1993 provides the provision of human right commission in two tire system, but parallel in application. The National Human Rights Commission(NHRC) and the State Human Right Commission(SHRCs) in the state level for the adjudication of the cases of violation of human rights. The persons whose human rights have been violated can move either to NHRC or to SHRC of jurisdiction, but cannot use the forum of NHRC as an appellate body.

7.3.1 National Human Rights Commission (NHRC)

The National Human Rights Commission (NHRC) of India is a Statutory public body constituted on 12 October 1993 under the Protection of Human Rights Ordinance of 28 September 1993.[1] It was given a statutory basis by the Protection of Human Rights Act, 1993 (PHRA). [2] The NHRC is the National Human Rights Commission of India,[3] responsible for the protection and promotion of human rights, defined by the Act as «Rights Relating To Life, liberty, equality and dignity of the individual guaranteed by the Constitution or embodied in the International Covenants and enforceable by courts in India."

Chapter II to IV of the Act deals with the National Human Rights Commission. Section 3 of the Chapter II lays down that Central Government shall constitute a body to be known as the National Human Rights Commission.

7.3.1.1 Composition

The NHRC consists of the Chairman and four members (excluding the ex-officio members)

A Chairperson, who has been a Chief Justice of India or a Judge of the Supreme Court

One member who is, or has been, a Judge of the Supreme Court of India, or, One member who is, or has been, the Chief Justice of a High Court

Three Members, out of which at least one shall be a woman to be appointed from amongst persons having knowledge of, or practical experience in, matters relating to human rights

In addition, the Chairpersons of National Commissions viz., National Commission for Scheduled Castes, National Commission for Scheduled Tribes, National Commission for Women , National Commission for Minorities, National Commission for Backward Classes, National Commission for Protection of Child Rights; and the Chief Commissioner for Persons with Disabilities serve as ex officio members.

7.3.1.2 Appointments

The chairperson and the members of the commission shall be appointed by the president on a recommendation of a six-member committee headed by the Prime Minister[1]. The chairperson and the members shall hold office for a period of five years, from the date on which they enter upon their office. They shall be eligible for re-appointment for another term.[2]

A person can serve the commission until the age of 70 years. If any vacancy takes place in the office of the Chair Person by reason of his death, resignation on otherwise, the President may, by notification authorize one of the members to act until the appointment of a new member.

1 Section 4 Protection of Human Rights Act. other members of the commission shall be speaker of the House of the People, Minister-in-Charge of the Ministry of Home affairs in the Government of India, leader of the opposition in the House of the People, leaders of the opposition in the council of states and the Deputy Chairman of the Council of States

2 Section 6 of the Protection of Human Rights Act.

The chairperson or any other member of the commission may be removed from his office by an order of the President on the ground of provide misbehavior or incapacity after the Supreme Court, on reference being made by the by President. The President may remove from the office of the Chairperson or any other Member if (a) he is adjudged on insolvent; or (b) he is engaged during his office; or (c) he has become unfit to continue his office by reason of infirmity of mind or body or (d) he has been declared by a competent Court a person of unsound mind; (e) he has been convicted and sentenced to imprisonment for any offence which in the opinion of the President involves moral turpitude. The Chairperson or any member may, by notice in writing under his hand addressed to the President of India, resign his office.[3]

In addition to the above, the Central Government shall make available to the Commission an officer of the rank of the Secretary to the Government of India who shall be the Secretary General of the Commission, and such police and investigative staff as may be necessary on the efficient performance of the function of the Commission.[4] The Commission shall have its headquarters in New Delhi and with the permission of the Central Government may establish office in other places in India.[5]

7.3.1.3 Power of NHRC

NHRC holds the power to investigate grievances related to the violation of human rights either *suomoto* or after receiving a petition.

It has the power to interfere in any judicial proceedings involving any allegation of violation of human rights.

It can visit any jail or other government-controlled facility to see the prisoners' living conditions and make recommendations on them.

3 Section 5(1) of the Protection of Human Rights (Amendment) Act. 2006.
4 Section 11 of the Protection of Human Rights (Amendment) Act. 2006
5 Section 3 of the Protection of Human Rights (Amendment) Act. 2006

It can review the protections provided for in the constitution or any human rights protection legislation and can recommend effective remedial steps.

NHRC also undertakes and promotes research in the field of human rights. It works to spread human rights literacy among various sections of society and promotes awareness of the safeguards available for the protection of these rights through publications, media, seminars, and other means.

The Commission takes an independent stance while, for the time being, giving advice on the defense of human rights in the constitutional parlance or in the statute.

NHRC has the powers of a civil court and can grant interim relief.

It also has the authority to recommend payment of compensation or damages.

It can recommend to both the central and state governments to take suitable steps to prevent the violation of Human Rights.

NHRC submits its annual report to the President of India who causes it to be laid before each House of Parliament.

7.3.1.4 Functions of the NHRC

The functions of the National Human Right Commission are laid down under section 12 of the Act.

The Commission shall inquire '*Suomoto*' or on a petition presented to it by a victim or any person on his behalf, into complaints of (a) violation of human rights or abatement thereof; (b) negligence in the prevention of such violation by a public servant.

The Commission may intervene in any proceedings involving any allegation of violation of human rights pending before a court with the approval of such court.

The commission shall visit under intimation to the State Government, where persons are detained or lodged for purposes of treatment, reformation or protection to study the living conditions of the inmates and make recommendations thereon.

The commission shall review the safeguards provided by or under the Constitution or any law for the time being in force for the protection of human rights and will recommended measures for their effective implementation.

The Commission shall review the factors, including acts of terrorism, which inhibit exercise of one's human rights as well as the safeguards currently in force and make appropriate recommendations.

The Commission shall study the treaties and other international instruments on human rights and make recommendations for their effective implementation.

The Commission will undertake and promote research in the field of human rights.

The Commission shall spread human rights literacy among various sections of society and promote awareness of the safeguards available for the protection of those rights through publications, the media, seminars and other available means.

The Commission shall encourage the efforts of non-governmental organizations and institutions working in the field of human rights.

The Commission may perform any other function as it may consider necessary for the promotion of human rights.

The Commission shall have submit an annual report to the Central Government and to the State Government concerned and may at any time submit special reports on any matter which, in its opinion is of such urgency or importance that it shall not be deferred till submission of the annual report. The Central Government and the Staff shall cause the annual and special reports of the Commission to be laid before each House of Parliament or the State Legislature respectively along with a memorandum of action taken or proposed to be taken on the recommendations of the commission and the reasons for non-acceptance of the recommendations, if any[6].

The Commission shall perform functions pursuant to the directions issued by the Supreme Court in exercise of the jurisdiction under Article 32 of the Constitution. The Supreme Court in ***Premjit Kaur Vs. State of Punjab***[7], stated that the Commission would function pursuant to the directions issued by this Court. National Human Rights Commission is given a free hand and is not circumscribed by any conditions. Therefore the jurisdiction exercised by the National Human Rights Commission in these matters is of a special nature not covered by enactment or law, and thus acts '*Sui Generuis*'.

7.3.2 State Human Rights Commissions (SHRCs)

The Protection of Human Right Act 1993 also provided under Chapter-V for the setting up of State Human Rights Commission in states.

7.3.2.1 Composition

Human Rights (Amendment) Act, 2006 consists of three members including achairperson:

The chairperson should be a retired Chief Justice of a High Court.

A serving or retired judge of a High Court or a District Judge in the state with a minimum of seven years experience as District judge.

A person having practical experience or knowledge related to human rights.

7.3.2.2 Appointment

The Governor of the state appoints the chairperson and other members on the recommendations of a committee

6 Section 20 the Protection of Human Rights (Amendment) Act. 2006

7 AIR 1999 Supreme Court.

consisting of the Chief Minister as its head, the speaker of the Legislative Assembly, the state home minister and the leader of the opposition in the Legislative Assembly. The chairman and the leader of the opposition of legislative council would also be the members of the committee, in case the state has legislative council.All the members of the Commission shall hold office for a period of five years from the date of assumption of office or at the age of 70 years. Whichever is earlier. A member is eligible for re-appointment for another term of five years subject to the age of 70 years[8]. The Chairperson or a member of a State Commission may, by notice in writing under his hand addressed to the Governor, resign his office. The Chairperson or a member of a State Commission shall only be removed from his office by order of the President on those grounds on which the Chairperson or a member of the National Human Rights Commission is removed.

7.3.2.3 Power of the State Commissions

The Commission exercises the following powers while enquiring into the complaints of violations of human rights:

The Commission while enquiring into complaints shall have all the powers of a civil court trying a suit under the Code of Civil Procedure of 1998., in particular in respect of the following matters :

Summoning and enforcing the attendance of witnesses and examining them on both; (b) discovery and production of any document; (c) receiving evidence on affidavits; (d) requisitioning any public record or copy thereof from any Court or office; (e) issuing Commissions for the examination of witnesses or documents; (i) any other matter which may be prescribed.[9]

The Commission shall have power to require any person to furnish information on such points or matters as in the opinion of the Commission may be useful for, or relevant to the subject-matter of inquiry and any person so required shall

8 Section 24 the Protection of Human Rights (Amendment) Act, 2006
9 Section 13 (1) the Protection of Human Rights (Amendment) Act. 2006

be deemed to be legally bound to furnish such information within the meaning of Section 176 and Section 177 of the Indian Penal Code.[10]

The Commission or any other officer not below the rank of Gazetted Officer, specially authorized in this behalf by the Commission, may enter any building or place where the Commission has reason to believe that any document relating to the subject-matter of the inquiry may be found, and may seize any such document or take extracts or copies therefrom.[11]

The Commission is though empowered to exercise the powers of a Civil Court only during the Course of inquiry into complaints, it can also records the facts constituting the offence and statement of the accused person as is described in Sections 175, 178,179,180 and 228 of the I.P.C. The Commission after recording the facts constituting the offence and statement of the accused as provided in the Code of Criminal Procedure (1973) has to forward the case to a Magistrate having jurisdiction to conduct the trial. The Magistrate to whom any case is forwarded shall proceed to hear the complaint against the accused as if the case has been forwarded to him under Section 346 of the Code of Criminal Procedure, 1973.[12]

The Commission may, after completing the enquiry recommended to the appropriate Government or authority to take action against the person concerned where the inquiry discloses the violation of human rights.[13] It may also recommended the appropriate government or authority for grant of necessary interim relief to the victim or his family members.[14] The Commission may approach the Supreme Court or the Concerned High Court to pass such directions, orders or writes as the Court may deem necessary,[15] The Commission provides a copy of the inquiry report to the

10 Section 13 (2) the Protection of Human Rights (Amendment) Act. 2006
11 Section 13 (3) the Protection of Human Rights (Amendment) Act. 2006
12 Section 13 (4) the Protection of Human Rights (Amendment) Act, 2006
13 Section 18(1) the Protection of Human Rights (Amendment) Act, 2006
14 Section 18 (3) the Protection of Human Rights (Amendment) Act, 2006
15 Section 18 (2) the Protection of Human Rights (Amendment) Act, 2006

petitioner or his representative. It shall also send a copy of its inquiry report together with its recommendations to the concerned Government or authority who shall, within a month forward to the Commission its comments on the report including the action taken or proposed to be taken. The Commission shall publish its inquiry report together with the comments of the concerned Government or authority, if any, and the action taken or proposed to be taken by the appropriate authority on the recommendations of the Commission.

7.3.2.4 Functions of the State Human Rights Commissions

The State Commission is empowered to perform all those functions which have been entrusted to the National Human Rights Commission, However Para 'C' of Section 29 excludes the study of treaties and other international instrument on human rights from the purview of the SHRC's as the 'study' of such ferities and the eligibility to make recommendations for their effective implementation has been made as the exclusive domain of NHRC. The state Commission may inquire into violation of human rights only in respect of matters related to any of the entries enumerated in List II and III in the Seventh Schedule to the constitution.[16] Section 36(1) of the Act, however, States that the N.H.R.C. shall not enquire into any matter which is pending before the State Commission duly constituted under any law in force. It implies that the Act gives priority to the State Commission dealing with a problem if the matter is filed before it and the National Human Rights Commission. The Commission is required to submit its annual reports to the State Government and it may submit at any time special report on any matter which in its opinion is of such urgency or importance that it should not be deferred till submission of the annual report.[17] The State Government shall submit these reports before each House of the State Legislature

16 Section 21(5) the Protection of Human Rights (Amendment) At, 2006
17 Section 28 (1) the Protection of Human Rights (Amendment) Act, 2006

with a memorandum of action taken or / and the reason for non-acceptance of the recommendations, if any.[18]

The State Human Rights Commission have been established in 16 States, namely, Jammu and Kashmir, Himachal Pradesh, Punjab, Rajasthan, Madhya Pradesh, Chhattisgarh, Maharashtra, Kerala, Tamil Nadu, West Bengal, Assam, Manipur, Andhra Pradesh, Orissa, Karnataka and Uttar Pradesh. It may be noted that certain State Government have informed the N.H.R.C. of their difficulty in establishing the Commissions because of financial constraints or because of the non-availability of retired Chief Justice or Justices of the High Court whose presence is essential to the proper composition of the five member commissions envisaged under provisions of section 21(2) of the protection of Human Rights Act of 1993. Hence, and amendment therefore is required to be made in the Act to remove the difficulty. Through the N.H.R.C. in its 1999-2000 report again emphasized the need for the early setting up of the State Commission, but some States have failed to constitute State Human Rights commission even after fifteen years of the enactment of the Act. Further some of those Commissions have already been either non-functional or ineffective where they exist. The commission itself has noted that not all the State Human Rights Commission, that have been established, are being appropriately supported through the provision of adequate financial and man power resources. Greater political will is required at the State-level Combined with encouragement from the Central Government and the major political parties to proceed conclusively in this direction.

It is desirable and important that if the State Human Rights Commissions are established in different States their work is coordinated with that of the NHRC so that confusion and duplication does not occur.

7.3.3 Human Rights Court in Districts

Chapter VI of the Act comprising of Sections 30 and 31 makes the provisions relating to the creation of Human

18 Section 28 the Protection of Human Rights (Amendment) Act, 2006

Rights Courts in each district. The setting up of Human Rights Courts in every district of the country for the speedy trial of fences arising out of violation of human rights is a novel provision of the Act. Section 30 of the Act provides that Human Rights Courts may be set up by the State Government, with a concurrence of the Chief Justice of the High Court, by notification, specifying for each district a Court of Session to be a Human Rights Court[19]. For every Human Rights Court, Section 31 provides that the State Government in accordance with Section 31 of the Act shall appoint a Public Prosecutor or an advocate who has been in practice as an advocate who has been in practice as an advocate for not less than seven years for the purpose of conducting cases in the Human Rights Courts[20]. Such a person shall be called a special Public Prosecutor.

A question arises as to what cases shall be decided by such Courts. Will these Courts decide the cases involving human rights violations which are referred to Supreme Court under Article 32 or the High Courts under Article 226 of the Constitution? The ambiguity exists as to precise nature of the offences that should be tried in such Courts and other details regarding the conduct of their business in view of the fact that Section 30 of the Protection of Human Rights Act of 1993 does not lay down the jurisdiction and procedure to be followed by such courts. Provisions relating to the creation of Human Rights Courts in Districts are therefore inadequate and defective and require modifications without which Human Rights Court at the district level, even formed cannot function efficiently.

The National Human Rights Commission in its 1998-99 report has drawn attention to the ambiguity as to the precise nature of offences that could be tried by those Courts. It recognized that substantive amendments of Section 30 of the Act are necessary to enable to courts to fulfill the expectation that they would provide speedy trial of offences arising out of

19 Section 30 the Protection of Human Rights (Amendment) Act, 2006
20 Section 31 the Protection of Human Rights (Amendment) Act, 2006

violations of human rights. It therefore recommended to the Central Government to undertake the necessary legislation for this purpose at an early date. The Commission in its Annual Report of 2000-2001 stated that in the absence of action being taken on the proposed amendment, these Courts are not adequately discharging the purpose for which they are designated.

❑❑❑

CHAPTER

8 Women Rights under Personal Laws

8.1 Introduction

Personal laws are personal in terms of religion, customs and practices. In India it is based on religion and practices. Personal laws like Hindu law, Mohammadan Law, Christian law, Persian law are prevailing in India. Personal laws regulate marriage, divorce, maintenance, inheritance and succession for Indian citizens. These laws are largely influenced by religious customs of different communities. However they are criticized for perpetuating gender inequality and discriminatory attitudes. While Muslim personal laws receive the most flak for being discriminatory, some argue that Hindu laws are of no different, in many a situations, though the things have received social need and are under a paradigm shift in recent days due to judicial intervention and other social reasons.

The core controversy surrounding this issue has been the conflict between personal laws and gender justice. In this context, there has been continued demand for a constitutional objects laid down under Article 44 of the Constitution i.e. Uniform Civil Code (UCC), a standardized law regulating all aspects of personal law irrespective of any religious touch.

Sharaya Bano Vs. Union of India,[1] a case in which the Supreme Court invalidated divorces resulting from Triple

1 2017 SCC On Line SC 963, decided on 22.08.2017

Talaq, reignited this issue. Though the case did not touch upon UCC, it delved into issues regarding personal laws and gender justice.

Inspite of conservative foundation of Personal laws in favour of women, still some remarkable provisions are there, which certainly improves the position of women in terms of growth of rights and protection of interest of women in India.

8.2 Protection under Personal Laws

India has yet not achieved the dream of the constitution makes in the form of uniform civil code; therefore, there are particular family or personal laws applicable according to the faith of the particular community. The personal laws are basically depending upon the practices, conventions and precedents of the particular faith, for which the laws are made for.

8.2.1 Succession and Maintenance

That during last 70 years, various legislative amendments have been effected so as to provide gender justice in property rights to Hindu woman. In 1937, the Hindu Women's right to Property Act, 1937 was enacted which provided equal status to the wife when partition was effected in join Hindu family property.

That with the passing of Hindu Succession Act, 1956 it provides for the first time those daughters would have an equal right of inheritance in the father's self acquired property. However, it did not apply to ancestral property which was governed by the concept of Mitakshara coparcenary property. The Hindu coparcenary did not include a female member of the family.

The legislature has now passed a further amendment to S. 6 of the Hindu Succession Act, 1956 on September 9, 2005 whereby daughters have an equal right in coparcenary property, as that of a son.

Dowry and presents at the time of marriage are the exclusive property of a married woman, and do not become the joint property of both the spouses. The supreme Court held in the case of ***Pratibha Rani Vs. Suraj Kumar***[2] that refusal to return Stridhan of the wife, amounts to criminal breach of trust, and can be prosecuted under S. 406 of IPC.

The jurisdiction clause in the Hindu Marriage Act, 1955 was amended whereby in S. 19 clause (iii) (a) was incorporated, so as to provide that where a wife is a petitioner, then the place where she is residing on the date of the presentation of the petition, the district Court of such place would also be a court of competent jurisdiction.

Section 18 (2) of the Hindu Adoption and Maintenance Act, 1955 provides that a wife can live separately from the husband , and still claim maintenance if the husband is guilty of cruelty, bigamy, desertion etc.

Section 24 of the Hindu Marriage Act, 1955 provides that a spouse liable to be maintained during the pendency of the proceedings before the Court if he/she does not have sufficient independent source of income. S 25 provides that the dependent spouse can claim for permanent alimony and maintenance from the other spouse.

Section 125 of the Criminal Procedure code, 1973 gives effect to the natural duty of a man to maintain his wife, children and parents. This is a legal obligation of his being a husband or father.

The provisions of Section 125 of Cr.PC are equally applicable to spouses of all religion. However, now the ceiling of Rs. 500 is removed, and under Section 125 of the codes parties may pursue both criminal and civil proceedings simultaneously as there is no legal bar to it.

That the Courts have normally been following the norm that the husband is required to pay maintenance which is generally 1/3rd of his income or salary to his wife and child, unless the wife has her independent income. There are certain

2 (1985) 2 SCC 370: AIR 1978 SC 961

criteria which are taken into account before deciding the amount of maintenance payable like, the position and status of the parties, the reasonable requirements of the claimant, the income of the husband, the claimants own earnings, the number of persons entitled to be maintained.

That even though there is provision for interim maintenance, the inordinate delays in Court procedures, makes it extremely difficult and hard for woman, particularly when they are unemployed, and dependent. The expense of litigation and delay in obtaining relief, defeats they very purpose, which is intended by these provisions. It is necessary that the judicial process is streamlined so that relief becomes available within a time bound period.

Legal recognition should be given to the economic value of the contribution made by the wife through household work for purpose of determining ownership of matrimonial property, acquired after marriage so as to ensure an equitable share in family wealth.

8.2.2 Adoptions

We know that the Hindus have regarded the institution of sonship as important as the institution of marriage. To have son was considered a 'must' for every Hindu. Son is called putra because the son delivers his father from hell, called 'put'[3]. Baudhayana declared:

"Through son one conquers the world, through a grand-son one obtains the immortality, and through the great-grand son one ascends to the highest heaven."[4]

Accordingly to manu, sons are classified into two categories. The sons in category (I)are Kiusmen as well as heirs, while in category (II) they are only Kinsmen. Most of the above sons became obsolete in the port- 'Smriti' period. The aurasa, the putrikaputra and dattaka remained. During the Raj, the putrikaputra also became obsolete, and there remained, only the natural born son and the adopted

3 1Manu V 138
4 2,6,16 Manu IX, 137-138 Vishnu XV, 44,46; Yajnavalkya 1,78,

son. Hindu law had never recognized legistimization. It is submitted that the recognition of so many secondary sons was something akin to the process of legitimization. All the secondary sons were the sons of the man only if he recognized them.

Looked at broadly, the self-given son, the son made, bought son and given son were all adopted sons. Since in most of these cases, there was a breach of some moral principle, the secondary sons, except the adopted son which is essentially a gift of a son, became obsolete. Predominautly, adoption was considered as a sacramental act. Under the old Hindu law, there were many rules relating to adoption which could be supported only on the basis that adoption was a sacramental act.

In the present submission, the Hindu Adoptions and Maintenance Act 1956, has steered of clearly from all the religious and sacramental aspects of adoption, and has made adoption a secular institution and secular act, so much so that even a religious ceremony is not necessary for adoptions. All adoptions after 1956 are secular, and to be valid, must conform to the requirement of the Act.

The law of adoption enables a childless person to make somebody else's child as his own. Hindus foresaw this at the down of their civilization. The adopted sons will be treated as natural son. Both Hindu male and female can make adoption. It is not necessary to enquire into the motive of adoption[5]. No person can make an adoption unless he or she is (a) major and (b) of sound mind. Majority means completion of 18 yrs, and it seems, this is the age even fore person to whom guardian has been appointed under the Guardians and words act, 1890 (in case a guardian is appointed for a minor; the age of majority is extended to the completion of 21 years).

A major Hindu male of sound mind can adopt whether he is a bachelor, widower, divorcee or married person. But for a married Hindu male, it is obligatory to obtain the consent of his wife. In case, he has more than one wife, can sent

5 Naidu Vs. Naidu, 1970 SC 1673.

of all the wives is necessary[6]. An adoption is made without the consent of the wife is void[7]. If consent of a wife living with the husband is taken but the consent of the other wife living separately is not taken, the adoption will be void[8]. The consent of the wife may be express or implied.

8.2.3 Restrictive Conditions of Adoption

Just because a person has capacity to adopt, it is not necessary that he has also the right to make and adoption; certain restrictive conditions exist there;

Adoption of son-Adopter must not have a Hindu son, son's son or son's son. If he has any one of these, he cannot make an adoption. Son or son's son or son's son's son may be by legitimate birth or a by adoption. If the son, son's son or son's son's son has ceased to be Hindu, an adoption of a son to be valid.[9]

Adoption of daughter : if a Hindu wants to adopta daughter, it is necessary that he must not have a Hindu daughter, or a son's daughter, existence of an adopted daughter or son's adopted daughter will also bar the adoption of a daughter. But if daughter or son's daughter has ceased to be a Hindu, adoption of a daughter can be validly made.[10]

8.2.4 Who may Give in Adoption

The father cannot now give the child in adoption without the consent of the mother of the child (i) if she has been judicially declared to be of unsound mind (ii) if she has finally and completely renounced the world or (iii) if she has ceased to be a Hindu.

The mother of an illegitimate child has power to give the child in adoption and no question arises of putative father's consent. But the mother of a legitimate child has during

6 Proviso s.7
7 section 5(1)
8 Bholooram Vs. Ramlal, 1989 M.P. 198
9 Secrtion II (i) Hindu adoption and maintenance Act. 1956
10 Section II (ii)

the lifetime of the father, no power to give the child in adoption even with the consent of the father. But mother of a legitimate child can give the child in adoption during the life time of the father in the following cases (i)if the father has ceased to be a Hindu, (ii) if he as finally and completely renounced the world or (iii) if he has judicially declared to be of unsound mind. But a remarried woman has no right to give away in adoption her son born to her from her deceased husband. But she can only enjoy the guardian ship of the son according to sec. 3 of the Hindu Remarriage Act,1956. The mother has power to give her legitimate child in adoption after the death of the father. Even, if a father, before his death expressed himself categorically that his child should not be given in adoption, the mother can, after his death validly give the child in adoption. But we remember, the expression 'mother' does not include adoptive mother or stepmother. But, a mother on conversion to another religionwill not lose her right to give the child in adoption in case the parent has ceased to be a Hindu [Section 9(4)]. Mother also does not lose her right of given the child in adoption on divorce.

Two persons cannot adopt the same child. The child, who may be taken by adoption, must be Hindu. The Hindu adoption and Maintenance Act, 1956 makes a provision for the adoption of orphans. Further, if the parents have renounced the world or have been judicially declared to be unsound mind, the child can be given in adoption by the guardian. Adoption of an abandoned child can be made.[11]

8.2.5 Guardianship

Guardianship as conceived originally was, in most systems, an extension of paternal power, but in modern law, it essentially implies and idea of protection, under the Hindu Minority and Guardianship Act 1956, sec 4(b), minor means a person who has not completed the age of age of eighteen years. A minor is considered to be a person who is physically

11 Jandumani Vs. Haji Oijh, (1974) 40 CLR 70

and intellectually imperfect and immature and hence needs some one's protection. Guardian is,

"a person having the care of the person of the minor or his property or both person and property."[12]

Guardians may be of the following kinds:

- Natural Guardians
- Testamentary guardians
- Guardian appointed or declared by the Court.

Under the lunacy law also, guardians can be appointed for lunatic or idiots even if they are guardians in litigation who are entrusted with the duty of protecting the interest of minor-plain life or minor defendant. These guardians do not fall within the preview of the work. According to section 19 of the Guardian and words Act, 1890, father cannot be deprived of the natural guardianship of his minor children unless he has been found unfit. Hence, father is the natural guardian of his minor legitimate children, sons and daughters. Section 13 of the Act, lays down that welfare of the minor is of paramount consideration and father's right of guardianship is subordinate to the welfare of the child.[13] Before 1956, the father could prevent the mother form assuming the guardianship of her minor children even after his death by appointing testamentary guardian. This cannot be done now. The Act lays down that if father appoints a testamentary guardian and the mother survives him, the appointment of testamentary guardian will be ineffective so long as the mother is alive. If the mother dies after appointing a testamentary guardian, the mother's appointee will take over the charge over the child as a guardian and the father's appointee will be ineffective.[14] The position of adopted children is at par with natural born children. Where the father is alive but he is non-functioning natural guardian, the mother can act as the natural guardian. Vaidyalingam. J. said that in the particular circumstances of this case,

12 Hindu Minority and Guardian ship Act. 1956
13 Lilita Vs. Ganga, 1973, Raj 93.
14 Section 9 (2) of the Act

"the mother could be considered as the natural guardian of her minor daughter. In that case, the father and mother of a minor child had fallen out and the mother was living separately from the father for over twenty years. The mother had been looking after the affairs of her minor daughter and managing her properties. The child was all along under her protection and care.[15]*Thus , it seems that where the father fails to function or refuses to function or is incapable of functioning as guardian, the mother will be able to exercise all powers and functions of a natural guardian without being appointed guardian by the Court."*[16]

When a minor brings a suit against the father to set aside improper alienation, the mother can act as a guardian of minor even without seeking permission of Court.[17]

8.2.5.1 Mother

The mother is the natural guardian of the minor illegitimate children even if the father is alive. However, she is the natural guardian of her minor legitimate children only if the father is dead or otherwise is incapable of acting as guardian. Remarriage of the mother with a person of different faith cannot disqualify her to be a guardian of her minor child, especially when the child was being looked after extremely will be the mother.[18] Proviso to clause (a) of section 6 of this Act lays down that the custody of a minor who has not completed the age of five shall ordinarily be with the mother. Thus the mother is entitled to the custody of the child below five years, unless the welfare of the minor requires otherwise.[19] But this does not mean that she is not entitled to custody thereafter. Mother's right of guardianship is not lost on her conversion to another religion so long as she is able to provide a congenial, comfortable and happy home.[20] The position of mother's guardianship of her adopted children is

15 Jijabai Vs. Pathan, 1971, S.C.. 315
16 Narayan Vs. Sapurna, 1968. Pat, 318
17 Rajendra Kumar Vs. Deepak Markwana, 2008
18 Lakshmi Vs. Vasantha Kumari, 2005 Ker. 249
19 Chandra Vs. Prem (1969) del.283 & Santha Kumari Vs. Natarajan,(1973)2 M.L. J. 286
20 Sheela Vs. Soli, 1981, Bom. 175

the same as those natural born children. It is submitted that if would be a better proposition of law if is laid down that percents are equal and co-ordinate guardians of their minor children.

Step-parents are not entitled to guardian ship, unless they are specifically appointed by the Court.[21] Once a child goes in adoption, natural parents cease to be natural guardians of the child. Natural parents could be guardians of the child only if so appointed by the adoptive parents or by the court.[22]

Further, the Hindu Minority and Guardianship Act, 1956, also lays down that husband is the natural guardian of the person and property of the minor wife. It is submitted that it is open to the Courts not to give custody of a minor wife to a husband, if they are satisfied that it will not be for the welfare of the minor wife. This is the important of sec-13 of the Act which lays down the welfare of the minor is of paramount consideration.

It is submitted that it would be in the interest of the minor wife if it laid down that the guardianship of the person and property of the minor wife should continue to vest in the parents and the husband will not be entitled to have the custody of his minor wife so long as she is not physically fit to have marital intercourse.

8.2.5.2 Rights of Guardian of a Person

The natural guardian has the following rights in respect of minor children:

- Right to Custody
- Right to determine the religion of children.
- Right to control education,
- Right to control movement, and
- Right to reasonable chastisement.

21 A. Angurbala Vs. Debabrata, (1949), 8, Cal 278
22 KumarsuManikayala Rao Vs. KumarsuNagabhushanam, 2001, A.P. 531 G.

These rights are conferred on the guardian in the interest of the minor children and therefore exercise of each of these rights is subject to the welfare of the minor children.

8.2.5.3 Testamentary Guardians

Since shastric law did not contemplate testamentary disposition of property, wills were practically unknown to Hindus. When, during the Raj, testamentary were conferred on Hindus, the testamentary guardians also came into existence. Then testamentary power in respect of appointment of guardians was considered to be nothing but a manifestation of paternal power and therefore father alone had this power, Mother had no such power. Under the Hindu Minority and Guardianship Act, 1956, testamentary power of appointing a guardian has now been conferred on both parents. Parents have power of testamentary appointment of guardians in all cases where they are competent to act as natural guardians.[23]

It seems that a Hindu father cannot appoint a guardian of his minor illegitimate children even when he is entitled to act as their natural guardian, as Sec. 9(1) confers testamentary power on him in respect of legitimate children. In case of illegitimate children, Sec. 9(4) confers the power on the mother only.

8.2.5.4 Guardians Appointed by the Court

The appointment of guardians of Hindu children is still regulated by the guardians and wards Act. 1890. The District Court may appoint or declare any person as the guardian whenever it considers it necessary in the welfare of the child.[24] In appointing a guardian, the Court takes into consideration various factors, including age, sex, wishes of the child, the wishes of the parents and the personal law of the child.[25]

23 Section 9 (1) of the Act.
24 Section 17, Bimala Vs. Subhash, 1992 pat 96
25 Section 13, Hindu Minority and Guardianship Act 1956;

The welfare of the children is of paramount consideration. The Court has the power to remove any guardian from the guardianship, if it comes to the conclusion that the do so will be in the interest of the minor.

The guardian by affinity is the guardian of a minor widow. The textual source of the guardianship of minor widow is the same a relating to the guardianship of a minor wife. Further, a de facto guardian means a self-appointed guardian. A de facto guardian is a person who takes continuous interest in the welfare of the minor's property without any authority of law. The term 'de facto guardian' as such it is not mentioned in any of the texts, but his existence has never been denied in Hindu Law. In some cases it has been held that in view of Sec. 11, a de-facto guardian cannot alienate a minor's property.[26] Hence, minor child, minor wife, minor widow, orphans etc are entitled to get the umbrella of the guardianship by Hindu law.

❑❑❑

26 Amrik Rai Vs. Satpadisood, 1983 P& H 301: Sohrab Khan Vs. Deputy Director of Consolidation(1970) All, L.J. 288.

CHAPTER

9 Women Rights and Protection under Criminal Laws

9.1 Introduction

India is a country known for its rich beautiful culture and tradition. Women are given the place of goddess Lakshmi in the Indian culture. But by seeing the last few year crimes against women, there seems the safety and security of women are at stake. As we can literally observe that crimes against women occur every minute in India. There has been a decline in the women status from ancient to medieval period which is continued in such an advanced era.

Each day a single woman, a girl child, a young girl, a mother and women from all walks of life are being assaulted, molested, and violated. The streets, public transport, public spaces, in particular, have become the territory of the hunters. There are certain common crimes against women are rape, dowry deaths, sexual harassment at home or workplace, kidnapping and abduction, cruelty by husband, relatives, assault on a woman, child and sex, trafficking, attack, child marriages and many more.

Though the Constitution of India has given the equal rights of dignity, equality, and freedom from gender discrimination but in practical filed no one bothers to follow such law until and unless the people's mindset towards a woman does not change. There are many activities are done against women do undermined their status and life by application of force and by other means, but at the same time there are multiple laws and policies are there under which women are given lots of right and authority to take action against the offender or perpetrator in India.

9.2 Protections under Criminal Law

The various amendments to the Cr.P.C. I.P.C. and Evidence Act have been incorporated to curb crimes against Women, both perpetrated by strangers, as well as domestic violence in the four corners of the home.

Sec. 304B was incorporated in the IPC where the death of a woman is caused by any burns or bodily injury, or occurs otherwise in unnatural circumstances, within 7 years of her marriage, in connection with, any demand for dowry, such death shall be called a “dowry death” and the husband or relative shall be deemed to have caused her death, and is punishable with imprisonment for not less than 7 years. By an amendment to the First Schedule of the Cr.P.C., these offences have been made cognizable, non-bailable and can be tried by Sessions Court.

Chapter XXA which contains Sec. 498A, was incorporated in the Indian Penal Code on 25.12.83 to deal with respect to cruelty by husband or his relatives which is likely to drive a woman to commit suicide or to cause grave injury or danger to life, or harassment to a woman to coerce her to meet any lawful demand for property, is liable to be punished with imprisonment.

Sec. 113A and Sec. 113B have been incorporated in the Indian Evidence Act, 1872. Sec. 113A provides that if a married woman commits suicide within 7 years of marriage and it is shown that her husband and his relatives subjected her to cruelty, then the Court may hold that such suicide has been abetted by the husband or such relative of her husband.

Sec. 113B provides that when the question is whether a person has Committed the dowry of a woman, and it is shown that soon before her death such woman had been subjected by such person to cruelty or harassment for, or in connection with, any demand for dowry, the Court shall presume that such person had caused the dowry death.

Sect. 228A was incorporated in the IPC w.e.f. 25.12.1983 whereby disclosure of the identity of a victim of rape under Sec. 376, 376A. 376B. 376C and 376D was made punishable with imprisonment and fine.

That with the effect from 25.12.1983, in the Indian Penal Code, whereby Sections 375 and 376 were amended and Sec. A-D were inserted in the IPC, And Sec. 114-A was incorporated in the Indian Evidence Act., 1872.

Section 376-A of the Indian Penal Code, 1860 provides that if a man has sexual intercourse with his own wife without her consent, if she is living separately from him under a decree of separation, or under any custom or usage then he shall be punished with imprisonment which may extend to 2 years or fine.

Section 376B of the Indian Penal Code, 1860 provides for imprisonment of a public servant who takes advantage of his official position and induces or seduces any woman, who is in his custody to have sexual intercourse with hi, such sexual intercourse not amounting to the offence of rape.

Section 376C of the Indian Penal Code, 1860 provides for imprisonment of a Superintendent/Manager of Jail/Remand home/or other place as specified in the Section, if he induces or seduces any female intimate of the jail, remand home, place or institution to have sexual intercourse with him, such sexual intercourse not amounting to the offence of rape.

Section 376D of the Indian Penal Code, 1860 provides that if any member of the management or staff of a hospital or being on the staff or a hospital takes advantage of his position and has sexual intercourse with ant woman in that hospital, not amounting to rape, shall be punishable with imprisonment.

Section 114A of the Indian Evidence Act 1872, provides that in a prosecution for rape under Sec 376 of Indian Penal Code, where sexual intercourse is proved and the question is whether it was without the consent of woman alleged to have been raped, and she starts in her evidence before the Court that she did not consent, the Court shall presume that she did not consent.

Section 16(1) CrPC requires the witnesses to attend the Police Station as is required by the Investigation officer. But clause (2) thereof provides an exemption from such requisition, for women and males under the age of fifteen years. The Investigating Officer has to go to the place of residence where the women resides to gather information from her. Thus, a woman cannot be compelled to visit Police Station as witness.

Section 46 of the CrPC was amended in 2005, which provides safeguards for women in terms of bar on arrest after sunset, and before sunrise, except in exceptional circumstances.

To address the problem of increasing domestic violence, but has remained largely invisible in the public domain. The protection of woman from Domestic Violence an Act was passed in 2005 to provide civil remedies to women in abusive / violent relationship and empower Magistrates to grant protection to victim of domestic violence and provide other relief.[1]

9.2.1 Domestic Violence

The position of women in Indian Society is very melancholy. Woman has become a weaker section of human population in the patriarchal society. Her functions have been relegated to mere recreation and attending to household chores. But it is very painful to write that this so called queen of the household, the Ardhangini, the Sahadharmini and equal participator with her husband in all sacrifices has become a

1 State of Mysore Vs. Workers of Gold Mines, AIR 1958 SC, 923 when the Industrial Disputes Act 1947 was amended in 1956.

worst target of social and economic exploitation. Now a day the life of a woman is no structured that she has become sub-servant to the needs of man and has become a victim of social and personal aggression. Even in the era of equality of sexes, equality before law and equal protection of laws, if us ironical that cruelty to women and problem of battered wives has become almost a worldwide phenomenon.

When we drafted the constitution, we were aware of the problem of woman who has been by centuries of exploitation, rendered. 'Weaker Section' of the society, while guaranteeing equal protection and equality of Law[2] and enacting non-discrimination clause, the constitutions a specific clause for protective discrimination in favour of women and children. Following provisions of the constitution may be quoted in this context:

Clause 3 of Article 15 says that,

"Nothing in this article shall prevent the state from making any special provision for the women and children."[3]

Clause 4 of Article 15 says that,

"Nothing this Article or in clause (2) of Article 29 shall prevent the state from making any special provision for the advancement of any socially and educationally backward classes of citizens or for the scheduled castes and scheduled tribes"[4]

9.2.2 Protection of Women against Medical Termination of Pregnancy

The Medical Termination of Pregnancy Act, 1971 provides for the termination of certain Pregnancies by Registered medical practitioners and for matters connected therewith or incidental thereto.

Sec. 3 provides that pregnancies can be terminated by registered medical practitioners where the pregnancy is not

2 Muir Mills Ltd. Vs. Suti Mill Mazdoor Union (1955) I LLJ 1 (SC)
3 Clause 3 of Article 15 of the Constitution
4 Clause 4 of Article 15 of the Constitution

more than 12 weeks or where the pregnancy is more than 12 weeks but less than 20 weeks at least two medical practitioners are of opinion that the continuance of the pregnancy would involve to a risk to the a lo the life of the pregnancy woman or of grave injury to her physical or mental health or of there is substantial risk that if the child was born, it would suffer from such physical or mental abnormalities as to be seriously handicapped.

The Indian Penal code 1860, which was enacted more than fifty years ago, on the basis of the then British Law, contained some provisions regarding the termination to pregnancy. Abortion was a crime, for which the mother as well as the abortionist could be punished except where it has to be induced in order to save the life of the mother. This strict law had been absorbed in the benches all over the country. The object of law, which went unnoticed, was one of the major factors for the untimely death of pregnant mothers. Moreover, during the then prevailing circumstances medical facilities were not adequate. In recent years health services have expanded and the services of hospital are being availed of by all classes of society. Doctors have often been confronted with gravely ill or dying pregnant women whose pregnant uterus have been tampered with a view to causing an abortion and consequently have suffered very severely. In order to save the pregnant women's health, strength and sometimes life. The Medical Termination to Pregnancy Bill was introduced in the Parliament.

The Medical Termination Act, 1971 provides for the termination of certain pregnancies by registered medical practitioners and for matters connected therewith or incidental thereto.

9.2.2.1 When Pregnancies may be Terminated by Registered Medical Practitioners

In terms of Section 3 of the Medical Termination of Pregnancy Act, 1971, a pregnancy may be terminated by a registered medical practitioner under the following circumstances:-

- where the length of the pregnancy does not exceed twelve weeks, if a medical practitioner is; or
- where the length of the pregnancy exceed twelve weeks but does not exceed twenty weeks, if not less than two registered medical practitioners are, of the opinion formed in good faith; that
- the continuance of the pregnancy would involve a risk to the life of the pregnant woman or of grave injury to her physical or mental health; or
- there is substantial risk that if the child was born, it would suffer from such physical or mental abnormalities as to be seriously handicapped.

In other words pregnancies can be terminated by registered medical practitioners where the pregnancy is not more than 12 weeks, or where the pregnancy is more than 12 weeks but less than 20 weeks at least two medical practitioners are of the opinion that the continuance of the pregnancy would involve a risk to the life of the pregnant woman or of grave injury to her physical or mental health or there is substantial risk that if the child was born, it would suffer from such physical or mental abnormalities as to be seriously handicapped.

Pregnancy of any woman who is less than 18 years or who is a mentally ill person can be terminated only, with the consent in writing of her guardian [Section 3(3)]

9.2.2.2 Place where Pregnancy may be Terminated

According to Section 4 of the Medical Termination of Pregnancy Act, 1971 pregnancy can be terminated either at a hospital established or maintained by the Government or at a place which is approved by the Government or district level constituted by that Government.

9.2.2.3 Protection of Action Taken Good Faith

According to Section 8 of the Medical Termination of Pregnancy Act, 1971 if any registered medical practitioner causes any damage by anything which is, in good faith, done or intended to be done under the Medical Termination of Pregnancy Act 1971, no suit or other legal proceedings can be instituted against him.

9.2.3 Protection of Women from the Pre-Conception and Pre-Natal Sex Selection or Determination

9.2.3.1 Protective Law and Procedure

The Pre-Conception and Pre-Natal Diagnostic Techniques (Prohibition of Sex Selection) Act, 1994 was passed with an object to provide for the prohibition of sex selection, before or after conception and for regulation of pre-natal diagnostic techniques for the purposes of detecting genetic abnormalities or metabolic disorders or chromosomal abnormalities or certain congenital malformations or sex linked disorders and for the prevention of their misuse for sex determination leading to female foeticide and for matters connected therewith or incidental thereto.

9.2.3.2 Scheme of Prohibitory Legislation

The newly named, The pre-conception and Pre-natal Diagnostic techniques (Prohibition of Sex Selection) Act, 1994 consists a total of 34 Sections and 8 Chapters. This Act regulates the use of pre-conception and pre-natal Diagnostic Techniques and it also prohibits pre-sex selection not only by individuals such as medical practitioners, gynecologists and pediatricians but also by any genetic counseling centre or genetic laboratory or clinic.

9.2.3.3 Regulation of Genetic Counseling Centers, Genetic Laboratories and Genetic Clinic

According to Section 3 of the pre-conception and Pre-natal Diagnostics Techniques (Prohibition of Sex Selection) Act, 1994 genetic counseling centers, genetic laboratories, genetic clinics, unless registered under said Act, cannot conduct or associated with, or help in, conducting activities relating to pre-natal diagnostic techniques.

They cannot employ or cause to be employed or take services of any person whether on honorary basis or on payment who does not possess the prescribed qualification, medical geneticist, gynecologist, pediatrician, registered medical practitioner or any other person and cannot conduct or cause to be conducted or aid in conducting by himself or through any other person, any pre-natal diagnostic techniques at a place other than a registered place.

9.2.3.4 Prohibition of Sex Selection

In terms of newly added Section 3-A of the Act sex selection on a woman or a man or on both or on any issue, embryo, conceptus, fluid or gametes destined from either or both of them is prohibited.

9.2.3.5 Prohibition on State of Ultrasound Machine etc.

According to new Section 3-B of the Act sale of any ultrasound machine or imaging machine or scanner or any other equipment capable of detecting sex of fetus to any genetic counseling centre, genetic laboratory, genetic clinic or any other person not registered under the Act is prohibited.

9.2.3.6 Regulation of Pre-natal Diagnostic Techniques

In terms of Section 4(2) of the Act of 1994 no pre-natal diagnostic techniques shall be conducted except for the purposes of detection of any of the following abnormalities, namely,

- chromosomal abnormalities;
- genetic metabolic disease;
- hemoglobinopathis;
- sex-liked genetic diseases;
- congenital anomalies;

- any other abnormalities or disease as may be specified by the Central Supervisory Board.

9.2.3.7 Pre-condition to use Pre-natal Diagnostic Techniques

As provided under Section 4(3) of the Act, no pre-natal diagnostic techniques shall be used or conducted unless the person qualified to do so is satisfied for reasons to be recorded in writing that any of the following conditions are fulfilled, namely:-

- age of the pregnant women is above 35 years;
- the pregnant women has undergone two or more spontaneous abortions or fetal loss;
- the pregnant woman had been exposed to potentially teratogenic agents such as drugs, radiation, infection or chemicals;
- the pregnant woman or her spouse has a family history of mental retardation or physical deformities such as, spastically or any other genetic disease;
- any other condition as may be specified by the Central supervisory Board:

Provided that the person conducting ultrasonography on a pregnant woman shall keep complete record thereof in the clinic in such manner, as may be prescribed and any deficiency or inaccuracy found therein shall amount of contravention of the provisions of Section 6 (determination of sex prohibited), unless contrary is proved by the person conducting such ultrasonography.

No person including a relative or husband of the pregnant woman shall, seek or encourage the conduct of pre-natal diagnostic techniques on her expect for the purpose as mentioned above.

9.2.3.8 Consent of and Communication to Pregnant Woman

By virtue of Section 5 of the Act, 1994 pre-natal diagnostic procedure cannot be conducted unless:

- all side and after effects of such procedures have been explained to the concerned pregnant woman;
- her written consent to undergo such procedure that has been explained in the language which she understands; and
- a copy of her written consent is given to the concerned pregnant woman.
- Communication of sex of the fetus by words, signs or in any other manner to the concerned pregnant women or her relations or any other person is prohibited.

9.2.3.9 Determination of Sex Prohibited

According to Section 6 of the Act no genetic counseling centers or Genetic laboratories or genetic clinic or any person can conduct or cause to be conducted pre-natal diagnostic techniques including ultrasonography for the purpose of determining the sex of fetus. No person can cause or allow to be, caused selection of sex before or after conception. Despite the intent and purpose of the Act being wide and all encompassing, it has been interpreted by the ultrasonologists, the abortionists, the doctors and more shockingly the government alike to exclude pre-conceptual sex selection. This male practice should be stopped immediately for making a beautiful country in future.

9.2.4 Protection of Women against Sexual Harassment at Workplace

Close to half the population of the country is female and based on that approximately half the hypothetical potential workforce would then be female. Therefore as rightly put by the National Commission on Labour in 2002, *"any social, economic or industrial system that ignores the potentials, talents and special attitudes of this half will be flawed on many counts. It is, therefore, necessary to ensure equal opportunities and protection from indignities."*[5]

Sexual Harassment in the workplace refers to any unwanted sexual advances, be it verbal or physical, as long as it is of sexual nature and is either used as leverage for favourable treatment at work or is interfering with an individual's performance at work by creating a hostile work environment. Sexual harassment is inclusive [xiii] of:

- Inappropriate remarks, jokes, or insinuations of a lewd or sexual nature:
- Unwanted physical contact, including assault
- Lewd gestures and lecherous looks
- Compromising invitations.

Requests or demands for sexual favours-including implicit or explicit threats of dismissal or other unfavorable treatment if such favours are refuse; also incentive of favourable treatment in return for such favours.

Sexual harassment is not only viewed as a discrimination problem related to safety and health, but also as a violation of fundamental rights and human rights. It is offensive at a very personal level and in a way undermines the right to equal opportunity and equal treatment of women at the workplace. The first and foremost effort ought to be to prevent the occurrence of such harassment in the first place, but in the event that such harassment does occur, it ought to be punished and the victims protected. Women are often unaware of their rights and also many a time keep things quiet in fear of losing their jobs. Employers need to be more proactive about spreading awareness and fighting against sexual harassment at the workplace. Contrary to popular belief sexual harassment at the workplace does not only have an impact on the victim alone, but affects the productivity of the industry/company as a whole. It can also

5 Annual Report of National Commission on Labour in 2002

ruin the reputation of a company, leading to a tarnished public image, which may in turn affect sales and profits. Employers and trade unions ought to take more active steps towards the prevention and punishment of such activities. This can be done through policies and procedures adopted within the industry itself. There should be an adequate complaint mechanism, disciplinary rules, sexual harassment awareness, defence training, and communication strategy. The 71st Session of the ILO Conference 1985 adopted a resolution on the matter, which states,

"sexual harassment at the workplace is detrimental to employee's working conditions and to employment and promotion prospects. Policies for the advancement of equality should therefore include measures to combat and prevent sexual harassment."

Multiple countries have penal provisions to deal with sexual harassment in the workplace, for example the UK's Employment Equality Regulations 2005, the EU Equal Treatment Directive 2002, Germany's Employees Protect Act 1995, etc.

Women because of their second-class citizen treatment at workplaces are often vulnerable and targets of sexual harassment and sexual violence. This is the harsh reality regardless of whether they are domestic workers in the unorganized sector or highly paid executives in an urban setting.

In India no legislation regarding this existed until the case of ***Vishaka Vs. the State of Rajasthan.***[6] In the Vishaka case the Supreme Court laid down guidelines regarding sexual harassment at the workplace. Post the Vishaka case a Bill for the prevention of sexual harassment at the workplace developed over the years – Protection of Women against Sexual Harassment at Workplace Bill; from the year 2000 to 2010 there have been 9 different attempts by different drafting committees. In 2012, the final Bill on the subject, The Sexual Harassment of Women at Workplace (Prevention,

6 (1997) 6 SCC 241 : 1997 AIR SC 3043

Prohibition and Redressal) Bill drafted by the Women and Child Development (WCD) Ministry was proposed and was passed by both houses in 2013. The Sexual Harassment of Women at Workplace (Prevention, Prohibition and Redressal) Act came into force on the 9th of December 2013.

In the Indian context the position on sexual harassment at the workplace as introduced through the multiple Bills on the matter, and finally the Sexual Harassment of Women at Workplace (Prevention, Prohibition and Redressal) Act 2013, post the Vishaka case is about the same as mentioned above keeping with the ILO guidelines; in fact touching and extreme behaviour amounts to attempted rape or rape.

The current position in India with regards to sexual harassment at the workplace as under the Act of 2013 is a more improved version of the guidelines laid down in the Vishaka case. The Act defines sexual harassment, and not only provides a mechanism for redressal of complaints, but also allows for safeguards against malicious complaints. It defines "aggrieved woman" to include all women, regardless of their age or area/ sector of employment. It includes public servants to domestic workers. Unlike the guidelines set up in Vishaka it also includes workers that are not employed under a traditional office set up where the lines between employer and employee are not very clearly drawn. It includes any place that an employee may visit in the course of her employment, inclusive of transportation. It makes a mandatory provision for an Internal Complaints Committee, where there are any more than 10 workers at an office or branch. This committee is required to complete any inquiry regarding a sexual harassment complaint within 90 days and send a report regarding the same to the employer as well as the District Officer, who on receipt of the report are to take requisite action within 60 days. The District Officer if he deems appropriate can make provision for a Local Complaints committee at district as well as block level. These Committees have the powers of a Civil Court in terms of evidence gathering, and are also required to provide conciliatory assistance before inquiry proceedings if so requested by the complainant. The Act also has penal provisions in terms of the employer. A failure to comply with the provisions of the Act will result in a fine up to Rs.50000, which can be increased in the case of repeat offences. Also repeat offences can result in termination of licence or registration to conduct business.

9.3 National Commission for Women

In January 1992, the National Commission for Women was set up by Act of Parliament with the specific mandate to study and monitor all matters relating to the constitutional and legal safeguards provided for women, review the existing legislation, to suggest amendments wherever necessary, and safeguards the rights and entitlements of women. The Commission extends financial support to NGOs and educational institutions to conduct legal awareness programme to enable women to become aware of their rights. The National Commission has also made suggestion for various amendments to the IPC, Cr PC and Evidence Act.

9.4 The National Plan of Action for Girl Child (1991-2000)

The Plan of Action is to ensure survival, protection and development of the girl child with the ultimate objective of building up a better future for the girl child.

9.5 National Policy for the Empowerment of Women, 2001

The principle of gender equality is enshrined in the Indian Constitution in its Preamble, Fundamental Rights, Fundamental Duties and Directive Principles. The Constitution not only grants equality to women, but also empowers the State to adopt measures of positive discrimination in favour of women.

Within the framework of a democratic polity, our laws, development policies, Plans and programmes have aimed at women's advancement in different spheres. From the Fifth Five Year Plan (1974-78) onwards has been a marked shift in the approach to women's issues from welfare to development. In recent years, the empowerment of women has been recognized as the central issue in determining the status of women. The National Commission for Women was set up by an Act of Parliament in 1990 to safeguard the rights and legal entitlements of women. The 73rd and 74th Amendments (1993) to the Constitution of India have provided for reservation of seats in the local bodies of panchayats and Municipalities for women, laying a strong foundation for their participation in decision making at the local levels.

India has also ratified various international conventions and human rights instruments committing to secure equal rights of women. Key among them is the ratification of the Convention on Elimination of All Forms of Discrimination Against Women (CEDAW) in 1993.

The Mexico Plan of Action (1975), the Nairobi Forward Looking Strategies (1985), the Beijing Declaration as well as the Platform for Action (1995) and the Outcome Document adopted by the UNGA Session on Gender Equality and Development & Peace for the 21st century, titled "Further actions and initiatives to implement the Beijing Declaration and the Platform for Action" have been unreservedly endorsed by India for appropriate follow up.

The Policy also takes note of the commitments of the Ninth Five Year Plan and the other Sectoral Policies relating to empowerment of Women.

The women's movement and a wide-spread network of non-Government Organisations which have strong grass-roots presence and deep insight into women's concerns have contributed in inspiring initiatives for the empowerment of women.

However, there still exists a wide gap between the goals enunciated in the Constitution, legislation, policies, plans, programmes, and related mechanisms on the one hand and the situational reality of the status of women in India, on the other. This has been analyzed extensively in the Report of the Committee on the Status of Women in India, 'Towards Equality', 1974 and highlighted in the National Perspective Plan for Women, 1988-2000, the Shramshakti Report, 1988 and the Platform for Action, Five Years After- An assessment.

Gender disparity manifests itself in various forms, the most obvious being the trend of continuously declining female ratio in the population in the last few decades. Social stereotyping and violence at the domestic and societal levels are some of the other manifestations. Discrimination against girl children, adolescent girls and women persists in parts of the country.

The underlying causes of gender inequality are related to social and economic structure, which is based on informal and formal norms, and practices.

India has also ratified various international conventions including the convention on Elimination of all Forms of Discrimination against Women (CEDAW) in 1993.

Consequently, the access of women particularly those belonging to weaker sections including Scheduled Castes/ Scheduled Tribes/ Other backward Classes and minorities, majority of whom are in the rural areas and in the informal, unorganized sector – to education, health and productive resources, among others, is inadequate. Therefore, they remain largely marginalized, poor and socially excluded.

❑❑❑

CHAPTER

10 Human Rights and Women in India

10.1 Introduction

In its 1994 statement to the United Nations Human Rights Commission, the Government of India recognized the diversity of women in Indian society, *"It is not easy to talk in general terms about the socio-economic or legal status of women in India because women cut across a number of socio-economic, cultural and religious groups in the country and enjoy status depending upon the section or group to which these women belong. We, therefore, have women who are highly educated, well trained, commanding respect in society and occupying positions of authority. At the other end of the spectrum we have women who are illiterate and poor."*[1]

Seventy-five per cent of Indian women live in rural areas.[2] There are differences between the lives of rural women and urban women. For example, women's literacy in rural areas is approximately 25 per cent[3], whereas in urban regions it is approximately 54 per cent.[4] India exhibits strong regional differences, as well as divisions formed by the deeply entrenched caste system.[5] Economic divisions also exist: 40 per cent of the inhabitants of urban areas and 51 per cent

1 Permanent Mission of India 28 Feb. 1994, 1; see also CJWL 1993, 280, 283
2 CJWL 1993, 280
3 IPS 30 Sept. 1992
4 Bose Jan. 1992, 28
5 Country Reports 1992 1993, 1144

of the inhabitants of rural areas live below the poverty line, and, while poverty is not restricted to the women of India, there is evidence that it has a disproportionate effect on them due to their inferior socio-economic status and the division of labour based on gender.[6]

10.2 Legal Rights

The human rights of women is not made in a day throughout the globe, rather it is gradual development of social structure and thought in the society. Following are some of the important documents or global activities through which the human rights of women developed globally including India:

10.2.1 International Obligations

India has ratified the International Covenant on Economic, Social and Cultural Rights,[7] the International Covenant on Civil and Political Rights,[8] the Convention for the Suppression of the Traffic in Persons, the Convention on the Exploitation of the Prostitution of Others, the International Labour Organization Convention No. 100 on Equal Remuneration and the Convention on the Political Rights of Women.[9]

India has also ratified the Convention on the Elimination of All Forms of Discrimination against Women.[10] The government made at least one reservation to the convention by way of a declaration, stating it will not interfere in the "personal affairs" of any community without that community's initiative or consent.[11] This has been interpreted by at least one source as an indication that the government is unwilling to change the religion-specific personal laws that discriminate against women in such areas as marriage, divorce and inheritance (ibid.).

6 ibid., 1134
7 1979
8 1979
9 Johnston 3 Jan. 1994, 3; HRLJ 1 Jan. 1993, 64, 67, 70
10 Johnston 3 Jan. 1994, 3
11 CJTL 1990, 486

10.2.2 The Constitution

The constitution of India, which came into effect in 1949, contains a provision on fundamental rights for all citizens. Article 14 provides that "the State shall not deny to any person equality before the law or the equal protection of the laws within the territory of India".[12] Article 15(1) prohibits state discrimination based on the grounds of religion, race, caste, sex or place of birth, and Article 15(2) adds that no one is to be denied access to public and state-funded services and facilities. Article 15(3) states that the government may make special provision for women and children.[13]

10.2.3 The Indian Penal Code

Indian criminal law is set out in the Indian Penal Code. The penal code addresses crimes against women in several sections and deals with such things as voluntarily causing a miscarriage for reasons other than the health of the woman (s. 312); assaulting a woman with the intent of outrag[ing] her modesty (s. 354); enticing a minor out of the keeping of the lawful guardian (s. 361); abducting a woman and compelling her to marry or forcing or seducing her to engage in illicit intercourse (s. 366); exporting girls under 18 (s. 366a) and importing girls under 21 (s. 366b) for the purposes of prostitution; dealing in slaves (s. 370) and selling or buying a minor for the purposes of prostitution, including the dedication of girls as Devadasi [Devadasi is a religious practice in which young girls are dedicated to the service of a goddess. Their "service" takes the form of prostitution.[14]

The penal code has a section on offences relating to marriage. These offences include deceiving a woman to believe she is married and then cohabiting with her (s. 493), committing bigamy (s. 494) and committing adultery with a married woman (s. 497). An adulterous married woman is not punished as an abettor (s. 497). Section 498(a) of the

12 Article 14 of the Indian Constitution
13 Ibid
14 Women Magazine July 1993, 64

penal code makes it a crime for a husband or his relatives to act in such a way as to drive his spouse to commit suicide or to cause her harm or injury. The crime carries a punishment of up to three years imprisonment and a fine.

The penal code also addresses rape (see section 4.5) and domestic violence (see section 4.1).

Other Legislation

Other legislation addressing women's rights includes the Equal Remuneration Act 1976, the Maternity Benefits Act 1961, the Medical Termination of Pregnancy Act 1971 and certain provisions of the Hindu Marriage Act 1955. These acts are dealt with elsewhere under sub-sections 3.5, 3.6, and 4.3.

Although the legislation cited above is intended to protect women's rights, critics note that it does not affect the majority of Indian women.[15] Country Reports 1993, states that the laws are not always enforced, especially in rural areas, due to social and religious practices.[16] One report states that laws prohibiting violence against women, although strong, are "widely ignored".[17]

10.3 Status of Women

A number of sources indicate that women generally occupy a lower social status than men in India.[18] In traditional Hindu law, the son is the "sole object of worship" and the daughter is to be "despised and detested" according to one report *"much of the law fails under the weight of 3,000 years of celebrating sons and despising daughters."*[19]

There is a marked preference for boy children.[20] One of the reasons given for this preference is that *"... a girl is paraya dhan (some one else's wealth)"* as she, and everything

15 BCTWLJ 1993, 64; CJWL 1993, 290, 293
16 Country Reports 1993 1994, 1350
17 Dallas Morning News 7 Mar. 1993, 6
18 The Toronto Star 4 Feb. 1993, A17; Liddle and Joshi 1986, 177-185; BCTWLJ 1993, 63;
19 Dallas Morning News 7 Mar. 1993, 2
20 NPR 11 Sept. 1994; The New York Times 27 Aug. 1994; WIN News Summer 1993, 61; Kelkar 1992, 81

invested in her training or education, is lost when she moves to her husband's home upon marriage.[21] According to one author, this attitude plays a large role in the treatment of female children.[22]

10.3.1 Casteism

The caste system, which is over 2,000 years old, is integral to Indian social and cultural relations. It is a part not only of Hindu society but of Muslim, Sikh and Christian societies as well. Within the four principal castes (Brahmin, Kshatriya, Vaishaya and Sudra) there are thousands of sub-castes, which differ from region to region.[23]

One group, formerly referred to as "untouchables" or "outcasts" is considered to be "beyond the pale of the caste system".[24] These terms are seldom used now and members of this group, who make up 15 per cent of the population,[25] are commonly referred to as scheduled castes as the concept of untouchability was banned in Article 17 of the constitution and in the Untouchability (Offenses) Act 1955.[26] They are also called harijans or Dalits, although Dalits refers to an economic category and is not exclusive to scheduled castes. Along with the "levelling effects of urbanization, industrialization, education and the numerical superiority of the lower castes at the polls," the legislation on untouchability has, according to one source, contributed to a less rigid social climate.[27] Country Reports 1993 states, however, that untouchability "remains very much a part of life in India."[28] According to Women Magazine, Dalit women face double discrimination because of their gender and caste.[29]

The caste system comprises a hierarchy of values with the higher castes generally considered to be the most pure.

21 Widows, Abandoned and Destitute Women 1989, 4
22 Ibid
23 MRG 1982, 4; Liddle and Joshi 1986, 58
24 ibid
25 Encyclopedia of the Third World 1992, 811
26 MRG 1982, 7
27 Encyclopedia of the Third World 1992, 811
28 Country Reports 1993 1994, 1351
29 Women Magazine July 1993, 63

Economic power alone is not enough to move up in the caste hierarchy; a group must also emulate the signs of purity of the highest castes, one of which is tight constraints on women.[30] These constraints take various forms such as the tradition of purdah (the veiling and seclusion of women), arranged marriages, prohibitions on divorce, sati (widow burning) and the removal of women from public life, including the workforce.

The tradition of purdah is practised by both Muslim and Hindu communities.[31] The purdah tradition is much stronger in the north (ibid.). One study found that in the northern state of Uttar Pradesh, 45 per cent of the women were veiled, in comparison to 5 per cent in the southern state of Tamil Nadu. It also found that women were more socially active in Tamil Nadu than in Uttar Pradesh.[32]Tensions between castes often erupt in violent clashes[33]. According to sources, much of the violence is directed at the lower castes by the higher castes.[34]), and reports of rapes and murders of lower-caste women have increased.[35] In January 1994, a harijan woman was stripped and paraded naked in the street of a village in Uttar Pradesh; no one intervened. The state government compensated her and suspended the local police inspector after the incident was reported in the media and aroused a public outcry. This was the third such incident within a month.[36] In 1988, during a raid on a Bihar village, some policemen took part in a mass rape of lower caste women.[37] The accused were later acquitted because, according to defence council, the women were engaged in menial jobs and therefore of questionable character. For this reason, according to reports, their testimony was not considered to be believable. Agricultural labourers are reportedly often

30 ibid
31 Ibid,
32 Basu 1992, 60-62
33 UPI 10 Feb. 1994; International Herald Tribune 18 Feb. 1994: see also Asia Watch 20 Sept. 1992
34 Encyclopedia of the Third World 1992, 815
35 Kelkar 1992, 80; International Herald Tribune 18 Feb. 1994
36 ibid
37 Kelkar 1992, 80

victims of the upper-caste landowners who use mass rapes to repress the poor, landless castes .

10.3.2 Women in the Workforce

The Constitution of India contains a number of provisions of benefit to women in the workplace. Article 16 (1) of the constitution prohibits sex discrimination in matters relating to employment or appointment to government jobs, while article 39(d) supports the principle of equal pay for equal work.[38] Article 42 makes clear the state's obligation to *"make provision for securing just and humane conditions of work and for maternity relief."*[39].

Two pieces of legislation that directly address the situation of women in the workforce are the 1961 Maternity Benefit Act and the Equal Remuneration Act, 1976.[40] The Maternity Benefit Act prohibits employers from requiring that women work while pregnant and requires that they provide 12 weeks paid maternity leave and breaks for working mothers to nurse their children. The Equal Remuneration Act, 1976 and Equal Remuneration (Amendment) Act 1987 not only oblige an employer to pay men and women equally for the same work or "work of a similar nature," but also prohibit discriminatory practices in hiring, training and promotions;[41]. The Domestic Workers Service Bill of 1990 sets maximum limits for hours of work and stipulates minimum wages for domestic workers.[42]

Since the early twentieth century the participation of women in the paid workforce has been declining, both in absolute numbers and as a percentage of the total labour force.[43] Between 1911 and 1971 the percentage of women in the organized labour force declined from 34.4 per cent to 17.3 per cent.[44] This trend has accelerated in recent years as employers in the unionized industrial sector have pursued

38 Blaustein Oct. 1990, 49, 62
39 Ibid,
40 CJWL 1993, 291-92
41 Human Rights in Developing Countries Yearbook 1991 1991, 182
42 WIN News Autumn 1990b, 58
43 Calman 1992, 58; Manushi July-Aug. 1991, 11
44 ibid

a deliberate policy of reducing their reliance on organized labour.[45] Census figures indicate that by 1981 only 6 per cent of the female labour force was employed in the organized sector.[46] More recent statistics are not available among the sources consulted by DIRB. As women workers are generally the first to be terminated,[47] women have become increasingly reliant on employment in the unorganized sector, where wages are lower than in industry and workers are largely outside the reach of most legislation designed to protect them from unsafe working conditions.[48] Although legislation protecting women in the organized sector does exist, Leslie Calman, director of the Barnard Center for Research on Women, describes it as "nearly useless." Minimum wage laws are often ignored by employers, and poverty, illiteracy and the casual nature of employment further contributes to the problem.

One example of the economic exploitation of women workers in the industrial sector can be found in the match and fireworks factories of Tamil Nadu state. The work is dangerous, the pay low and the factories are non-union and staffed almost exclusively with girls and women. In 1993, the Tamil Nadu government began a five-year project to eliminate child labour in the match and fireworks industries. The DIRB has no information on the progress of this project at the time of writing.

Family-run businesses and cottage-industries, in which the majority of workers are women and children, are exempt from much of the labour standards legislation.[49] The contractual system allows many industries to evade the requirements of the Factories Act, Minimum Wages Act and Child Labour Act, while subcontracting, by keeping the number of full-time workers to a minimum, enables employers to hide the true size of their enterprises.[50]Gathia indicates

45 ibid
46 Calman 1992, 58
47 Manushi July-Aug. 1991, 11
48 Calman 1992, 59
49 Gathia 1990b, 197, 199; Encyclopedia of the Third World 1992, 826
50 Gathia 1990, 197

that the participation rate in home-based industries is higher for girls than for boys, with more boys than girls attending school (ibid., 199). He also points out that women and girls are seen as *"fit to do only the most routine and unskilled low-paid jobs,"* are invariably employed in piece-work and are more often exposed to hazardous working conditions than are boys.[51]

A United Nations study entitled Women's Education and Fertility Behaviour found that Indian women's economic activity decreases as they become more educated, suggesting that, at least for women, there is a greater correlation between poverty and workforce participation than between education and workforce participation (United Nations 1993b, 10). The study did note that there was an upswing in women's participation in the workforce at the top levels of education, which was mainly due to their participation in non-agricultural activities.[52] One report indicates that new employment opportunities are more readily available for middle-class women than for unskilled or semi-skilled workers.[53] Women's employment in transport, communications and financial services has increased as these sectors have grown, but workers in these fields comprise only a fraction of the total workforce.[54]

10.3.3 Women in Political Life

Women were granted the right to vote in 1950.[55] Their representation in government is approximately ten per cent in the Council of States (Rajya Sabha or upper house) and approximately seven per cent in the House of the People (Lok Sabha or lower house).[56] Despite their low numbers in government, women have been highly visible participants in Indian politics although some sources point out that women politicians are frequently not representative of Indian women

51 Ibid
52 ibid.; see also Liddle and Joshi 1986, 72-73
53 Manushi July-Aug. 1991, 10
54 Ibid
55 United Nations 1991, 416
56 Inter-Parliamentary Union 1991, 98-99; see also UNDP 1992, 145

as a whole.[57] A May 1993 study on women parliamentarians concluded that "not many women from the grass-roots level are coming up to the National Legislature".[58] Vibhuti Patel, in an article in Women in Action,[59] writes that most women wanting to enter politics face opposition from family, community and male political leaders. According to her, "the present political leadership, in spite of its populist rhetorics, wants to keep women out of the political scene. Women politicians are still looked upon as appendages to the males in the political arena".[60]

Patel notes that many women politicians are from the "elite" and that their "political presence" derives from male relatives also involved in politics.[61] A number of other sources also indicate that the women who are elected to office are often relatives of prominent politicians, past and present.[62] The result, according to some observers, is that the interests of women are not well represented. Women's groups complain that the issues they raise are appropriated by the parties only when they are politically expedient (IPS 19 Nov. 1993). The May 1993 study on women parliamentarians found that within political parties there is a "marked non-involvement" of women in the decision-making bodies and that women's issues tend to be considered as social rather than political issues.[63]

Women in rural areas in particular "play only marginal roles in politics," according to one report.[64] Until recently, men had a monopoly over village councils, or panchayats, and over decision-making in practically every part of the country.[65] Members of the panchayats are now elected, and 30 per cent of the seats are reserved for women. Ratna Kapur, a

57 CSR Newsletter Sept. 1993, 7; Women in Action 1994, 15
58 CSR Newsletter Sept. 1993, 7
59 published by ISIS, an international women's rights organization which coordinates the International Feminist Network
60 ibid.,
61 ibid.,
62 CSR Newsletter Sept. 1993, 7; IPS 19 Nov. 1993; The Economist 17 Dec. 1993, 82; Calman 1992, 61
63 Ibid
64 IPS 19 Nov. 1993
65 India Today 15 Apr. 1993, 52

feminist lawyer in New Delhi, notes that men on the councils have not always been representative of the community and points out that, as such is also the case with the new female members, reserving seats for women may not make much difference .

10.3.4 Education Issues

Section 45 of the Constitution requires the Indian government to undertake a programme of compulsory education for everyone up to the age of fourteen. Tamil Nadu is the only Indian state that has indicated it will introduce legislation to enforce this requirement. The state has, however, passed a bill that imposes a fine on parents who do not send their children under 14 to school.

India's 1991 census report showed the female literacy rate to be 40 per cent,[66] with considerable differences between regions.[67] For example, in Kerala the female literacy rate is reportedly between 70 and 80 per cent.[68] In Rajasthan, Uttar Pradesh, Madhya Pradesh and Bihar, whose populations together account for 40 per cent of India's total population, the female literacy rate is reported to be below 30 per cent. Generally, literacy is highest among Brahmins, Christians, Parsis and Jains, and is higher in the south than in the north.[69]

Overall, females in India receive less education than males[70]. In Tamil Nadu, for example, it is reported that 70 per cent of the boys go to school while 80 per cent of the girls work full time.[71] The UNDP reports that in 1990 Indian female children received approximately one-third the schooling of male children.[72] The Ministry of Education, cited in a report by A. B. Bose, indicates that there has been a drastic improvement in enrolment figures since mid-century,

66 IPS 30 Sept. 1992; Xinhua 4 Nov. 1993
67 Bose Jan. 1992, 28
68 Kapur 1991, 10; The Globe and Mail 20 Nov. 1993b, D-1
69 Encyclopedia of the Third World 1992, 831; see also Gathia 1990a, 9
70 United Nations 1993b, 7
71 The Globe and Mail 20 Nov. 1993b, D-1; Child Asia 1993a, 9
72 UNDP 1992, 145; see also The Toronto Star 4 Feb. 1993, A17

both in absolute numbers and the percentage of children in school.[73] The ratios for girls remain lower than those for boys, however.

Girls in rural areas are much less likely to go to school than those in urban areas.[74] The 1981 census showed that female literacy in rural areas was approximately 18 per cent compared to 48 per cent in urban areas; these figures had risen to 25 and 54 per cent by the time of the 1991 census.[75] Dropout rates for both boys and girls are high, especially in the high schools. The rates for girls at the lower levels, however, are reportedly higher and increase as a girl approaches puberty; primary school enrolment of girls as a percentage of that of boys was 97 for 1988-89 but dropped to 45 per cent for tertiary enrolment.[76] One reason advanced for the drop in attendance is that, once a girl reaches puberty, she is often restricted by custom to her home and is expected to marry.[77] Higher education is usually available only for girls from the upper and middle classes, most of who are from urban areas.

10.3.5 Health Issues

The preference for male children has an impact on female health. Parents often give nutritional and health care priority to male children.[78] Girls receive less breast milk, are weaned earlier, are given less food and receive medical services less frequently. In addition, there is a marked disparity between male and female infant mortality rates.

Another factor contributing to women's poor health is the tradition of early marriages, and subsequent early and frequent childbirth and lactation.[79] The average fertility rate

73 Bose comments, however, that these figures are affected by over-reporting, under-age and over-age of children in a class, and grade repetition
74 Calman 1992, 62; The Globe and Mail 20 Nov. 1993, D-1
75 IPS 30 Sept. 1992; Bose Jan. 1992, 28
76 UNDP 1992, 145; Bose Jan. 1992, 32
77 Gathia 1990a, 10; The Toronto Star 4 Feb. 1993, A17
78 NPR 11 Sept. 1994; The New York Times 27 Aug. 1994; Country Reports 1993 1994, 1351; Gathia 1990a, 7
79 Calman 1992, 61; The Globe and Mail 3 Mar. 1994

in 1990 was 3.8 children per woman.[80] Because they are often malnourished, women are at risk of dying in childbirth. The national maternal mortality rate in India in 1988 was 550 per 100,000. The average rate for all developing countries was 420 per 100,000 and for industrial countries, 26 per 100,000. A United Nations study on abortion policies notes that the high number of unsafe abortions in India contributes to the high rates of maternal..

Prior to 1977 the Indian government had a strict three-child policy that included mandatory sterilization after the third child.[81] Although all elements of compulsion have been removed, the government continues to promote two-child families by means of incentives and direct support for contraceptive use. Nevertheless, contraceptive use is apparently not widespread. The Medical Termination of Pregnancy Act 1971, which significantly liberalized abortion laws in India, was meant to reduce the number of illegal abortions. Studies show, however, that while educated, urban, middle-class families use the approved facilities, the majority of abortions performed remain illegal and unregistered. It is estimated that there are between two and six million illegal abortions per year, compared to approximately one million abortions in approved facilities.

10.3.6 Personal Laws

Although all Indians are governed by national criminal law, some private matters, such as marriage, divorce and property, are covered by their respective religious laws. Hindus comprise the majority of the population of India (78.8 per cent), followed by Muslims (11.6 per cent), Christians (3.9 per cent), Sikhs (2 per cent), Buddhists (0.8 per cent), Jainists (0.5 per cent), Parsis and Jews. The aboriginal inhabitants of the country make up three per cent of the population.[82] Country Reports 1992 states that “the family, marriage and inheritance laws of several of India’s religious communities

80 Encyclopedia of the Third World 1992, 809
81 Encyclopedia of the Third World 1992, 810
82 Encyclopedia of the Third World 1992, 810-811

manifest legally sanctioned gender discrimination"[83]; Country Reports 1993 1994, 351). There have been legal challenges to some of the personal laws, especially those provisions addressing property, based on the constitutional guarantee of equality, but reportedly the courts have been reluctant to apply the constitution in domestic economic matters. In the early 1980s the concept of public interest litigation was introduced.[84] According to Manushi, a women's newsletter published in New Delhi, while human rights advocates were enthusiastic about pursuing several cases dealing with gender equality and property and inheritance rights, the results were disappointing. For women in the lower economic classes, basic necessities and survival come before family law matters (ibid.).

10.3.6.1 Marriage

Each religious community in India has a set of rules governing the formalities and procedures that constitute marriage in that community. As it is not within the scope of this paper to detail these formalities, this section primarily indicates which legislation, if any, regulates marriage for each community.

Marriage for Hindus, Buddhists, Jains and Sikhs is covered by the Hindu Marriage Act 1955 and the Hindu Adoptions and Maintenance Act 1956. The latter requires a husband to maintain his wife (section 18). If her husband is bigamous or guilty of desertion, has treated her so cruelly that she fears harm if she were to stay with him, suffers from leprosy, keeps a concubine in the house or has ceased to be Hindu, a wife may receive maintenance while living apart from her husband (section 18(2)). Section 18(3) removes the right to maintenance if the wife has been unchaste or ceases to be Hindu. Muslim personal law is not codified in India; marriage and property laws are prescribed by the Koran and Shariah law. Divorce for Muslims, however, is covered by the Dissolution of Muslim Marriages Act 1939.

83 Country Reports 1992 1993, 1144; see also Calman 1992, 53; BCTWLJ 1993, 67
84 CJWL 1993, 288-289

The procedures and formalities for marriage for Christian Indians are covered by the Indian Christian Marriage Act 1872. The Indian government enacted the Special Marriage Act in 1954 to provide an option for those not wishing to be married under one of the religious acts.

Shortly after independence the Hindu Code, which was originally meant to reform all aspects of personal law, such as marriage and inheritance, and included provisions for sexual equality, was passed.[85] The controversy surrounding its adoption during the first post-independence election resulted in the least controversial parts of the bill being passed and those relating to personal laws being left aside to a certain extent (ibid.). Joanna Liddle and Rama Joshi note that, although the constitution and Hindu Code addressed some aspects of discrimination, *"it was in precisely the area which characterises [sic] women's subordination, the very feature which distinguishes gender oppression from other forms, namely in personal, domestic, sexual and family relations, that the men resisted conceding their privilege"*[86]

According to Leslie Calman, marriage is considered a social necessity for women of all religions and regions in India. An article in Manushi points out that it is quite unusual for a woman to remain unmarried[87] as the sexes are not encouraged to mix prior to marriage.[88] In the south, intra-village or intra-family marriages are encouraged in order to strengthen existing family networks, while the northern communities encourage marriage outside the community to expand the family network. The result of these traditions is that women in the north have little contact with their natal families, whereas in the south they tend to have greater access to their family of birth. Calman states that the patri-local system, whereby a daughter leaves her natal home to live with her husband's family, is characterized by the subordination of the bride to men and to older women. The

85 Liddle and Joshi 1986, 36-38
86 Ibid
87 Press Association News file 5 May 1994, 6
88 Kumari 1989, 15; Calman 1992, 55, 124

bride finds herself at the bottom of the power structure and is expected to be submissive.[89] According to many sources, the dowry tradition continues to be a prevalent and integral part of marriage in Indian society.[90]

10.3.6.2 Divorce

Divorce is available to all Indian citizens but the form of, and procedure for, the divorce depend on the personal law applicable to the individual. Under the Hindu Marriage Act the parties have the right to dissolve the marriage according to their custom. Under Muslim law, extra-judicial divorces are permitted. The marriage may be dissolved by the husband at his will (by talaq) or by mutual consent.[91] The Dissolution of Muslim Marriages Act 1939 permits a woman to apply to the courts on her own for a divorce decree.[92]

The Indian Divorce Act 1969 governs Christian marriages and permits any husband to present a petition to the court to dissolve his marriage on the basis of adultery. Under the act a woman may petition the court for a divorce on one or more of several grounds, including bigamy and rape. The divorce law applying to secular marriages is included in the Special Marriage Act and provides for the possibility of divorce by mutual consent as well as by a petition presented to the court.[93]

Despite these legal provisions, divorce remains socially unacceptable for women.[94] A divorced woman is often ostracized by her community and even her family,[95] in part because of the high value society places on female chastity. Calman notes that a single woman may find it difficult to acquire housing. Divorce may also not be a realistic option,

89 ibid.; see also Kumari 1989, 15
90 FEER 28 Oct. 1993; India Today 15 Apr. 1993, 52; Country Reports 1993 1994, 1350
91 Ibid
92 Indian Legal Documents, 8 Sept. 1987, 18
93 Ibid
94 BCTWLJ 1993, 75
95 CJTL 1990, 474, 482; ILHR Mar. 1991, 7; Widows, Abandoned and Destitute Women 1989, 43

according to Gita Gopal, due to the economic dependence of women on their husbands.[96]

Under the Hindu Marriage Act (section 24) and the Hindu Adoptions and Maintenance Act (section 18) either spouse has the right to request maintenance.[97] Before granting a maintenance order, however, the court must inquire into the woman's chastity. Muslim law requires that, upon divorce, the husband pay back the wife her meher (dowry). A Christian woman is entitled to maintenance of up to one-fifth of her husband's net income during the divorce proceedings and unlimited permanent maintenance following the divorce.[98]

Section 125 of the Code of Criminal Procedure requires that all divorced husbands support destitute ex-wives. A controversy arose when a Muslim woman named Shah Bano sued her ex-husband for support under this section.[99] The court consulted Muslim personal law and ruled that section 125 should apply to Muslims. Muslim religious leaders protested that the court was overstepping its boundaries by interpreting Muslim law

The Muslim Women (Protection of Rights on Divorce) Act was passed in 1986 under pressure from Muslim leaders, including demonstrations and the defeat of several government candidates in national elections, during and after the ***Shah Bano Case***[100] decision. This act is seen to effectively exempt all Muslims from the requirement of section 125 of the Code of Criminal Procedure. It has been denounced by one author as a *"triumph of religious rights over women's rights in India"*. Calman asserts that it constitutes *"a step away from the equal treatment of women under the law"*.[101] The act fails to provide for the return of property owned by the wife and may require that her family support her after the iddat period.[102] According to Anika Rahman, writing in the Columbia Journal

96 BCTWLJ 1993, 75
97 Calman 1992, 153
98 CJWL 1993, 287-288; Calman 1992, 153
99 For further details, see the following: Engineer, Ashghar Ali. 1987. The Shah Bano Controversy. Bombay: Orient Longman.
100 AIR 1985 SC 945
101 Calman 1992, 161
102 A three month period during which she cannot remarry

of Transnational Law, it is unlikely that she would receive this support.[103] Rahman further states that although the act provides for institutional support, it is equally unlikely to be given to a divorced woman. She also criticizes the act for not promoting a divorced woman's self-sufficiency but rather encouraging dependence.[104]

With respect to custody of children, the Hindu Minority and Guardianship Act 1956 declares the mother to be the legal guardian of a child until the child's fifth birthday at which time the father becomes the guardian. Under the Hindu Marriage Act 1955, a court may make orders concerning custody. In Muslim law, a mother has custody of a male child until he reaches seven years of age and of a female child until she reaches puberty. If the mother remarries, however, custody of all children reverts to the father (ibid., 24).

10.3.6.3 Property

Property is also governed by the religious laws of each community. The Hindu Succession Act grants equal inheritance rights to Hindu women[105]. However, according to Country Reports 1993, in practice married daughters rarely inherit a share of their parents' property. The most prevalent system of property control (co-parcenary) is an arrangement which, according to one source, creates an inequality of access to property for women.[106]

According to several reports, in late July 1994 the *"wealthiest and most progressive state"*, Maharashtra, amended the Hindu Succession Act 1966 to *"enable a daughter to inherit property in the same manner as a son"*.[107] A government spokesman said the law was intended to *"help tackle gender bias and the practice of dowry"* . There is no mention in the reports of changes to the inheritance rights of widows.

103 CJTL 1990, 481 n.1
104 Ibid
105 Country Reports 1993 1994, 1351
106 BCTWLJ 1993, 80-88
107 The Gazette 22 Aug. 1994; Chicago Tribune 14 Aug. 1994; The Washington Times 6 August 1994; AP 1 Aug. 1994

Wives are reported to have little or no control over their husbands' property.[108] Under the Hindu Succession Act, which tried to make some provision for women, when a Hindu male dies intestate the surviving widow, sons, daughters and mother all take one share; however, the sons receive this share in addition to the share that they acquire at the time of their birth. As well, daughters have no right to partition the family home until the male heirs decide to divide their shares. Muslim personal law specifies that a daughter should receive half of a son's share of the parental property.[109]

10.4 Domestic Violence

10.4.1 Spousal Abuse

According to the report written by the voluntary organization Integrated Human Development Services Foundation (IHDSF) on a conference entitled "National Workshop on Family Violence Against Females", held in New Delhi in 1988, wife beating is widespread in India.[110] It is said to be the most common but least reported crime,[111] cutting across all castes, classes, religions and education level[112] Author Rubia Bhuiyan notes that women are often reluctant to report battering to the authorities since they risk being thrown out of their homes and accused of adultery.

The majority of the women who went to the Bombay Women's Centre, a women's shelter, between April 1990 and April 1991, had been abused and sometimes brutally beaten by their husbands or in-laws.[113] Others had been thrown out of their marital homes, deserted by their husbands, or harassed by their husband and in-laws, or they had left because their husbands had committed bigamy or had extra-marital affairs.

108 BCTWLJ 1993, 73; see also Country Reports 1992 1993, 1144
109 Country Reports 1993 1994, 1351
110 IHDSF 15-18 Feb. 1988, 20
111 Lawyers Collective Apr. 1991, 4
112 IHSDF 15-18 Feb. 1988, 20; Bhuiyan 1991, 36
113 Manushi Jan.-Feb. 1992, 19; see also IHDSF 15-18 Feb. 1988, 19

10.4.2 Dowry Violence

The government officially banned dowry in 1961 with the Dowry Prohibition Act, but this law proved ineffective.[114] In fact, the practice is reported to be on the increase.[115] The director general of the Anthropological Survey of India, K.S. Singh, in his report on an eight-year study of Indian habits and customs, indicates that 40 per cent of the 4,635 communities in the study believed in dowry giving. While it was formerly the practice only among Brahmins, dowry giving has spread to all castes as well as other religions.[116]

The pressure to provide a dowry is keenly felt by families. Female foeticide and infanticide are said to occur in part because families consider girl children to be poor investments.[117]

The Dowry Prohibition Act was amended in 1984 [The Dowry Prohibition (Amendment) Act of 1984 was strongly criticized by women's groups and in the media.. The 1986 amendments reverse the burden of proving that there was no demand for dowry to the person accused of taking or abetting the taking of dowry.[118]

The 1993 census indicates that approximately 5,000 dowry-related deaths, including suicides, were reported in eight states and the capital. The highest number were recorded in Uttar Pradesh (1952), followed by Maharashtra (746), Andhra Pradesh (575), Madhya Pradesh (370), Bihar (336), Rajasthan (271), Karnataka (266) and Punjab (147). New Delhi reported 107 dowry-related deaths for that year (The Irish Times 30 May 1994; Press Association 5 May 1994). Official estimates are believed to under-report the actual number of cases, and numerous cases are dismissed

114 The New York Times 30 Dec. 1993; ILSA Journal of International Law 1992, 115-116; Calman 1992, 132

115 San Francisco Chronicle 7 Mar. 1995; Dallas Morning News 7 Mar. 1993, 3; The New York Times 30 Dec. 1993

116 FEER 28 Oct. 1993, 41; India Today 15 Apr. 1993, 52; Calman 1992, 56; Kumari 1989, 7-8

117 WIN News Autumn 1990a, 22; Calman 1992, 126v

118 ILSA Journal of International Law 1992, 115-116; Calman 1992, 132, 134-137

as attempted suicides or accidental deaths.[119] Many of the deaths are attributed to accidental burns caused by kerosene stove explosions or "mysterious kitchen fires".[120]

Critics suggest that there is tacit acceptance of the dowry system by the largely male-dominated establishment and accuse the police of deliberate inaction in dowry cases

The 1986 amendments to the Dowry Prohibition Act call for the appointment of regional dowry prohibition officers to investigate claims of dowry abuse. Another attempt to address the issue has been made by the Delhi Administration Directorate of Social Welfare, which set up a reconciliation-cum-guidance bureau and Anti-Dowry Cell to educate the public and to provide counselling and mediation services or legal assistance. The Anti-Dowry Cells are intended to provide a place for women who are victims of dowry violence to discuss their situation in private. The organization has, however, been described as "ineffective"; complaints reportedly remain unattended for too long and counselling lacks privacy and professional. According to Naina Kapur, some people have criticized the Anti-Dowry Cells for merely espousing "traditional family values" and counselling women to return to their husbands. She states that there are often complaints that the officers involved do not believe the women who approach them and will not file the case in the appropriate police records.[121]

10.4.3 Female Foeticide and Infanticide

There has been a steady decrease over the last century in the ratio of females to males in India.[122] In 1991 there were 927 females per 1,000 males, although the ratio varies widely among regions. For example, according to a 1988 article in India Today, among the Bhati people there are only 550 women to every 1,000 males.[123] Two reasons advanced for the

119 ILHR Mar. 1991, 5; Calman 1992, 127; ILSA Journal of International Law 1992, 113
120 ibid.; The New York Times 27 Aug. 1994; Kumari 1989, 2; Calman 1992, 127
121 Kapur 8 Aug. 1994
122 Country Reports 1993 1994, 1351; Human Rights in Developing Countries Yearbook 1991 1991, 183; ILSA Journal of International Law 1992, 111
123 Rhoodie 1989, 395

distorted sex ratios, both linked to the cultural preference for sons, are the practices of abortion of female foetuses (female foeticide) and female infanticide).

It is reported that amniocentesis tests are widely used to determine the sex of an unborn child, resulting in a disproportionate percentage of female foetus abortions. Sex-determination tests have been banned in Punjab, Maharashtra and Rajasthan.[124] A letter from the Embassy of India in the United States, printed in The Washington Times, states that the tests are also banned in Haryana. WIN News reported in 1990 that the results of a ban in Maharashtra had not been very successful and other reports state that many doctors in Bombay, the capital of Maharashtra, still perform the tests and the subsequent abortions.

The Pre-Natal Diagnostic Techniques (Regulation and Prevention of Misuse) Act was passed by parliament on 26 July 1994 and took effect in December 1994. The India-wide law provides for fines of about $US 320.00 and up to three years in prison for advertising gender determination tests or working in a testing centre. Only women over the age of 35 or those who have certificates stating there are medical reasons for the tests are permitted to have them; women who take the tests simply to determine the gender of the foetus can be prosecuted and fined or imprisoned.

One of the criticisms of the law is that it does not provide for the registration of ultrasound machines, many of which are put into vans and driven from village to village. Madhu Kishwar, the editor of Manushi and a professor of literature at the University of Delhi, does not believe the national law will be more effective than the state laws which were passed earlier: *"All you are doing with this new law is giving the police a new potential for extorting bribes ... from doctors"*[125] The director of policy research at Population Action International qualified her praise for the law by adding: *"It remains to be seen whether it can be enforced."*[126]

124 AP 23 May 1994; The Irish Times 30 May 1994; Country Reports 1993, 1144
125 Ibid
126 Chicago Tribune 11 Dec. 1994

Section 318 of the Indian Penal Code states that it is an offence to conceal the birth of a child by secretly disposing of the dead body, the penalty being a fine or imprisonment of up to two years or both. Annotations on this section by Ranchhoddas and Thakore note that this particular provision was intended to prevent infanticide.[127] Section 317 of the penal code also makes it an offence to expose or leave a child with the intention of wholly abandoning it. [128]

The governments of some states have tried to stop the practice of female infanticide, although an article in The Times claims that there is little political will to stop infanticide.. One programme in Tamil Nadu establishes a trust fund at the registration of a girl's birth. That fund, which comes to maturity when she reaches marrying age, is meant to be enough to pay for her dowry as the pressure to provide a dowry is said to be part of the reason for the practice of female foeticide and infanticide. The programme, however, requires that the mother be sterilized. As a result only 40 girls were registered in the first year of its operation. Some NGOs have been offering direct incentives, such as credit schemes, loans for sewing machines, dairy cows, and goats to women to keep their girl children alive for six months or longer. The programme managers believe that once a child is six months old the risk of it being killed is greatly reduced. Naina Kapur states that there are several women's organizations working on eliminating the practice.[129]

10.4.4 Child Brides

The Child Marriage Restraint (Amendment) Act was passed in 1976, making 18 the minimum age of marriage for women.[130] Country Reports 1993 notes, however, that enforcement of the act is "uneven". While one United Nations report indicates the national average of marriage is 18.7, The New York Times reports that child marriages are quite

127 Ranchhoddas and Thakore 1987, 197
128 Ibid
129 Kapur 8 Aug. 1994
130 Country Reports 1993 1994, 1351

common. It quotes an Indian columnist who says, *"90 percent of girls in villages get married before 13"*. The United Nations also indicates that there continue to be cases of girls married at very young ages, particularly in rural areas.

Child marriages are reportedly most common in Rajasthan. In 1992, the state's chief minister appeared on television, as part of a campaign against child marriage, to order an end to the practice. One campaign activist and her husband were attacked and she was raped by people opposing the campaign.[131]

The selling of child brides, some as young as ten, to foreigners has become increasingly common in recent years in Muslim-dominated, impoverished areas of India and particularly in Hyderabad.[132] In 1991 the case of a ten-year old girl named Ameena attracted national and international attention. She was married against her will, by her parents, to a sixty-year old Saudi Arabian man. He was arrested when flight attendants found her crying on the plane that was to take them to New Delhi. He was charged with kidnapping, fraudulent marriage, forgery and use of forged documents.[133]

Recently, the Indian government imposed special marriage restrictions on foreigners to deter the increasing number of men who are buying Muslim child brides and using them in the sex-slave trade outside of India. The new regulations require that the Muslim Wakf Board, which overseas Muslim personal laws, clear all marriages of Indian women to foreigners.

10.4.5 Rape

Reports of violence against women, in particular rape, have been increasing over the last few years.[134] According

131 Ibid
132 UPI 3 Jan. 1994; ibid. 10 Dec. 1993
133 The New York Times 21 Oct. 1991, A7), but he was released on bail and returned to Saudi Arabia (UPI 10 Dec. 1993)
134 India Alert Bulletin 1992, 18

to a 1985 review by the Bureau of Police Research and Development, approximately 20,000 rapes were committed per year. Police state that only one-quarter of the actual total number of rapes are reported.[135]

Sections 375 and 376 of the Indian Penal Code, which were substantially changed by the Criminal Law (Amendment) Act 1983, deal with sexual offences. Section 375 defines rape as sexual intercourse with a woman against her will and without her consent, and identifies certain conditions in which, even with a woman's consent, sexual intercourse constitutes rape. It also stipulates that *"sexual intercourse by a man with his own wife, the wife not being under fifteen years of age, is not rape"*; the code punishes sexual intercourse by a husband with his unconsenting wife only if the couple is separated. Section 376 provides for a minimum punishment of seven years' imprisonment for rape, ten for custodial rape, gang rape, and rape of a pregnant woman or girl under 12. A court may impose a lesser sentence *"for adequate and special reasons to be mentioned in the judgement"*.[136]

The Criminal Law (Amendment) Act also made an important change to section 114(a) of the Indian Evidence Act. Previously, a woman was required to provide corroborative evidence to support her claim that she had been raped, and the onus was on her to prove that she did not consent to the sexual act. The Evidence Act now states that, provided the prosecution has established that the sexual act took place and the woman states that she did not consent, the court *"shall presume that she did not consent"*. Ranchhodas and Thakore, in their commentary on the penal code, suggest that this change acknowledges the fact that *"in India ... a disclosure of this nature is likely to ruin the prospect of a girl's rehabilitation in society for all times to come and unless her story was painfully true she would not have taken such a grave risk merely to malign the accused"*.[137] Indeed, Asia Watch and Physicians for Human Rights, in a report on Kashmir, state

135 Kelkar 1992, 80
136 Ranchhoddas and Thakore 1987, 218-220; see also PUDR May 1994, 8-15
137 Ranchhoddas and Takore 1987, 219

that *"victims of rape are often stigmatized, and their testimony and integrity impugned"*.[138]

Amnesty International adds that, in addition to the physical and emotional effects of rape, such abuse has *"considerable social repercussions for the position and status of women in the community"*.[139] The mother of two young women victims of rape was reported to have feared for the marriageability of her daughters after they had been attacked.

The Peoples Union for Democratic Rights (PUDR), in its publication Custodial Rape: A Report on the Aftermath, comments, however, that *"the presumption in favour of the complainant can effectively be diluted if not totally eroded by the grounds available to the defence"*. The accused can counter the court's presumption by bringing in evidence that the woman's testimony is unreliable. In some cases, medical evidence, needed to prove injury, may be lacking or inconclusive. The woman may have willingly accompanied the accused, may not have cried out, or may have delayed in reporting the incident. Such factors can all be used to undermine the prosecution's case. Moreover, the 1983 amendments did not delete the provision in the Evidence Act that in a prosecution for rape, *"it may be shown that the prosecutrix was of generally immoral character"*. In numerous cases, the women's testimony was held to have little or no value.[140]

10.4.6 Custodial Rape

Women, who make up from two to six per cent of the prison population, are particularly vulnerable to attack and rape while in custody whether in prison or in other forms of official custody. Country Reports 1993 adds that women prisoners have in some instances been sold to brothels.

While there have been convictions for custodial rape, they are not common or well publicized. Amnesty International expresses concern over what it calls *"the lack of official determination to bring the perpetrators of custodial crimes*

138 Asia Watch and PHR 9 May 1993, 1 n.3; see also Varadarajan Aug. 1992, 9
139 AI Dec. 1991; see also Varadarajan Aug. 1992, 9; Asia Watch and PHR 9 May 1993, 16
140 For examples for such cases see sections 3.1 and 4.5.1 as well as PUDR May 1994, 8-9, 11 14, 18-19; Asia Watch and PURD 9 May 1993, 6; and Calman 1992, 119

to justice". The PUDR report published on 24th May, 1994, which reviews a number of cases of custodial rape and the legal action taken in each, concludes that *"while the letter of the law has changed [with the 1983 Criminal Law (Amendment) Act], the attitudes of police and judicial authorities have remained the same"*.

In one case in 1989, the supreme court reduced by one-half the sentence of two police officers convicted of custodial rape. The court reasoned that, because the victim was considered to be of "dubious virtue," there was not any great degree of harm inflicted upon her by the multiple rapes she suffered.[141] The convicted rapists were released. Ten years earlier the supreme court had, partly for similar reasons, overturned a decision convicting two officers of raping a young woman named Mathura, who was being held in their custody. In its decision, the court stated that the fact that the woman did not initially resist meant that she consented, despite the belief of a lower court of appeal that she could not have successfully resisted her assailants. Traces of semen found on her clothes after the attack were considered to be evidence of previous sexual encounters, indicating to the court that she was of poor moral character.

A March 1988 Amnesty International report states that between one and two-thirds of custodial rapes are suffered by women of scheduled castes and tribes.[142] Country Reports 1993 also indicate that most of the above appears to be directed at the poor and the uneducated lower castes who do not understand their right to redress. According to the International League for Human Rights, convictions for custodial rape are not only rare, but when they do occur they generally involve upper caste women.

10.4.6.1 Rape by Police, Security Forces and Militants in Areas of Conflict

Abuses by security forces, militant forces and police, including rape and other violence against women, have

141 Kapur 1991, 8
142 ILHR Mar. 1991, 11; see also AI 1993, 159; PUDR May 1994

been recorded all over India, but particularly in regions where there is armed conflict, such as Jammu and Kashmir and the Punjab.[143] Women appear to be particular targets of security forces during counter-insurgency operations in Kashmir.[144] Amnesty International reports that in Jammu and Kashmir women, in their testimony about abuses during such operations, mention only occasionally any attempt by the security forces to extract information from them. Rather they appear to have been victimized simply because they live in an area where armed opposition groups are active, or as punishment for perceived support of the separatist cause, or simply because they were Muslims.

A report on Kashmir by Asia Watch and Physicians for Human Rights adds that *"both security forces and armed militants have used rape as a weapon: to punish, intimidate, coerce, humiliate and degrade"*

10.4.7 Prostitution

Child prostitution in India is reportedly "rampant".[145] Country Reports 1992 estimates that there are approximately 100,000 prostitutes in Bombay alone, many of whom are minors held in bondage at brothels.[146]

The Immoral Traffic (Prevention) Act (formerly the Suppression of Immoral Traffic in Women and Girls Act 1956) was amended in 1986. The act, which provides for the imprisonment and fining of persons who are supported by the avails of prostitution, has nonetheless been criticized for allowing police enough latitude to harass prostitutes and even extort money from them.[147]

According to some sources, prostitution is often supported, even encouraged, by the families of the prostitutes.[148] Often those who enter the "industry" are tribal people who have traditionally performed the most degrading

143 HRW 1992, 409; Asia Watch Aug. 1991, 113, 118-119
144 ILHR Mar. 1991, 10; AI Dec. 1991; Asia Watch and PHR 9 May 1993, 1
145 Country Reports 1993 1994, 1351
146 Country Reports 1992 1993, 1144; see also Dallas Morning News 7 Mar. 1993, 4
147 Bhandari et al. 1990, 45
148 Rhoodie 1989, 396; Manchester Guardian Weekly 3 Jan. 1993

work, are landless or have been allotted the worst land. The Manchester Guardian Weekly reports that in one Rajasthan village many girls are prostituted by their fathers, who do little work and use their daughters as their only significant source of income.

The Karnataka Devadasi (Prohibition of Dedication) Act 1982 forbids the practice of Devadasi (Widows, Abandoned and Destitute Women 1989, 33). Deep-rooted religious and cultural customs are not easily eliminated by legislation however, and although the practice is declining, it is estimated that over 10,000 girls are still dedicated each year. Although Devadasi is supposed to be the dedication of a young girl to the service of a deity, the present-day practice, according to several sources, is merely religiously-sanctioned prostitution. While the national percentage of prostitutes who are Devadasi is 15 per cent, in Karnataka and Maharashtra the number rises to between 80 and 90 per cent.[149] Girls who have been dedicated are forbidden to marry and are more often than not sold into prostitution upon reaching puberty when they can start making "good money". A majority of the families who dedicate their daughters are from the poorer economic strata and lower castes and material gain is an important reason for the practice.[150] In addition to the money a girl brings in as a prostitute, the fact that she remains unmarried means that she can inherit family property and thereby keep it in the family.

A study on women and AIDS in India says that prostitutes are being blamed in large part for the spread of the disease, engendering further discrimination against an already disadvantaged group.

10.5 Alternatives Available to Women

According to Ratna Kapur, the alternatives available to women who are victims of gender discrimination depend on many factors, including caste, socio-economic class,

149 Widows, Abandoned and Destitute Women 1989, 34
150 Widows, Abandoned and Destitute Women 1989, 30

religion, marital status and the region in which they live.[151] Women who are knowledgable in regard to their rights are more likely to take advantage of those recourses which are available.

10.5.1 Family Support

As women are, for the most part, financially dependent on their husbands, it is difficult for them to leave their homes. In addition, although citizens are permitted to travel freely within the country (except in certain border areas) and foreign travel and emigration are not generally restricted, Ratna Kapur remarks on the lack of mobility for women and notes that the financial constraints on those who wish to leave their homes are severe. According to a 1988 report by the Integrated Human Development Services Foundation, when she marries, a bride leaves her natal home to live with her husband's family and should she be abused, her natal parents will frequently discourage her from leaving, or even send her back to an abusive husband.[152] Calman states that a married woman who leaves her home will often receive no help from her parents, will not have many opportunities to remarry and will face widespread social opprobrium. Naina Kapur says that a woman who returns to her family for support when she is a victim of domestic violence will often be told to return to her husband to try to work out the problems because her family does not want to interfere. She does state, however, that if after several attempts to return to her husband she still wishes to leave, the woman will be able to return to her parents home.[153]

10.5.2 Panchayats (Village Councils)

Advice is often given to rural women by the panchayat on the treatment they receive at home.[154] As noted earlier, the panchayats used to be male institutions; however, now 30 per

151 Kapur 29 Apr. 1994
152 IHDSF 15-18 Feb. 1988, 9
153 Kapur 8 Aug. 1994
154 Women Magazine July 1993, 64

cent of the seats in the panchayat are reserved for women.[155] Ratna Kapur believes that, with further education concerning the role of the panchayats and their accountability to the people who have elected them, they could become effective recourses for women.

10.5.3 Shelters

There are very few shelters for women in India;[156] in 1992, there were only 26 "short-stay homes" for battered women in the entire country. Finding housing is difficult for single women, whether they are victims of abuse or divorced women trying to live independently, especially if they have children. In 1985 one shelter was opened in Delhi that accepts children. A 1991 Article in the Lawyers Collective, in which several people working with battered women were interviewed, reported that those shelters which do exist have such lengthy and detailed requirements for admission that, in fact, in an emergency there is no shelter to be found.[157] The article further reports that the *"serious lack of shelters leaves no option to women but to stick on in a violent situation at home"*. Naina Kapur notes that one of the reasons that there are not many shelters is that, as a final resort, a woman's family will generally provide shelter for her.[158]

10.5.4 Legal Recourse

Article 14 of the constitution provides that all persons are equal before the law and shall have equal protection of the law. Country Reports 1993 states that the Indian judiciary is independent with "strong constitutional safeguards".[159] It adds, however, that in Punjab and Kashmir the judicial systems "barely function". One report, quoting a family court lawyer in India, states that there have been no convictions for wife-battering in the last ten years.

155 India Today 15 Apr. 1993, 52
156 Dallas Morning News 7 Mar. 1993, 40
157 The Lawyers Collective Apr. 1991, 6
158 Kapur 8 Aug. 1994
159 Country Reports 1993 1994, 1344

A woman subject to violence, including domestic violence, has recourse under matrimonial (personal) law, or through civil or criminal courts. Under most of the personal, religious laws governing marriage, she can file for divorce or separation based on cruelty. A Christian woman whose marriage is governed by the Indian Divorce Act cannot obtain a divorce for cruelty, however, unless she can also prove adultery.

A civil suit for injunctive relief can be undertaken under the Civil Procedure Code and the Special Relief Act and the common law, in which a woman can request measures preventing her husband from taking further injurious action (e.g., an order for non-molestation). This type of relief can also be obtained under the Family Courts Act. In both cases the only remedy for non-compliance is further legal action for contempt of court.

In criminal law, a woman victim of violence, including in some cases emotional abuse or demands for dowry, can seek redress under several sections of the Indian Penal Code: "323 (hurt), 324 (hurt by dangerous weapons or means), 325 (grievous hurt), 326 (grievous hurt by dangerous weapons or means), 352 (assault), 337 (assault in order to confine a person), 342 (wrongful confinement), 346 (wrongful confinement in secret), 506 (criminal intimidation)" (Lawyers Collective Apr. 1991, 8). With the exception of Section 326, all of the sections cover bailable offences whereby the offender is immediately released upon posting bail (ibid.). Section 498(a), which makes domestic violence a non-bailable offence, can be invoked by the victim against her husband as well as his relatives. Its use is limited, however, as only the victim herself or a relative through blood or marriage can file a complaint.

Several sources state that, while it is true that there is a strong judiciary in India, many factors make the courts a difficult recourse for women. Women often lack economic,[160] geographic and even political access to the legal system.[161] Liddle and Joshi write that *"a majority of women are both*

160 Lawyers Collective Apr. 1991, 7; CJWL 1993, 289
161 CJWL 1993, 289

illiterate and poor, unaware of their legal rights, and without the resources to fight for them through the courts".[162] An article in The Lawyers Collective points out lawyers are excluded, except with permission of the court, from representing plaintiffs in family courts and women, who are generally less educated than their husbands, thus have more difficulty in presenting their cases. As well, many women are not accustomed to dealing with public institutions: *"Women ... find it extremely difficult to follow procedures and explain their problems to a male judge while constantly being intimidated by their angry husbands".*[163]

Many sources report that women are often subject to the negative attitudes of the male-dominated judiciary.[164] An article in Manushi, a women's newsletter published in Delhi, reports that there have been instances in the family courts where judges have asked women litigants to stand outside the courtroom while they discuss the case with the husband.[165] Country Reports 1993 states that, according to lawyers who deal with dowry cases, judges and prosecutors are not interested in the issue of dowry deaths. Asia Watch and Physicians for Human Rights have reported that *"social attitudes which cast the woman, and not her attacker, as the guilty party pervade the judiciary, making rape cases difficult to prosecute and leaving the women unwilling to press charges".*[166] CJWL also reports that women face many social pressures not to make claims. Additionally, due to a backlog of cases it can take years before a case is heard.[167]

10.5 Women's Organizations

Country Reports 1993 states that there are thousands of organizations working at the grassroots level for the development and advancement of women. Inter Press

---

162 Liddle and Joshi 1986, 75; see also Kumari 1989, 86; Lawyers Collective Apr. 1991, 7
163 Manushi Sept.-Oct. 1991, 13
164 Liddle and Joshi 1986, 75; Manushi Sept.-Oct. 1991, 13; AI Mar. 1994, 6; Calman 1992, 119
165 Manushi Sept.-Oct. 1991, 13
166 Asia Watch and PHR 9 May 1993, 1 n.3
167 LCHR June 1993, 11; Dallas Morning News 7 Mar. 1993, 6

Service reports that women in Rajasthan, a traditionally conservative region of the country, have become more active and vocal in recent years.[168] Naina Kapur points to the Women's Development Programme in that state as a "model" for empowering rural women by giving them the means to articulate their concerns and to be active with respect to issues including domestic violence. According to Ratna Kapur, women's groups are involved in a wide variety of issues which vary from region to region.[169] For example, in Tamil Nadu and Andhra Pradesh there are strong anti-liquor campaigns led by women.[170] The Washington Post reports that these campaigns constitute the first widespread movement started by rural women. Naina Kapur comments that these campaigns have been very successful and that those two states are now "dry" states. In Uttar Pradesh women's groups have been involved in the issue of religious freedom. Ratna Kapur says that one of the major issues women's groups are addressing is that of population policies resulting from the government's attempts to conform to the structural adjustment policies of international donor agencies.

A September 1994 broadcast on National Public Radio in the United States interviewed members of a women's group called "Mahila Samatya" (Women's Empowerment) which travels from village to village in five states to assist women in empowering themselves and raise their status in their traditional culture.[171] The broadcast focuses on the efforts of a lawyer and feminist activist, Tulika Shlevastrava, to change the attitudes of women towards issues such as education for daughters and the favouring of sons. To this end, the organization has set up a network of village schools where girls can fit education into their daily household routines. Progress is slow, in one village in which women traditionally blamed the victim of violence such as rape or domestic abuse,

168 Inter Press Service (IPS) Reports 23 June 1994
169 Kapur 29 Apr. 1994
170 India Alert Bulletin Summer/Fall 1993, 28
171 NPR 11 Sept. 1994

it took the organization many meetings and discussions "to introduce new ideas so women know there is another way to live". The women of the group no longer tolerate domestic violence and, on the day of the broadcast, using the power of peer pressure, they convince a mother-in-law to refrain from beating her daughter-in-law.

Indian women's organizations are working on various projects, including an anti-dowry campaign that began in the 1970s and was strong in the early 1980s;[172] an anti-rape campaign;[173] and grassroots union activity. Women's role in development continues to be an important issue for women's groups and rural women's groups are beginning to form.[174]

The women's movement in India is not homogenous, and according to the India Alert Bulletin there has been an increasing emphasis on religious and caste identities that may endanger the creation of necessary links between women's groups.[175] There has also been resistance to women's participation in organizations from their families, as well as from the traditionally privileged groups.[176]

10.7 Governmental Initiatives

The Indian government has taken some steps that could have far reaching implications for women in India.[177] According to a June 1994 report by Xinhua News Agency, it had "finalized a proposal" to establish a national resource centre for women. The main purpose of the centre will be to focus on empowering women.[178] The National Commission on Women's Rights has also been involved in the preparation of legislation dealing with child sexual abuse and more recently with legislation on sexual harassment.[179]

172 Calman 1992, 63; Matsui 1987, 81
173 Women in Action 1994, 14
174 Calman 1992, 176
175 India Alert Bulletin Apr. 1991, 23
176 Country Reports 1993 1994, 1351
177 See sections 3.6.2 on inheritance; 4.1.2 on dowry cells; and 4.3 on gender determination tests
178 The Washington Times 13 July 1994, A18
179 Kapur 8 Aug. 1994

In August 1994 the state government of Maharashtra announced a policy to reserve 30 per cent of government jobs and 25 per cent of police station commands for women, as well as abolishing court fees in cases of violence against women.

❑❑❑

CHAPTER

11

The Paving Ways for Women Rights and Protection

"Fight for gender equality is note fight against men. It is fight against traditions that lives chained them a fight against attitudes that are ingrained in the society it is a fight against system a fight against proverbial "Lakshman Rekha" which is different for men and different for women. The society must rise to the occasion. It must recognized and accept the fact that men and women are equal partners in life. They are individuals who have their own identity".

–Justice Dr. A.S. Anand.[1]

11.1 Perceptive

It is known to all that in India about half of the Indian population are women.[2] They have always been discriminated against and have suffered and are suffering discrimination in silence in the civilized as well as the primitive society. Even thought self-sacrifice and self denial are their nobility and virtue, yet they have been made the victims of all inequalities, indignities, inequity and discrimination from time immemorial.

The question of gender equality is a very old and burning problem. Twenty five years ago in Mexico the First World Conference on Women inspired a movement, which has helped to reduce gender inequality worldwide. Illiteracy among women is declining maternity, morality and total fertility rates are beginning to fall and more women are

1 Justice (Dr) A S Anand

2 The Population; female (% of total) in India was last reported at 48.37 in 2011, according to a World Bank report published in 2012.

participating in the labour force than even before, however, much rooming to be alone. Persistent inequality between women and men constraints as society's productivity and ultimately shows its rate of economic growth. Although this problem has been generally recognized evidence on the need for corrective action is more compelling today than ever.

The exploitation and discrimination of women has been multifaceted, all around and all pervading. There has been hardly any job, employment or engagement in which women were not given wages less than the men, even when they have been engaged in the same type of work and for the same duration. Despite the constitutional mandate that women will not be discriminated in any sphere, discrimination has continued. The social justice enshrined in the constitution enjoins the sate that exploitation of weaker section of the society should cease. And despite the constitutional guarantee of equality of sexes and constitutional mandate of social justice, rampant discrimination and exploitation of women continues. The incidents of bridge burning, women haltering, molestation and rape, and brazen ill treatment of women is on the increase. Their discrimination and exploitation in father's house and in in-law's abode and at work place are still the order of the day.

It is an established fact that the Gender Justice is enshrined in the Indian constitution on its preamble, fundamental rights, fundamental duties and directive principles. The constitution not only grants equality to women, but also empowers the state to adopt measures of positive discrimination in favour of women but the illiteracy and lack of social awareness making these provisions dormant and sometime useless particularly for unprivileged women, which is a real challenge before law.

This intense craving, coupled with avarice, made the middle classes seek new avenues for getting rich quickly. They restored to coercion and blackmail by compelling young birds' parent to dish-out money, and more money after marriage. Thus women, who has been traditionally regarded as the preserver of social order and the standard-bearer of decency and social morality, is now subjected to inhuman and immoral treatment in case her parents failed to meet the ever-increasing demands of her husband and his parents. Needless to say, such treatment of women, which is the outcome of dowry syndrome, is a bolt on our society. Bride burning is still going on in our society.

These are some of factors that prompted the legislature to make various laws to give the women their due share. The Constitution of India prohibits any discrimination solely based on the ground of sex in general and in the matter of public employment. The prohibition of gender-based discrimination has been given the status of a Fundamental Right. Various others laws have been enacted to deal with the personal matters like marriage, divorce and succession of the women. The criminal law also contains numerous provisions to deal with the crimes committed against women; enactments like the Dowry Prohibition Act supplement the existing criminal laws to combat the evil of dowry. Further, numbers of labour and industrial laws provide for the protection and welfare of the women, which include maternity benefit, equal pay for equal work, Domestic violence Act, Factories Act, Compensation Act, Bonus Act, prohibition of employment of women in dangerous activities and crèche facility for the children of working women and legal service Authority Act 1987. In order to curb the immoral and anti-social practice of prostitution, the Immoral Traffic (Prevention) Act has been enacted. The female foeticide and the infanticide have assumed dangerous proportions and the determination of sex of the fetus which became possible due to the advanced scientific inventions, abetted the Commission of these inhuman acts. The parliament has passed the Pre-natal Diagnostic Techniques (Regulation & Prevention of Misuse) Act 1994 to arrest this undesirable trend. Latest parliament has passed the Sexual Harassment of Women at Work Place (Prevention, Prohibition and Redressal) Act, 2013 to protect the women at work place to protect the women from one of the recurring evils the modern society is the sexual harassment caused to the women particularly the working women by their male counterpart and other members of the society, after a long gap of the guidelines given by a Division Bench of Supreme Court speaking through Chief Justice J. S. Verma (as he then was) in ***Vishaka Vs. State of Rajasthan,***[3] but the ***Case of Nirbhaya***[4] and ***Mumbai Rape Case***[5] proved that work has not been done completely.

Various other laws have been enacted to deal with the personal matters like marriage, divorce and succession etc., of the women. Unfortunately, only a few such laws could be codified and made uniform. The criminal law may also contain numerous provisions to deal with the crimes committed against women; enactments like the Dowry Prohibition Act supplement the existing criminal laws to combat the civil of dowry. Number of labour and industrial laws provide for the protection and welfare of the women, which include maternity benefit, prohibition of employment of women in dangerous activities and crèche facilities for the children of working women. In order to curb the immoral and anti social practice of prostitution, the Immoral Traffic (Prevention) Act has been enacted. The female feticide and infanticide have assumed dangerous proportions and the discrimination of sex of the fetus which became possible due to the advanced scientific inventions, abetted the Commission of these inhuman acts. These legislative measures aforementioned are only illustrative in nature and not at all exhaustive.

In order to curb the pervading evil of dowry, the Dowry Prohibition Act 1961was passed. However, this Act could not arrest the rising fide of violence against women. Indian Penal Code also supplemented with drastic provisions. Section 304 B of the Indian Penal code defines dowry death in the following words:

"Where the death of a woman caused by any burns or bodily injury or occurs otherwise than under normal circumstances

3 AIR (1997) 6 SCC 241

4 State Through Reference Vs. Ram Singh & Ors, Judgement delivered on 13 March, 2014 : Mukesh & Anr. Vs. State For NCT of Delhi & Ors, Judgement delivered on 5 May, 2017

5 Mumbai gang-rape case: Rapists assaulted 4 other women in past 6 months, Times of India, August, 28, 2013

within seven years of marriage and it shown that soon before her death she was subjected to cruelty or harassment by her husband or any relatives of her husband for or in connection with any demand for dowry, such husband or relative shall be deemed to have caused her death."[6]

Lots of protective measures have been kept under various labour laws also. The principal of equal pay for equal work is contained in clause (d) of Article 39 of the Indian Constitution, is now playing a vital role in this regard. Further, the equal pay for equal work finds its place in the Directive principal of state policy and it is an accompaniment of equality clause enshrined in Article 14 and 16 of the of the constitution of India. The Equal Remuneration Act, 1976 provides for the payment of equal remuneration to men and women workers and for prevention of discrimination, on the ground sex against women in the matter of employment and for matters connected therewith or incidental thereto. The Act ensures against discrimination in recruitment and promotion of men and women. To protect the working women, another important Act, i.e. Maternity Benefit Act 1961, was enacted to regulate the employment of women in certain establishments for certain periods before and after child birth and to provide for maternity benefit and certain other benefits. This Act extends to the whole of India except the State of Jammu and Kashmir. The Employees' Compensation Act 1923 is one of the earliest measures adopted to benefit the labourers. It was passed in 1923 and enforced on 1st July 1924. Since then, a number of amendments have been made from time to time so as to suit the changing needs and conditions of the employees. Another important Act to protect the women workers is, Protection of Women under ‗The Factories Act, 194'. This Act was amended in the year 1954 to prohibit the employment of the young persons including women during the night shift. Child marriage has been one of the biggest injustices committed against a child. In the process of child marriage, we have deprived the young girl to be an educated

6 304 B of Indian Penal Code, 1973

and a capable citizen and also deprived a new generation of children from getting care by a well informed and healthy mother. The potential loss to society, both socially and economically, will be hard to quantify but it would be enormous. Women have historically always constituted an exploited class in the society. The English Common Law created wife as the chattel of husband. Since then law has tried to address the problems of the status of women by means of legislation. Legal Service Authority Act1987 was passed to provide free and competent legal services to the weaker sections of our society in order to ensure proper justices for the poor and needy people and to see that they are not denied of such rights. We can refer an interesting case in this connection ***Kesavananda Bharati Vs. State of Kerala***[7]. We are living in the 21st century, i.e., in the modern era. It could hardly be denied that women of our country are the weaker section of our society till date. Lok Adalats are playing a vital role to protect the women's right in our country. After fifty-sixth year of the Republic of India, the parliament has enacted an important Act to provide more effective protection of the rights of women under the Constitution, who are victims of violence of any kind within the family and for matters connected therewith or incidental thereto. That Act was entitled as —Protection of Women from Domestic Violence Act 2005. This Act is very important Act of our Country to protect the women from domestic violence, but honest implementation of this Act is necessary. Despite of these Acts there are no protective Acts for the Domestic servants (men & women) who are working, usually, morning to night at his/her master's house year after year. Many men and women workers are working in many hotels, food plaza and Big Bazar etc. They are working from 8 a.m. to 8 p.m. There is another important Act to protect the women to save their lives, e.g. Medical treatment of pregnancy Act 1971.

Apart from the protection through the Constitution and other legislations the Parliament of India realized

7 AIR 1973 SC

the importance of a monitoring institution to examine and investigate all the matters relating to the safe guards provided for woman under the Constitution and other laws. This realization has led to the enactment of the National Commission for Women Act, 1990 which came into force with effect from 31-01-1992, which has been burdened with the laborious responsibility of reporting to the Government as to the efficacy and effective implementation of the safeguards for improving the conditions of woman by the Government and for monitoring the socio-economic development of women in all walks of their life. Unfortunately, the Commission can make only recommendations and send the same to the respective authority for action. It has no Judicial Powers for making it an effective instrument for providing relief to woman and distress. Justice V. R. Krishna Iyer, aptly remarked that a National Commission for Women has hardly any teeth or nail[8]. Number of other commissions and committees on women's problem has also set up which came with reports and numerous suggestions and many solutions had been offered. The result is that, their role as a housekeeper and keeper of children and that of second fiddle to man, unchanged. We need total transformation of the man's mind, and the outlook of the society towards women should be drastically changed, for the emancipation of women and that is our goal. Problems of women are not only the problems of the society but the problem of a country as well.

11.2 Attention Seeking Areas

According to the information provided by the office of Registrar General & Census Commissioner of India, As per Census 2011, India's labour force will soon become the largest in the world. According to, the total number of female workers in India is 149.8 million and female workers in rural and urban areas are 121.8 and 28.0 million respectively. Out of total 149.8 million female workers, 35.9 million females are working as cultivators and another 61.5 million

8 Justice V.R. Krishna Iyer on the role of National Commission for Women.

are agricultural laborers. Of the remaining female workers, 8.5 million are in household Industry and 43.7 million are classified as other workers. [9]

Labors are being Subject to misuse and discrimination and their human rights being damaged so the need emerged for an order of the laws for their assurance and security. Working ladies shape a noteworthy proportion of society. Among – workers, the states of women are especially helpless & hapless thus numerous administrative enactments have been given in all work resolutions which address issues of women who work. Women fundamentally require some protection due to the accompanying reasons, which are peculiar physical reasons:

- Physical Buildup
- Poor Health due to repeated pregnancies
- Home Drudger
- Due to nature of Occupation

Once our late Prime Minister Honorable Jawaharlal Nehru has righty observed that,

"to awaken the people it is the woman who must be awakened, once she is on the move, the family moves, the village moves, the nation moves."[10]

11.2.1 Women and Labour Law Need for Special Treatment

While women constitute a substantial chunk of the available workforce in India, they are still lacking in work participation (the percentage of women employed is still low) as well as quality of employment.[i] One of the reasons for this lack of this female labour participation is the lack of suitable jobs on offer, i.e. the disparity between what they can

9 https://labour.gov.in/womenlabour/about-women-labour

10 Taken from Souvenir Volume of the Silver Jubilee Celebrations of The Tata Institute of Social Sciences, the History and Philosophy of Social Work in India, Edited by Professor A. R. Wadia, Tata Institute of Social Sciences, Bombay, Published by Allied Publishers Private Ltd.,196, 1New Delhi,.

do and what is available to them.[ii] Another reason for the low female turnout in the field of employment is the issue of safety. Better governance and policing is a must if there is any intention of increasing the sense of security among women and thus encouraging more women to take up jobs. Another problem is that the sectors that women are employed in such as "domestic work" falls under the "unorganized sector" and this is problematic in the sense that there is no strong set of workplace rules in place; this again is a factor that leads to the lack of women in the active workforce, as it is incredibly hard to simply maintain a job let alone build a career.[iii] This vulnerable position of women in terms of adverse conditions is only worsened by any possible sudden negative impact upon the industry as they are already dealing with unequal intrinsic situations.[iv] They have to cope with childbirth and related issues, they have also to deal with domestic responsibility, which in a patriarchal society is not much of a concern to men, [v] etc. Thus in order to bring women up to par with their male counterparts, it is important that they are not only given equal rights in labour law, but also special protection.[vi]

11.3 Employment Opportunities and Wage Disparity

Equality of employment and occupation is not possible without equal opportunities and equal treatment. While equal opportunity refers to having an equal chance of applying for a particular job – equal access to employment, which includes, equal chance to acquire training in the field, eligibility for promotions, and eligibility to attain certain qualifications/ enter certain cadres; equal treatment refers to being entitled to equal pay, working conditions, social security, and social protection and quality of family life (in terms of the opposite sex). Promotion of equality in employment is a positive enforcement, unlike prevention of discrimination, which is a sort of negative right or negative equality. This involves breaking down both horizontal and vertical occupational segregation.[vii]

The principle of equal pay, the antithesis of wage disparity, is based on the recognition of an objective evaluation of work in order to determine pay; and elimination of "discriminatory structural gender bias in labour markets." A woman's income, on average, worldwide, per hour is 75% that of a man. One of the reasons this practice is still so prevalent even today is because of the popular view that the costs of employing women is higher than employing men, because due to the various positive discriminations provided for in statutes women work fewer overtime hours, women must be given maternity leave, etc. Wage disparity is so hard to combat because it is often very hard to detect. It operates through access to promotions and other similar indirect means, as such qualifications affect not only pay, but also perquisites. The ILO Constitution of 1919, and the ILO Convention on Equal Remuneration 1951, both recognise the principle of "equal pay for work of equal value." This is also enshrined in the Constitution of India under Articles 14 and 15, as well as the Equal Remuneration Act of 1976. Despite such recognition often the issue of equal pay for women workers goes un-championed, even by trade unions, as they often do not view this to be a problem that affects the workers as a whole.[viii]

One of the most basic reasons as to why there is an inequality in the employment opportunities available to women and the disparity in wages is that women are view as supplementary earners and men are viewed as primary breadwinners.[ix] This operates as a vicious cycle, as the low wages offered to women further entrenches them in lower cadres of employment and continues to perpetuate disparity. Additionally women accept jobs with lower pay in order to avoid sitting idle, and this differential wages works as a discouraging factor against enhanced performance and thus reduces an opportunity for career advancement.[x] Another cause for disparity in income is that a majority of the active female workforce is involved in the informal sector, such as agriculture and domestic work, which have very few regulations in terms of remuneration and social security.[xi]

11.4 Ways for Effective Improvement

We are at the eve of twenty first centuries. But we are sorry to say that, if one asks question to another, who are the educationally backward in our society? Who are socially and economically dependent in our society? The answer will be that these crippled creatures are noting but the women of our country. But one can hardly deny the un-parallel influence of women in shaping the society. They have had lived through suppression, exploitation and ill treatment at the hands of man. Woman‘s status is intertwined with sensual pleasure and her amorous potential, and less of respect, and least based on equality and other basic human values. She would have, from the very beginning, a code of conduct, intended, understandably, to make her grow physically and mentally as an inferior beings; it is discriminatory and obnoxious; and would ultimately be prepared for a life of constraints and constant cheeks, before and after marriage. She was never free. She has no role but an object of sex, and serves man and rear children, always a confined to the four walls of the house. In t he matter of marriage, she had no say, and upon death of the husband she had to burn herself at his pyre, and after the abolition of _sati‘, once a window always window– a life ‘of social stigma, ostracism, a humiliation and disgrace. Where as a man could re-marry after the death of his wife, and lead to a life without foregoing its quality and content; a windowed woman could not and was not a welcome presence on auspicious occasions and in social gatherings.

So, the plight of women not being much different from that of the down trodden, their mental and physical inhibitions being similar, their symptoms being same, their diagnosis and treatment could not be different. India, one of the largest democratic countries in the world. But democracy is a mere cry in the wideness in the absence of social equality.[11] The concept of democracy will be of no vital significance to the common man and woman of India unless it serves as a means to bring about a change in the socio-economic relations of the community to achieve the ideal of social equality.

The first thing we must do is be content with political democracy. We must make our political democracy a social democracy as well. Political democracy cannot last unless there lies at the basis of it social democracy. What does social democracy mean? It means a way of life, which recognizes liberty, equality and fraternity are not to be treated as separate items in a trinity. They form a union of trinity in the sense that to divorce one form the other is to defeat the very purpose of democracy. Liberty cannot be divorced from equality; equality cannot be divorced from liberty. Nor can liberty and equality be divorced from fraternity. Without fraternity, liberty and equality not become a natural course of things. It would require a constable to enforce them.

We must begin by acknowledging the fact that there is complete absence of two things in Indian Society. One of these is equality. This equality 'can play a vital role for protecting women's right in every sphere of their life. But, on the social plane, we have in India, a society based on the principles of graded inequality which means elevation of some and degradation from others. On the economic plane, we have a society in which there are some who have immense wealth as against many who live in object poverty. In politics we will have equality and in social and economic life we will have inequality.

Article 14 of the constitution guarantees equality before the law and equal protection of the laws within the territory of India. Article 15 forbids discrimination by the state on grounds of religion, race, caste, sex and place of birth in terms of access to public places, like shops, restaurants, hotels, places of public entertainment or use of walls, tanks, bathing ghats etc. At the same time the article empowers the state to

11 Manju Kumar, Social Equality – The constitutional experiment in India (1982)

make special provision for the women that classification for the benefit of women.[12213]

Despite a number of constitutional guarantees and enactment of various laws, providing against exploitation of women, whenever and in whatever form it be like for instance, statutes prohibiting dowry granting equal treatment in matrimonial, divorce and succession matter, and in the matters of adoption, giving liberty to a window to re-marry, liberalizing maintenance laws. Laws prohibiting bride-burning and sati‘, Act relating to maternity benefit, Act relating to family pension etc, Act relating to medical termination of pregnancy so on and so forth, the woman still remains unequal; her role as a house-keeper and keeper of children, and that of second fiddle to man, unchanged.

The society, therefore, must be set for a much bigger role, with the State and its laws playing second fiddle, set only to create a congenial legal environment for the social change in bringing about social justice, realizing, it is human to treat every human being alike, without distinction on the ground of religion, caste, creed, race and sex, and inhuman to treat otherwise on any such ground, and to do that is no concession to anyone, but is a normal duty of one human being towards the other, and putting differently, is giving him what he is entitled to. Let hatred contempt vanish altogether.

It is true that gender justice is possible only through women‘s empowerment which involves economic and political opportunities, social equality and personal rights. Besides a lot needs to be done to elevate the status of women and put an end discriminatory, humiliating and torturous practices in the society.

It is a fact that about half of the population of India is women. So, one could hardly deny their great contribution to our society. The first thing, we have to provide proper education for then. Schooling shapes one‘s ideas. An educated woman can easily realize here right unless evil of exploitation of woman is addressed at eh grass –root level mere imposed

12 Article 15(3) of the Indian Constitution

changes on the top will be of no avail. We know that several non-legal measures have been suggested by the courts and jurists in different times.

Another non-legal measure is to augment the role of voluntary organizations. These voluntary groups by organizing camps work-shops, symposia, programmes in schools and colleges, both in rural and urban areas, can bring about awareness among the masses about the curse of women exploitations and penal consequences.

Media can also play an effective role. Tele-films, players, serials, talks by eminent persons, moral teachings highlighting the curse of women exploitations must be given preference both on T.V and Radio. Write-ups, opinion pieces, sentences awarded by the courts and lackadaisical approach, if any, of the law enforcing agencies must receive first page coverage in the national dailies.

We need total transformation of the men‘s mind, and the outlook of the society towards women drastically changed, for the emancipation of women and that is our goal. Promotion of education and awareness among men and women.

Women have a unique position in every society whether developed, developing or underdeveloped. This is known to all of us that they are playing vital role in various stages of their life, as a daughter, wife, mother and sister etc. in spite of her contribution in the every individual human being, she still belongs to a class or group of society which is in a disadvantaged position on account of several social barriers and impediments. She has been the victim of tyranny at the hand of men of dominate the society. The position of Indian Woman is not better compared to their counterparts in other parts of the world. Astonishing enough that, on one hand she is held in high esteem by one and all, worshipped, considered as the embodiment of tolerance and virtue. But on the other hand she has been the victim of untold miseries, hardships and atrocities caused and perpetuated by the male dominated society. The vulnerability of the women as a class has nothing to do with their economic independence.

In India almost help of the Indian population are women. They have always been discriminated against and have suffered and are suffering discrimination in silence in the civilized as well as the primitive society. Even thought self-sacrifice and self denial are their nobility and virtue, yet they have been made the victims of all inequalities, indignities, inequity and discrimination from time immemorial. These are some of factors that prompted the legislature to make various laws to give the women their due share. We know that the Constitution of India prohibits any discrimination solely based on the ground of sex in general and in the matter of public employment. The prohibition of gender-based discrimination has been given the status of a fundamental right. Various others laws have been enacted to deal with the personal matters like marriage, divorce and succession of the women. The criminal law also contains numerous provisions to deal with the crimes committed against women, enactments like the Dowry Prohibition Act supplement the existing criminal laws to combat the evil of dowry. Further, numbers of labour and industrial laws provide for the protection and welfare of the women, which include maternity benefit, equal pay for equal work, Domestic violence Act, Factories Act, Compensation Act, Bonus Act, prohibition of employment of women in dangerous activities and crèche facility for the children of working women and legal service Authority Act 1987. In order to curb the immoral and anti-social practice of prostitution, the Immoral Traffic (Prevention) Act has been enacted. The female foeticide and the infanticide have assumed dangerous proportions and the determination of sex of the fetus which became possible due to the advanced scientific inventions, abetted the Commission of these inhuman acts. The parliament has passed the Pre-natal Diagnostic Techniques (Regulation & Prevention of Misuse) Act 1994 to arrest this undesirable trend.

The parliament of Indian has realized the importance of a monitoring institution to examine and investigate all the matters relating to the safe guards provided for woman under the constitution and other laws. This realization has led to the enactment of the National Commission for women Act, 1990 which came into force with effect from 31-01-1992. This Commission is entrusted with the task of presenting to the Central Government the problems of women, deprivation of women's rights and the reports of the progress of the development of women under the Union and any State. This body has the responsibility of reporting to the Government as to the efficacy and effective implementation of the safeguards for improving the conditions of women by the Government and for monitoring the socio-economic development of women in all walks of their life. Unfortunately the Commission has no Judicial Powers for making it an effective instrument for providing relief to woman in distress. It is high time that the Commission has been given the Judicial Powers and also conferred the Constitutional status.

The question of gender equality is a very old and burning problem. Twenty five years ago in Mexico the First World Conference on Women inspired a movement that has helped to reduce gender inequality worldwide. Illiteracy among women is declining maternity, morality and total fertility rates are beginning to fall and more women are participating in the labour force than even before. However, much demoing is to be alone. Persistent inequality between women and men constraints as society's productivity and ultimately shows its rate of economic growth. Although this problem has been generally recognized evidence on the need for corrective action is more compelling today than ever.

The Employees Compensation Act 1923 in very old Act and also effective Act for the employees. This Act was framed with a view to provide for compensation to employees incapacitated by an injury from accident arising out of and in the course of employment. The main object of the Act was to make provision for payment of compensation to an employee only, i.e, the concerned employee himself in case of his surviving the injury in question and to his dependants in the case of his death, in review of section 2(1) (n) of the Act.[13]

13 In re, B, Habeebumah Periaswami AIR1977 Mad. 330

Important matter is that, it is not necessary that the accident should have caused by some wrongful act of the employer.

Protection of women under the factories Act, 1948 May play a vital role for all the workers including women workers by implementing the Act Properly. A new chapter dealing with "Annual Weave with wages" was substituted for chapter VIII of the Act. A prohibition against employment of women and young persons during the night has been enacted by this Act. [Factories (Amendment) Act 1954] this Act also prevented the young workers and women workers from doing hazardous and risky workers of the Factory.

The Minimum Wages Act (1948) was passed for the welfare of labourers. This Act has been enacted to secure the welfare of the workers in such a competitive market by providing for a minimum limit of wages in certain employments. The object of the Act is directed against exploitation of the ignorant less organized and less privilege members of the society by the employers. We know a large number of workers of plantation, Bidi factories, Brick factories etc are women in our country. So they may be exploited easily by the employer. This Act may prevent the workers from exploitation.[14] Another vital Act is enacted for protecting the working from financial exploitation. This Act is called the Employees' Provident Funds, family pension fund, and deposit linked insurance fund Act 1952. The main object of the Act is to provide for the institution of funds for employees in factories and other establishments. Employees' Provident Funds (Amendment) Act 1956 empowered the Government to expand the Act to non-factory establishments. In view of the Amendment Act 1976, this Act is now called Employees' Provident Funds and Miscellaneous Provisions Act 1952. In my opinion this Act is very helpful to all the workers including men and women.

Our parliament passed the Equal Remuneration Act 1976. It was further amended in the year 1987. Now the law makes a mandatory for the employer to pay equal wages to man and women workers and prohibits discrimination of

14 M/S Bhikas Yamasa Kshatriya Vs. Sangamner Akula Taluk Bidi Kamgar Union AIR 1963, S.C. 806.

women on the ground of sex in matter of recruitment, training and promotion. The amending Act also provides for stricture punishment for the violation of this mandate. But in practice we are observing that eighty percent of the working women hold on "Pink-Collar Jobs" and get paid about 6 to 65 percent salary in comparison with male workers of the same nature so, discrimination is going on till date. This scenario is same more or less, all over the world till the 21st century. Though in all interesting case[15], The Supreme Court has held that the State is competent under Art 15(3) , 16(2) and 16(4) of the constitution to give preference to women in Government jobs where they equally meritorious but more suited than men do. She has clearly stated that giving preference to women is only affirmative action and not a reservation, which normally implied a separate quota, which is reserved for a special category of persons who are less meritorious.

We are at the eve of twenty first centuries. But we are sorry to say that, if one asks question to another, who are the educationally backward in our society? Who are socially and economically dependent in our society? The answer will be that these crippled creatures are noting but the women of our country. But one can hardly deny the un-parallel influence of women in shaping the society. They have had lived through suppression, exploitation and ill treatment at the hands of man. Woman's status is intertwined with sensual pleasure and her amorous potential, and less of respect, and least based on equality and other basic human values. She would have, from the very beginning, a code of conduct, intended, understandably, to make her grow physically and mentally as an inferior beings; it is discriminatory and obnoxious; and would ultimately be prepared for a life of constraints and constant cheeks, before and after marriage. She was never free. She has not role but an object of sec, and serves man and rear children, always a confined to the four walls of the house. In the matter of marriage, she had no say, and upon death of the husband she had to burn herself at his pyre and after the abolition of 'sati', once a window always window – a

15 The Hindu Stautimes May 29, 1995.

life' of social stigma, ostracism, a humiliation and disgrace. Where as a man could re-marry after the death of his wife, and lead to a life without foregoing its quality and content; a windowed woman could not and was not a welcome presence on auspicious occasions and in social gatherings.

So, the plight of women not being much different from that of the down trodden, their mental and physical inhibitions being similar, their symptoms being same, their diagnosis and treatment could not be different .

India, one of the largest democratic country in the world. But democracy is a mere cry in the wideness in the absence of social equality[16]. The concept of democracy will be of no vital significance to the common man and woman of India unless it serves as a means to bring about a change in the socio-economic relations of the community to achieve the ideal of social equality.

The first thing we must do is be content with political democracy. We must make our political democracy a social democracy as well. Political democracy cannot last unless there lies at the basis of it social democracy. What does social democracy mean? It means a way of life, which recognizes liberty, equality and fraternity are not to be treated as separate items in a trinity. They form a union of trinity in the sense that to divorce one form the other is to defeat the very purpose of democracy. Liberty cannot be divorced from equality, equality cannot be divorced from liberty. Nor can liberty and equality be divorced from fraternity. Without fraternity, liberty and equality not become a natural course of things. It would require a constable to enforce them.

We must begin by acknowledging the fact that there is complete absence of two things in Indian Society. One of these is equality. This 'equality' can play a vital role for protecting women's right in every sphere of their life. But, on the social plane, we have in India, a society based on the principles of graded inequality which means elevation of some and degradation from others. On the economic plane, we have a

16 Manju Kumar, Social Equality – The constitutional experiment in India (1982) p-iii

society in which there are some who have immense wealth as against many who live in object poverty. In politics we will have equality and in social and economic life we will have inequality. How long shall we continue to deny equality in our social & economic life? How long shall we continue to live this life of contradictions? We must remove this contradiction at the earliest possible opportunity. We must go through the laws, enacted by the parliament and by the State also.

Article 14 of the constitution guarantees equality before t he law and equal protection of the laws within the territory of India. Article 15 forbids discrimination by the state on grounds of religion, race, caste, sex and place of birth. Sub-article (2) of this Article provides against any citizen being subject to any disability, restriction on condition with regard to access to public places, like shops, restaurants, hotels, places of public entertainment or use of walls, tanks, bathing ghats etc, only on the grounds of religion, race, sex, place of birth or any of them. Sub –article (3) provides that classification for the benefit of women[17] and depressed classes[18] can be made, thereby ensuring special status to said classes. Equitable distribution of national resources and compulsory education has been provided for in the directive principles.

The society, therefore, must be set for a much bigger role, with the State and its laws playing second fiddle, set only to create a congenial legal environment for the social change in bringing about social justice, realizing, it is human to treat every human being alike, without distinction on the ground of religion, caste, creed, race and sex, and inhuman to treat otherwise on any such ground, and to do that is no concession to anyone, but is a normal duty of one human being towards the other, and putting differently, is giving him what he is entitled to. Let hatred contempt vanish altogether.

There is no filed of human activity which the woman has not stormed here entry into; and none in which they have failed to perform equally well with men. Once entered any filed, they never stepped backward, rather, many

17 Article 15(3) of the Indian Constitution
18 Article 15(4) and Article 29 of the Indian Constitution

times overstepped their male colleagues forward. They are good educationalist teachers, scientists, politicians, administrators, business executive, artists, etc. and given an opportunity, can do any job, and carry out any assignment. She has attained some economic independence, one may say so. The status of woman has indisputably, in some respects, improved, and the constitutional guarantees have worked well to bring about that stat of things.

But, is that all we need do or be complacent about? Have we fully achieved what we committed ourselves to? Is the woman today fully emancipated; is she wholly free? Has she been able to cast off her household servility, shun household drudgery? Has the outlook of man changed – has he started looking upon her with respect for her qualities, and not merely as an object of sex, only to be seduced, or come to accept that she can do as well as, and sometimes better than he? Is a woman free to move around anywhere and at any hour of the day, without being eve-tested, humiliated and disgraced, and sometimes even molested? Does not she still full defence less and unprotected? Isn't she even today sexually assaulted, and sexually exploited? Is she entitled to get job in various Govt. office or in different establishment. Is she 100% free from the fear of physical and mental harassment at her work place? Is the dowry still not the integral part of the matrimonial system? Are not the women still burnt alive for dowry? Isn't remarriage of a window or a divorce still an unfavoured proposition? Isn't the birth of a girl in a family still unwelcome?

Despite a number of constitutional guarantees and enactment of various laws, providing against exploitation of women, whenever and in whatever form it be like for instance, statutes prohibiting dowry granting equal treatment in matrimonial, divorce and succession matter, and in the matters of adoption, giving liberty to a window to re-marry, liberalizing maintenance laws. Laws prohibiting bride-burning and 'sati', Act relating to maternity benefit, Act relating to family pension etc, Act relating to medical termination of pregnancy so on and so forth, the woman still remains unequal; her role as a house-keeper and rearer of children, and that of second fiddle to man, unchanged.

We know that the total population of our country is about 11 crores of which 50% are women. So, one could hardly deny their great contribution to our society. The first thing, we have to provide proper education for then. Schooling shapes one's ideas. An educated woman can easily realize here right unless evil of exploitation of woman is addressed at eh grass –root level mere imposed changes on the top will be of no avail. We know that several non-legal measures have been suggested by the courts and jurists in different times.

Secondly, another non-legal measure is to augment the role of voluntary organizations. These voluntary groups by organizing camps work-shops, symposia, programmes in schools and colleges, both in rural and urban areas, can bring about awareness among the masses about the curse of women exploitations and penal consequences.

Thirdly, Media can also play an effective role. Tele-films, players, serials, talks by eminent persons, moral teachings highlighting the curse of women exploitations must be given preference both on T.V and Radio. Write-ups, opinion pieces, sentences awarded by the courts and lackadaisical approach, if any, of the law enforcing agencies must receive first page coverage in the national dailies.

Fourthly, we need total transformation of the men's mind, and the outlook of the society towards women drastically changed, for the emancipation of women and that is our goal.

In fine, to me, it seems, education and a great lot of, at the grass-root level, is the surer means for obtaining the desired results, and not the naira of rules alone.

11.5 Legal Status of Women in India

After Independence there was have to acquaint some statutory laws with guarantee well-being and assurance of women.(Ashalatha.P et al. 2012) Keeping in see this prerequisite, much the same as established arrangements, different parliamentary advances have likewise been taken by the law of India with a specific end goal to guarantee stately life to the Indian Women. Parliamentary advances implies and incorporates the authorisation of different laws and statutory acts to secure the enthusiasm of ladies and to stop the wrongdoing against women. These demonstrations have demonstrated extremely helpful towards advance and security of women in the public eye. By and by I feel that equivalent rights ought to be granted to women which have just been delighted in by men in our general public as women shanoteworthy piece of Indian populace and for social and financial welfare on worldwide stage women welfare is especially required. Keeping in mind the end goal to guarantee adherence to established arrangements for women welfare, there was a need to order particular laws by the state and local Government. In spite of the fact that a women can be casualty of any wrongdoing in the public eye and in actuality all violations can't be delegated a wrongdoing against ladies with the exception of couple of violations which influences a women generally.

Anyway real advances have been taken by the enactment which has demonstrated as weapons for Women and helped them to remain in male ruling nation. Presently we will examine real wrongdoings against women alongside the legitimate arrangement which punish the criminal. Scarcely any wrongdoings which are perceived as wrongdoing against women may be:

11.5.1 Adultery

Adultery is an intense wrong doing against ladies in India and influences wedded women all things considered. In basic words infidelity implies having deliberate sexual association with a wedded individual other than the life partner. The offense of infidelity is managed by segment 497 of the Indian corrective Code, 1860, which says infidelity implies sex of a man with a wedded lady without the assent of her significant other when such sex does not add up to assault. Anyway we may discover diverse significance of infidelity in various laws in various nations. At first just men were rebuffed under the law of infidelity in India yet now people both are (The Indian corrective Code, 1860) similarly in charge of carrying out the wrongdoing of infidelity. According to segment 497 (the guilty party might be rebuffed with detainment for a term which may stretch out to five years, or with fine, or with both. In such case the spouse should not be culpable as a sly accomplice.

11.5.2 Child Marriage

Child marriage is a terrible offense against youngster as it doesn't just damages the fate of kid yet additionally harm social qualities. Facilitate the specialists have additionally uncovered that tyke marriage is a major purpose behind awful wellbeing condition for young lady tyke. Youngster marriage limits the social advancement alongside diminishment in the instructive and business openings in the worldwide market. It resembled a weight on society to hone this unwritten custom. The real advance was taken by the Law Commission of India by settling the base age for marriage which is 18 years for young women's and 21 years for young men.pes a Another real advance was obligatory essential training and also for young ladies arrangement with the expectation of complimentary instruction gave by the Government of India.

11.5.3 Female Infanticide

Female feticide implies distinguishing and murdering of female baby before they take birth. This is the most ruthless method for slaughtering ladies. The custom of female feticide is polished by the general public frame old circumstances and it is extremely disgraceful to take note of that even today, when we views ourselves as taught and humanized, this custom is rehearsed in a major way. Government has found a way to spread mindfulness among individuals about the outcomes of this wrongdoing. Numerous mindfulness programs are led by the Government to spread the mindfulness about the physical, mental and social impact of this training. Discipline of 3 years detainment and Rs. 10,000 fine has been recommended by Pre origination and Pre Natal Diagnostic Techniques (Prohibition of Sex determination) Act, 1994, for the offense of Female feticides. In an as of late improvement Maharashtra government has prescribe to the inside that the wrongdoing of female feticide ought to be dealt with as murder. To guarantee this revision in Pre origination and Pre Natal Diagnostic Techniques (Prohibition of Sex choice) Act, 1994, (PCPNDT Act, 1994) would end up vital (Pre origination and Pre Natal Diagnostic Techniques (Prohibition of Sex choice) Act, 1994. This arrangement will bring this wrongdoing inside the class of murder under segment 302 of the Indian Penal Code (IPC).

11.5.4 Trafficking and Prostitution:

Trafficking implies import and fare of people for sex business. It is for sure extremely tragic to discover that in India, where ladies are perceived as Devi and implored by all Indian's as Devi Shakti, they are additionally regarded as a wellspring of procuring by deceptive means.(Mehta 1987; Achchi et al. 2012) Prostitution is one of the most concerning issues in this world which is harming the ladies from various perspectives. By and large, the term prostitution implies offer of sexual administrations for acquiring cash. Prostitution (Suppression of Immoral Traffic (Prevention) Act 1956) is an issue which exists over the world. There are many laws in India keeping in mind the end goal to keep the wrongdoing of prostitution like Suppression of Immoral Traffic in Women and Girl Act 1956 and Immoral Traffic (Prevention) Act 1956. There are few commissions are made by state Government to spare ladies and uncommonly young women to shield them from this training.

11.5.5 Domestic Violence

Domestic viciousness (Domestic brutality Act, 2005) has turned into an intense issue for women. By and large the term Domestic savagery implies mental, physical, enthusiastic and conservative provocation of a lady by relatives. With the end goal of aggressive behaviour at home family incorporates mate, his mom, father, sibling, sister, his relatives and some of the time even companions. We call ourselves instructed and speak excessively about profound quality, morals and human progress and anticipate that others will regard make a fantasy world however overlook that without giving due regard to the ladies, a country's development is outlandish. Presently in India abusive behavior at home is perceived as a criminal offense

under area 498A of Indian Penal Code, 1860. Aggressive behavior at home means remorselessness by spouse towards ladies. Remorselessness should be possible by physically, rationally, monetarily or inwardly. A demonstration called Domestic brutality Act, 2005 was acquainted with handle the instances of Domestic savagery in India. This demonstration is an exceptionally important endeavor in India to perceive abusive behavior at home as a culpable offense. Prior to the presentation of this demonstration two sorts of cures were accessible to a ladies influenced by Domestic viciousness. These two cures were separate through common courts and utilization of area 498A through criminal courts.

11.5.6 Eve-Teasing

It is a general observation that eve prodding is certainly not a major wrongdoing like assault or kill and might be a direct result of that we don't consider it important. Yet, from a ladies' perspective eve prodding is likewise a major wrongdoing as this action makes her vibe awkward the greater part of the circumstances. Eve prodding as a rule includes prodding ladies, passing remarks on ladies and making revolting signs (eshare). A lady needs to confront this sort of chafing conduct and manage this on regular schedule. She can't battle back because of dread of lack of respect by others as everybody will reprimand her and say that you probably accomplished comment them. If there should arise an occurrence of eve prodding young lady ought not stay quiet and raise her voice. She ought to illuminate her relatives and all the while document a dissension in the closest police headquarters. For this situation family ought to likewise bolster the ladies as opposed to locking her at home.

11.5.7 Acid throwing

Recently the issue of corrosive tossing on young ladies has additionally turned into a major issue. There are few sorts of acids and all are extremely risky for human blaze and consume. This corrosive assault now and then is dangerous to the point that even bones and eyes are likewise got harmed because of corrosive. Scarcely any casualties are compelled to leave their training or occupation because of the aftereffects of corrosive tossing. Presently a days this has turned out to be simple for individuals to get these acids and the instances of corrosive tossing has turned out to be extremely general in every day life. It is very miserable that notwithstanding of such a large number of instances of corrosive assaults on ladies, we don't have a committed and particular law to manage such cases. The National Commission for Women (NCW) is requested a very much characterized law to manage such losses. The NCW has presented a draft of the Prevention of Offenses (by Acids) Act, 2008, which is with now with the Union Ministry of Women and Child Development to vet and last suggestions.

Once the Union Ministry of Women and Child Development endorsed the Bill, it will be sent to the law service to be tabled in Parliament. After the endorsement in Parliament it will wind up material as law.

11.5.8 Fraudulent Marriage

Before delving into the subtle elements of Fraudulent Marriage let me clarify the general importance of misrepresentation in connection to wrongdoing against ladies. Extortion implies concealing something or giving false impression about something which a man realizes that knowing the reality may hurt his planned marriage. The extent of false marriage has expanded in the ongoing past as in India guardians of a young lady are exceptionally enamored with NRI child in law. Guardians need to settle their girl with any rich NRI. Guardians of ladies don't ask excessively about the NRI prep as they are upbeat that their

little girl will wed a rich individual who will satisfy her everything requests and she will carry on with a lavish life in abroad. There dazzle confidence on NRI's may welcome issues like false responsibilities, false points of interest, second marriage and barrenness. This isn't fundamental that false relational unions just occurred in the event of NRI's even Indian grooms likewise do likewise for cash or for kid youngster or for some other reason.

11.5.9 Exploitation at Work Place

Though we as a whole acknowledge reality that in this day and age ladies has left her picture of house spouse and substantiated herself as a superior director then a man. In all divisions ladies are buckling down and getting honors and rewards for that. She has crossed every one of the limits and close the mouth of each one of those people groups who has ever scrutinized her working bore.

11.5.10 Rape, Murder

Rape is another intense wrongdoing against ladies and this wrongdoing is expanding step by step like anything. Revealing of assault and kidnapping cases has turned out to be exceptionally normal in print and electronic media which is to be sure an extremely tragic issue for every one of us. Expanding assault cases are sufficient to demonstrate that our ethical qualities are still low despite everything we to figure out how to regard the respect of ladies on the loose. In basic terms the word 'Assault' implies sex or sexual entrance, by someone else without the assent of the other individual or casualty. Arrangements identified with assault are given in segment 375 and 376 of the Indian Penal Code, 1860. Segment 375 clarifies the pre-condition which are vital tp demonstrate the offense of assault while area 376 gives discipline to the offense of assault. According to segment 376, whoever confers the offense of assault should be rebuffed with detainment of either for a term which might not be under seven years but rather which might be forever or for a term which may stretch out to ten years and might likewise be at risk to fine.

11.5.11 Dowry

The arrangement of settlement is another social insidiousness which dragging ladies once again from 100 of years as this underhandedness has a long history particularly in India. Different share based abusive behavior at home cases has been accounted for by media. There are sufficient lawful arrangements in India to give alleviation to ladies in the event of share based abusive behavior at home cases. Common law of India has restricted the installment of endowment in the year 1961. Promote Indian Penal Code, 1860 has presented Sections 304B and 498A, which enables ladies to record dissension and look for rebuilding of her rights from genuine provocation by the spouse's family (Security of Women from Domestic Violence Act 2005) . Settlement is one of the solid and main motivations of expanding abusive behavior at home. Consistently a huge number of endowment passings alongside mental injury cases detailed and enlisted in India. If there should arise an occurrence of lacking endowment, episodes like consuming, suicides, physical and mental torment of ladies is exceptionally normal by spouse and his family. Keeping in see the expanding instances of endowment passings another administrative arrangement called "Security of Women from Domestic Violence Act 2005", was acquainted all together with decrease abusive behavior home cases and to ensure women's rights.

11.5.12 Troll Patrol India

India is one of the largest and fastest growing audience markets globally for Twitter, a social media platform. Touted as a 'safe place for free expression', Twitter was envisioned to be a space where marginalised populations, including women, Dalits and religious minorities, would have an equal opportunity to make their voices heard. Over the years, the social media platform has evolved into an indispensable tool for political engagement, campaigning and activism, but has the vision translated into reality? Many women do not believe so. Every day, women on Twitter face a barrage of abuse: from racist and sexist attacks to rape and death threats. Online abuse has the power to belittle, demean, intimidate and eventually silence women.

It's what women have long been telling the world. We now have the data to back it up. With the help of 1,912 Decoders from 82 countries and 26 states in India, we analysed 114,716 tweets that mentioned 95 women politicians in India over a three-month period around the 2019 General Elections in India. This helped us conduct an unprecedented analysis of online abuse against Indian women politicians on Twitter!

11.5.13 Women and Education

It is a typical social faith in rustic India that, the training for young womens inconsequential since she will wind up working in the house or in cultivate. The uneducated and unpracticed young lady is considered as immaculate and virgin in numerous rustic regions and she eventually gets better proposition for her marriage. Cast framework likewise assumes an exceptionally fundamental part as an obstruction to a young lady kid's instructive rights.

Despite the fact that the constitution of India gifts women similar rights proportional to men, however there concealment takes after from the social custom, from religious standards and practices. Generally guardians need to put resources into the training of their child and ability improvement. Since, a young women is dependably a theme of her marriage and kids. While guys figure out how to wind up family supplier, female learn kid bearing and local obligations. Hitched young don't for the most part have instructive rights, in this way child marriage abuses the instructive privileges of a young women child . It denies them of potential freedom and also damaging the CRC (Convention on the Rights of the Child) arrangements. Islamic law, regularly known as Sharia Law, as deciphered by Islamic fundamentalists, requests that spouses submit to their better half. It likewise demands that young lady to wear a shroud on the off chance that they need to go out. It grants to have different spouses it likewise urges young ladies to wed in early age just to guarantee her virginity and extremely limits work chances of female. In every one of these conditions how a young lady tyke even hope to wind up a scholarly astuteness. Religion and social based imbalances in sharia law confines young lady's instruction by mingling. Fundamentalists of Islamic Law consider they the pioneers and utilize exacting translation of the sacred texts; they demonstrate female as troopers of heavenly war in which they need to battle to spare the convention and estimations of Islamic law. Fundamentalists of Islamic laws additionally trust that, 'instruction for a female decimates the conventional limits and meanings of sex parts and breaks up ladies' customary capacities are totally valid'. Religious laws devastate a young lady kid's instructive rights. The International Labor Organization (ILO) requested the anticipation of the shroud which makes break even with get to a young lady youngster to training. The absence of sex instruction in Muslim young ladies builds the danger of HIV/ AIDS on account of the recompense of hazardous polygamy framework in the religion. Much the same as the Quran, the Bible likewise contains the dialect to put ladies in subordinate position. For instance, Ephesians 5:22-24 peruses, 'spouses, submit to your significant other as the master. for the spouse is the leader of the congregation and his body is of which he is the deliverer, now as a congregation submit to Christ, so additionally wives should submit to their husbands in all things'. Hindu Dalit school kids' and instructors additionally experience the separation by the privileged individuals in India. It is exceptionally trying for a Dalit young lady to approach training in such condition. As per the report of 'India Education' in 2002, School participation of Dalit young ladies in 1993-94 was 46.2 percente while it was 61 percent from the young ladies of different gatherings.

Reservations in instructive organizations and grants for Dalit understudies mean a genuine segment in Dalit financial improvements.

It is an average social confidence in natural India that,(Political status of women in India; Shukla; Sibyl A. Schwarzanta; 2006) the preparation for youthful women irrelevant since she will end up working in the house or in develop. The uneducated and fresh young woman is considered as impeccable and virgin in various provincial districts and she in the long run shows signs of improvement recommendation for her marriage. Cast system similarly accept an outstandingly central part as a hindrance to a young woman child's educational rights.

Regardless of the way that the constitution of India endowments women Reservation for Women in Local Self -Government;73rd Constitutional Amendment, comparative rights corresponding to men, anyway there camouflage takes after from the social custom, from religious guidelines and practices. For the most part gatekeepers need to place assets into the preparation of their youngster and capacity change. Since, a young women is reliably a topic of her marriage and children. While folks make sense of how to twist up family provider, female learn kid bearing and neighbourhood commitments. Hitched young women don't generally have informative rights, along these lines kid marriage mishandle the informational benefits of a young women tyke . It precludes them from claiming potential flexibility and furthermore harming the CRC (Convention on the Rights of the Child) game plans. Islamic law, frequently known as Sharia Law, as deciphered by Islamic fundamentalists, asks for that mates submit to their significant other. It moreover requests that young woman to wear a cover if they have to go out. It gifts to have diverse life partners it in like manner urges young women to marry in early age just to promise her virginity and to a great degree limits work odds of female. In each one of these conditions how a young woman tyke even plan to twist up an insightful sagacity. Religion and social based uneven characters in sharia law limits young woman's direction by blending. Fundamentalists of Islamic Law consider they the pioneers and use demanding interpretation of the sacrosanct writings; they show female as troopers of magnificent war in which they have to fight to save the tradition and estimations of Islamic law. Fundamentalists of Islamic laws furthermore assume that, 'guideline for a female obliterates as far as possible and implications of sex parts and separates women's standard limits are absolutely substantial'. Religious laws crush a young woman child's educational rights. The International Labor Organization (ILO) asked for the expectation of the cover which makes earn backs the original investment with get to a young woman youth to preparing. The non appearance of sex direction in Muslim young women manufactures the peril of HIV/AIDS by virtue of the reward of perilous polygamy structure in the religion.

Much the same as the Quran, the Bible similarly contains the lingo to place women in subordinate position. For example, Ephesians 5:22-24 scrutinizes, 'companions, submit to your better half as the ace. for the life partner is the pioneer of the gathering and his body is of which he is the deliverer, now as an assembly submit to Christ, so also spouses should submit to their husbands no matter what'. Hindu Dalit school children's and educators also encounter the partition by the advantaged people in India. It is uncommonly striving for a Dalit young woman to approach preparing in such condition. According to the report of 'India Education' in 2002, School cooperation of Dalit young women in 1993-94 was 46.2 percente while it was 61 percent from the young women of various social events. Reservations The (constitutional bases of political and social change; Shlomo Slonim..........2007) in enlightening associations and awards for Dalit understudies mean a honest to goodness portion in Dalit amount related upgrades.

There has been seen significant improvement worldwide in propelling women's financial, social and social rights (The changing status of women; Jaso dhara Bagchi, Sarmistha Dulta Gupta; 2009). In the most recent decades, laws which deny oppression women in monetary and social life have been received in numerous nations, equality has been come to in the enrolment of young men and young women in essential instruction, and ladies have more access to work than previously.(G.R.Gangle et al. 2012) In any case, ladies still hate financial, social and social rights on an equivalent premise with men. Ladies keep on experiencing various infringement of their entitlement to wellbeing, including as prove by unsatisfactorily high maternal mortality and dreariness rates far and wide. There is inescapable oppression women in issues identifying with land, property and legacy (Constitutional context: women and their rights; Kathleen S. Sullivan, 1999). Women's business is all the time more problematic and less generously compensated than men's. Young Women's entrance to auxiliary training and a few territories of college instruction, generally held for men, isn't yet guaranteed.(Mogford 2011) Brutality against women has sensational outcomes on women's happiness regarding financial, social and social rights. At the point when infringement of these rights happen, women's equivalent access to equity isn't ensured. The Global Initiative works with its accomplices to raise the perceivability of women's ESC rights, and specifically land and property rights, at different universal and territorial gatherings, and to fortify the authorization of these rights. All the more for the most part, we likewise observe to give sexual orientation touchy investigations of substantive ESC rights(Mehta 1987) and their relationship to the satisfaction of women's entitlement to correspondence. Comparative work should likewise be possible at provincial and national levels. This incorporates recognizable proof of what the correct means for women as far as regard, ensure and satisfaction of rights and what sorts of particular measures should be considered by States for execution, including for ladies confronting intersectional segregation.

11.6 Media and Women

MAG Study (1994) revealed that there are now more women in the media workforce than they were twenty years ago. The decision making in these organizations remain overwhelmingly the domain of man. Senior decision makers with a gender sensitive perspective can use their persuasive power to empower others and change the image and status of women in print and electronic media organizations. As far as print media is concerned, late seventies and eighties in India witnessed the emergence of lot of women journalists. The choice of many educated women to take to this profession which was till recently considered a bastion of men is a sign of women of India joining the main stream decision making process in an important way. The last twenty years of print media is a story of women's participation in an area that focuses on the national agenda of great public interest. Communication researchers should take up studies on women's employment in various mass media. This may provide guidelines for bringing gender equality in the employment in mass media. It is true that women are lagging behind men in the media work force. At the same time, it is also a fact that there has been progress in this regard. There is more number of women employed now in media organizations and Government media of radio and Doordarshan in senior positions. Once they acquire positions of power in the media workforce, the task of improving women's images in media will become easier. There is a need for projecting the positive image of women in film media.

11.7 Awards

Government of India instituted five national awards which are to be called 'Stree Shakti Puraskar for recognition of achievements of individual women in the field of social development. These awards will be in the name of the eminent women personalities in the Indian history, who are famous for their personal courage and integrity like Devi Ahilya Bai Holkar, Kanngi, Mata Jijabai, Rani Gaidenlou Zeliang and Rani Lakshmi Bai. The award will carry a cash prize of Rupees one lakh and a citation. These awards will be given to women who have triumphed over difficult circumstances and have fought for and established the rights of women in various fields. Also, women achievers who have worked in the areas of education, health, agriculture and rural industry, protection of forests and environment and those who have created awareness and consciousness on women's issues through arts and media would be recognized and awarded by the Government. To extend respect and equal position to women 8th March is being observed as International Women's Day every year across the globe.

11.8 National Policy for Empowerment of Women

The National Policy for Empowerment of Women (NPEW) was formulated in 2001 as the blueprint for the future, with the expressive goal of bringing about the advancement, development and empowerment of women. The NPEW laid down detailed prescriptions to address discrimination against women, strengthen existing institutions which includes the legal system, provide better access to health care and other services, equal opportunities for women's participation in decision-making and mainstreaming gender concerns in the development process. The policies and programmes of the Government are directed towards achieving inclusive growth with special focus on women in line with the objective of the National Policy for Empowerment of Women. The Government introduced Gender Budgeting in 2005-06 in order to ensure that policy commitments are backed by financial outlays and that the gender perspective is incorporated in all stages of a policy or a programme. The objectives of Gender Budgeting are for committing to initiatives with the objective of influencing and effecting a change in the Ministries' policies, programmes in a way that could tackle gender imbalances, promote gender equality and development and ensure that public resources through the Ministries' budgets are allocated and managed accordingly. The government also made all efforts to ensure a definite flow of funds to women was the introduction of a Women's Component Plan (WCP) in the 9th Five Year Plan whereby all Ministries/Departments were directed to ensure at least 33 percent funds for women.

11.9 National Mission for Empowerment of Women

Government of India launched the National Mission for empowerment of women (NMEW) on International Women's Day in 2010 with the aim to strengthen overall processes that promote all-round development of women. It has the mandate to strengthen the inter-sector convergence; facilitate the process of coordinating all the women's welfare and socio-economic development programmes across ministries and departments. The Mission aims to provide a single window service for all programmes run by the Government for Women under aegis of various Central Ministries. The Mission has been named Mission Poorna Shakti, implying a vision for holistic empowerment of women. The Mission focussed on access to health, drinking water, sanitation and hygiene facilities for women, coverage of all girls especially those belonging to vulnerable groups in schools from primary to class 12th, higher and Professional education for girls, Skill development, Micro credit, vocational training, Entrepreneurship, Self-Help Groups development , Gender sensitization and dissemination of information and taking steps to prevent crimes against women and a safe environment for women.

All human rights are women's rights. The United Nations Organisation's International Covenant on civil and political rights, International Covenant on social, economic and cultural rights, Universal Declaration of human rights 1948, UN Convention on Complete Elimination of All Forms of Discrimination against women (CEDAW), several fundamental rights enshrined in Indian Constitution from articles 14 to 32 and directive principles of state policy from articles 36 to 51 describes the human rights of women. There are several legislative provisions and social security laws are also provides provisions for protection of human rights of women. The National Human Rights Commission constituted under the protection of human rights Act 1993 and National Commission' for women are actively working for protecting the woman's rights. The guidelines of supreme court of India in Vishakha case has to be followed for preventing sexual harassment of working women. The national policy for women and national mission for empowerment of women and national awards for eminent women working for protection of rights of women enables women empowerment and helps for protection of their human rights. The greatness of a civilization can be judged by the place given to women in the society. One of several factors that justify the greatness of India's ancient culture is the honorable place granted to women. The foreign influence on India caused considerable deterioration in the status of women. They were deprived of their rights of equality with men. Raja Ram Mohan Roy started a movement against this inequality and subjugation. The contact of Indian culture with that of the British also brought improvement in the status of women. The third factor in the revival of women's position was the influence of Mahatma Gandhi who induced women to participate in the Indian Freedom Struggle. The development of women is of paramount importance and sets the pace for overall development. There is a need for addressing gaps in state action for women on promoting inter-Ministerial and Inter Sector Convergence to create gender equitable and women centered policies and programmes. The Ministry of Women and Child Development has nodal responsibility to promote the human rights and concerns of women. We should have a vision of empowering women with human dignity and contributing as equal partners in development in an environment free from violence and discrimination. The Government and society should promote social, economic and political empowerment of women through policies, programmes and create awareness about their rights and facilitate institutional and legislative support for enabling them to realise their human rights and develop their full potential of human personality. Several social reformers like Mahatma Jyotirao Phule, Raja Ram Mohan Roy, Ishwar Chandra VidyaSagar, Narayan Guru and Periyar E.V. Ramasamy have fought for the human rights of women especially Right to Education, Right to Equality etc and removal of social evils like Abolition of Child Marriages, Sati and promotion of widow remarriages. Dr. B.R. Ambedkar, Chairman of the Drafting Committee of Indian Constitution and First Law Minister of independent India has introduced Hindu Code Bill in Parliament for liberating women from traditions and providing equal human rights for empowering them. Education, health employment and political power will empower the women and helps of protection of their human rights. 8th March is being observed as International Women's Day every year across the globe.

Bibliography

Books

Adhvaru Chari and Sharma, Firing Cost of Flexibility Evidence from Firms Employment Responses to Economic Shocks, Yale University Press, 2009.

Agarwal Dr. H.O., International Law & Human Rights,Central Law Publications, 15th Edn, 2008.

Ambedkar, B.R., Study in Law and Society, Ed. Mohammad Shabbir, Raw at Publications, Jaipur , 1997.

Bagehi Jasodhara, Co-ordinating Editor Dutta Gupta Sarmistha (Ed), The Changing Statues of Women in West Bengal, [1970-2000]The challenge Ahed, Serials Publications, New Delhi, 1st Edn., 2009.

Basu Kaushik, Fields Gory S. and Shub Debgupta, Retrenchment, Labour Laws and Government Policy; An Analysis with special Reference to India, Dept. of Labor Economics, Cornell University, 2000.

Basu, Alaka Malwade. 1992. Culture, the Status of Women, and Demographic Behaviour: Illustrated with the Case of India. Oxford: Clarendon Press.

Basu, Dr Durga Das, Constitutional Law of India, , Lexis Nexis Butterwoorths Wadhwa Nagpur, 8th Edn 2008.

Befort Stephen F. and Budd John W, Invisible Hands, Invisible objects: Bringing Work Place Law and Public Policy into Focus, Stand for University Press, 2009.

Beitz Charles R, The Idea of Human Rights, Oxford University Press, U.K, 2009.

Bhandari Asha and Mehta Rekha, Women, Justice and The Rule of Law, Serials Publications, New Delhi, 1st Edn., 2009.

Bhandari, Arun et al. 1990. Women and AIDS: Denial and Blame. New Delhi: Saraswati Art Press.

Bhuiyan, Rubia. 1991. Aspects of Violence Against Women. Dhaka: Institute of Democratic Rights.

Brownlie Ian, Principles of Public International Law, Oxford University Press, 6th Edn,2003.

Cassese, Antonio, Human Rights In a changing World, Oxford University Press, 2006.

Cassese, Antonio, International Criminal Law, Oxford University Press, May 2003.

Cassese, Antonio, International Law, Oxford University Press, Oxford University Press, 1st Edn, Feb. 10, 2005.

Chandrasekharan K.N., Pillai, Lectures on Criminal Procedure, Eastern Book Company, Lucknow, 4th Edn, 2006.

Chief Editor Sharma S.B. ,YOJANA, Women‘s Empowerment, (Oct. 2008) [VOL 52]

Devis Donald R, The Spirit of Hindu Law, Cambridge University Press, 2010.

Diwan Dr Paras and Peeyushi Modern Hindu Law , Allahbad Law Agency, New Delhi 20th Edn, 2009.

Ewing Keith Aileen McColn & Collins Hugh, Labour Laws, Texts and Material,Hart Publishing, 2005.

Gow Kailen, Never Say Never, Elge Books Com. Aug 13, 2012.

Grary, Christine, International Law and the Use Force, Oxford University Press, Oct. 21st , 2004.

Higgius, Rosalyn, Problems and Process, International Law How We Use it, Oxford University Press, Nov. 9, 1995.

Ishay Micheline R, The History of Human Rights: From Ancient Times to the Globalization, Univerity of Clifornia Press, 2008.

Kristof Nicholas D, Women's Empowerment Half the Sky: Turning Operation oppression into Opportunities for Women worldwide, Published by Knopf; September 2009.

Kumar, Manju Social Equality - The constitutional experiment in India, S. Chand, 1982.

Li Gorden XU, Labour Regulation, Economic Complexity and the China-India Gap, Himilton University Press, August 2010.

Lubin T., Devis D.R. and Krishnan, J.K.(ed), Hinduism and Law: An Introduction, Cambridge University Press, 2010.

Malcom, N. Shaw, International Law, Cambridge University Press, Oct. 13, 2013.

Mensik Werner, Hindu Law: Beyond Tradition and Modernity, Oxford University Press, 2003.

Misra Ranganath, Mayne's treatise on Hindu Law and Usage, Bharat Law House, New Delhi, 15th Edn, 2003.

Misra, Preeti, Domestic Violence Against Women, Legal Countrol and Judicial Response,Deep and Deep Publications Pvt. Ltd. , New Delhi – 110027.

Misra, S.N., Labour And Industrial Laws, Central Law Publication, 26th Edn, 2011.

Moyn Samual, The Last Utopia: Human Rights in History, Belknap Press of Harvard University, 2010.

Mulla, Sir Dinshow Framjee, Hindu Law, Lexis Nexis Butter Worth 17th Edn, 1998.

Olivelle, Patrick, The Law code of _Manu‘, Oxford University Press, 2004.

Pandey, Dr. J.N, The Constitutional Law of India, Central Law Agency, 49th Edn, 2012.

Parekh Parvin H., Human Rights, 2008, Universal Law Publishing.

Raghavachariar N.R, Hindu Law: Principles and Precedents 12th Edn, 2008.

Sharma Dr. Gokulesh, Human Rights and Social Justice, Deep & Deep Publications, New Delhi.

Takwani C.K. Civil Procedure, Eastern Book Company Publishing, Lucknow, 6th Edn,2009, Repriented 2011.

The Muslim Law of India, Lixis Nexis, New Delhi, 3rd Edn, 2002.

Tripathi, Dr S.C. and Arora Vibha, Law Relating to Women and children,Central Law Publications, 2nd Edn, 2006.

Walker Keshwan and Morell Arn, Labour and Employment, George Town University Press, U.S.A., 2005.

Articles

Gupta, Sadhama, Dowry Death : Law relating of dowry offences, Cr. L.J. 2006 Nov ; 112 (1283) at p. 289

Johannes Andeanes, The Morality of deterrence, in sentencing 194 (Hyman Gross and Andrew Von Hirscheds, New Work; AUP, 1981)

Justice V.R. Krishna Iyer on the role of National Commission for Women.

Kishwar, Madhu (1990): Women‘s Organisations-the Presence of Unrealistic Expectations, Manunshi, No.61 (November-December 1990).

Nandela, Krishnan, Gandhi on Women‘s Empowerment, www.sacred text.com.

Patil, Pratibha Singh, Empowerd Women-Empowered Nation, Yojana, Oct, 2008

Prof. P., Nirpama, Status of Women in Indian Society- Issues and Challenges in Process of Empowerment, Institute of Technology and Science, India, rupa@bitspilani.ac.in.

R.K., Growth and Development of Industrial Jurisprridence in India, Dr. Ram Manohar Lahiya National Law University, Lucknow

Siddhaaarth Barua, Supreme Court Views, New era, Law Publication 2005

Werner Menski, SOAS, University of London, –The Dowry Problem: Progress in Legal Remedies KLT(1997) 2 at page73

Electronic Resources

http://www.accesstoinsight.org/lib/authors/dewaraja/wheel280.h tm

http://www.accesstoinsight.org/lib/authors/horner/wheel030.htm

http://www.en.wikipedia. org/wiki/women in Hinduism.

International Conventions/ Commissions/ Covenants/ Conferences / Declarations Etc.

Commission on Human Rights, 1946.

Commission on the Status of Women,1946.

Convention and Recommendation on Consent to Marriage, Minimum age for Marriage and Registration of Marriage, 1962.

Convention on the Elimination of All Forms of Discrimination against Women, 1979.

Convention on the Nationality of Married Women, 1952.

Convention on the Political Rights of Women, 1952.

International Conference on Population and Development, 1994.

The Covenant on Civil and Political Rights,1966.

The Covenant on Economic, Social and Cultural Rights,1966.

The Discrimination (Employment and Occupation) Convention, 1958.

The Hague Adoption Convention on the Protection of Children and Co-operation in Respect of Inter-country Adoption, 1993

The Night Work (Women) Convention, 1951.

The Optional Protocol to the Covenant on Civil and Political Rights,1966.

The Underground World (Women) Convention, 1935.

The United Nations World Conference on Human Rights,1993.

The Universal Declaration of Human Rights, 1948.

United Nations Convention on the Rights of the Child, 1992.

United Nations Development Programme (UNDP). 1992. Human Development Report. New York: United Nations.

United Nations. 1989. World Population Policies. (ST/ESA/ SER.A/1&2/Add.1). Vol. 2. New York: United Nations.

United Nations. 5 October 1989. "Consideration of Reports Submitted by States Parties under Article 40 of the Covenant-Second Periodic Report of States Parties Due in 1985; Addendum-India." (CCPR/C/37/Add.13).

Statues/ Rules/ Regulations

- The 73rd Constitutional Amendment Act
- The 74th Constitutional Amendment Act
- The 92nd Constitutional Amendment Act
- The Child Marriage Restraint Act, 1929.
- The Commission of Sati (Prevention) Act, 1987.
- The Dowry Prohibition Act, 1961.
- The Equal Remuneration Act, 1976.
- The Factories Act, 1948.
- The Guardians and Wards Act, 1890.

- The Hindu Adoptions and Maintenance Act, 1956.
- The Hindu Law of Inheritance (Amendment) Act, 1929.
- The Hindu Marriage Act, 1955.
- The Hindu Marriage Amendment Act, 1976.
- The Hindu Minority and Guardianship Act, 1956.
- The Hindu Succession Act, 1956.
- The Hindu Women's Rights to Property Act, 1937.
- The Immoral Traffic (Prevention) Act, 1956.
- The Indecent Representation of Women (Prohibition) Act, 1986.
- The Indian Divorce (Amendment) Act, 2001.
- The Indian Divorce Act, 1869.
- The Indian Evidence Act, 1872.
- The Indian Penal Code, 1860.
- The Juvenile Justice (Care and Protection of Children) Act, 2000.
- The Juvenile Justice (Care and Protection of Children) Amendment Act, 2006.
- The Maternity Benefit Act, 1961.
- The Medical Termination of Pregnancy Act, 1971.
- The Minimum Wages Act, 1950.
- The Muslim Women (Protection of Rights on Divorce) Act, 1986.
- The National Commission for Women Act, 1990.
- The Payment of Wages Act, 1936.
- The Personal Laws (Amendment) Act, 2010.
- The Pre-Natal Diagnostic Techniques (Regulation and Prevention of Misuse) Act, 1994.
- The Protection of Human Rights (Amendment) Act, 2006.

- The Protection of Human Rights Act, 1993.
- The Protection of Women from Domestic Violence Act, 2005.
- The Sati Prohibition Act, 1829.
- The Special Marriage Act, 1954.

Constitutional Amendments

- 73rd Constitutional Amendment Act
- 74th Constitutional Amendment Act
- 92nd Constitutional Amendment Act

Newspapers/ Reports/ Magazines

Amnesty International (AI), December 1991. International Women's Day Action 1992. (AI Index: ACT 77/10/91). London: Amnesty International.

Anandabazar Patrika, Bangla Daily

Asia Watch, 20 September 1992. Police Killings and Rural Violence in Andhra Pradesh. New York: Human Rights Watch.

Inter Press Service (IPS). 19 November 1993. Manju Kak. "India Women: Politics Is a Man's Game." (NEXIS)

Inter Press Service (IPS). 23 June 1994. Neena Bhandari. "India: Rural Women Protest from Behind their Veils." (NEXIS)

Kurukshetra

Report of National Human Rights Commission

Report of the National Conference on Human Rights

Report of the National Conference on Human Rights and HIV/AIDS(2000)

The Hindu

The New York Times. 21 October 1991. Edward A. Gargan. "Tearful Bride, Just 10, Touches India." (NEXIS)

The New York Times. 30 December 1993. Edward A. Gargan. "For Many Brides in India, a Dowry Buys Death." (NEXIS)

The Statesman

The Times of India

The Washington Post. 18 February 1993. Molly Moore and John Ward Anderson. "Women Fed Up and Fighting Back." (NEXIS)

World Bank Report on Population, 2012.

❑❑❑

Made in the USA
Las Vegas, NV
30 March 2026

44475677R10213